ANY
CHILD
CAN
WRITE

OTHER BOOKS BY
Harvey S. Wiener

On Writing:
Creating Compositions
The English Skills Handbook
The Writing Lab
The Writing Room

On Reading:
Reading Skills Handbook
Basic Reading Skills Handbook

On Conversation:
Talk with Your Child

Anthologies:
Emerson and Thoreau
The Short Prose Reader
Great Writing
Enjoying Stories

ANY CHILD CAN WRITE

HARVEY S. WIENER

A
BANTAM
TRADE
PAPERBACK

BANTAM BOOKS
NEW YORK · TORONTO · LONDON · SYDNEY · AUCKLAND

ANY CHILD CAN WRITE
A Bantam Book / October 1990

Library of Congress Cataloging-in-Publication Data

Wiener, Harvey S.
    Any child can write / Harvey S. Wiener.
        p.   cm.
    ISBN 0-553-34958-9
    1. English language—Composition and exercises—Study and
teaching.   2. Language arts.   3. Education—Parent participation.
I. Title.
LB1576.W4874   1990
372.6'23—dc20   90-32424
                                                    CIP

Published simultaneously in the United States and Canada

Bantam Books are published by Bantam Books, a division of
Bantam Doubleday Dell Publishing Group, Inc. Its trademark,
consisting of the words "Bantam Books" and the portrayal of
a rooster, is Registered in U.S. Patent and Trademark Office
and in other countries. Marca Registrada. Bantam Books,
666 Fifth Avenue, New York, New York 10103.

PRINTED IN THE UNITED STATES OF AMERICA

CWO   0 9 8 7 6 5 4 3 2 1

To my wife,
my mother, my father,
and my sister,
for helping
writers grow.

Contents

ACKNOWLEDGMENTS   xiii

PREFACE   xv

1 Introduction: 1
THE SECOND "R"

Writing as Exploration
What's Happening in School
Some Basic Thoughts About Writing
Poor Writers: On the Question of Blame

2 Notes, Signs, and Shopping Lists: 11
HOW CAN A PARENT HELP?

Setting Examples
The Tools of the Trade
"I've Got a Little List"
Keep Out!: A Sign for Room or Door
Let's Leave a Note
Writing and Reading, Hand in Hand

3 Experience and Creative Expression   28

A View of Creative Expression
Autobiography: A Child's Experience
The Parent Sets the Stage
Mothers and Fathers as Storytellers

4

Pictures, Words, and Sentences: 36
LAYING FOUNDATIONS

Words and the Young Artist
Pictures and Words: Making Connections
Accent on Sentence Sense
Avoiding Bits and Pieces
Scissors, Paste, and Sentences
Seeing the Skill Advance

5

The Senses at Play: 55
IMAGES AS BUILDING BLOCKS

Sense Words Up Front
Four Writing Games and Variations
Two Longer Efforts
Comparisons for Solid Imagery

6

Correctness, Part 1: 79
AN OUTLOOK FOR YOUNG WRITERS AT HOME

The Writing Process
The Fever of Correctness
How Do Writers Write?
Reacting to Error
Your Code of Ethics: Writing for School
Proofreading, Hedge Against Mistake
Spotlight on Writing in the Grades

7

Correctness, Part 2: 111
WORD GAMES AND WORD AND SENTENCE CRAFT

Building Vocabulary
Words as Chameleons
Guesswork in the Limelight
Spelling Skills and Word Hot Spots
Sentences to Play With

8 Snapshots of Special Places 143

The Senses, Front and Center
Opinions in Focus
Subjectivity Leads the Way
Cameras and Crayons
Description Described

9 One Person in the Floodlights 157

One Person, One Sentence
A Party Riddle
Photo into Words
Self-Portraits for the Very Young
Expanding a Picture of Someone Close

10 A Moment Reborn in Language 170

What Is Narration? What Is a Moment?
A Moment in Focus
A Sense of Sequence
Narration: Sensory Language Leads the
    Way
Playing with Dialogue
A Short Story: Fiction for Thirteen-Year-
    Olds

11 Adventures in Make-Believe 193

Riddles and Games on Paper
Visits with Make-Believe
Animals on Parade
"I Am a Pizza": Personification and Delight
On Your Own in Fantasyland

12 **A Child's Message Through the Mails** 211

Using the Mails
Creative Letter Writing
"Come to My Party"
Let's Write Letters
Business Letters for Homebred Dynamos

13 **Words in Focus:** 229
CREATIVE DEFINITIONS FOR YOUR YOUNG WRITER

What Does It Mean? How Does It Feel?
Writing Clear Definitions
Personal Meanings, Personal Words

14 **Language Singing:** 243
YOUR CHILD AS POET

Talk-to-Me's and Word Whackies
What's Wrong with Jingling?
Language Singing, Sharp and Clear
Shapes and Rhythms for the Poet's Song
Why Poetry?

15 **A Report for School** 269

A Project in Stages
"What Do I Do?" First Questions First
Shaving the Topic Down
Your Friends: The Encyclopedia and Other
    Source Books
Getting Things in Order
Enter the Finished Product
Using Your Willpower

16   An Afterword for Too-Busy Parents   291

Appendix A.   One Hundred Ideas for Writing at
                 Home   293

Appendix B.   A Parent's Primer on Correctness   297

             Sentence Completeness
             One Hundred Words Most Often
                Misspelled
             Words Often Confused
             When to Use Capitals
             Some Punctuation Pointers

Appendix C.   Key Books for Young Writers and
                 Their Parents   317

             Children's Wordbooks
             Language Skills Books for Parents

INDEX   325

About the Author   334

Acknowledgments

The author acknowledges the use of the following previously published material.

The Bobbs-Merrill Company, Inc.: Selections from pages 83, 131, 159, and 129 from *Language Arts and Life Patterns: Grades 2 through 8,* by Don M. Wolfe. Copyright © 1961 by The Odyssey Press, Inc.; copyright © 1972 by the Bobbs-Merrill Company, Inc. Reprinted by permission of the publisher.

James I. Brown, "Master Word Chart." Reprinted by permission of James I. Brown.

Grolier Incorporated: Entry on "Hibernation." Reprinted from *The New Book of Knowledge,* 1974, by permission of the publisher, Grolier Incorporated.

Houghton Mifflin Co: Excerpt from page 149 of *The American Heritage First Dictionary.* Published by Houghton Mifflin Company, 1986.

Indiana Writes: Selections from pages 60 and 67. Copyright © 1976 by the Trustees of Indiana University.

McGraw-Hill Book Company: Selections from pages 45–46 and 173–174 and adaptations of pages 13–17, 45–50, 89–92, and 249–254. From *Creating Compositions, Second Edition,* by Harvey S. Wiener. Copyright © 1977 by Harvey S. Wiener. Used with permission of McGraw-Hill Book Company and the author.

The Macmillan Company: Excerpt from "What Is Pink" from *Sing-Song,* by Christina Rossetti. Copyright © 1924 by The Macmillan Company. Used with permission of the publisher.

Random House, Inc.: Selection from page 95 of *Enjoying English 6,* by Don M. Wolfe, Floy W. DeLaney, Lela T. Hamilton, and Ethel K. Howard. Published by L. W. Singer Co., Inc., 1969. Reprinted by permission of Random House, Inc.

The National Council of Teachers of English: Excerpt from page 97 of *Sentence Combining,* by Frank O'Hare. Research Report 15. Copyright © 1973 by the National Council of Teachers of English. Reprinted with permission: selection from page 660 of "The Single Narrative Paragraph and College Remediation." by Harvey S. Wiener, in *College English,* March 1972. Copyright © 1972 by the National Council of Teachers of English. Reprinted by permission; selection from page 571 of "Media Compositions: Preludes to Writing" by Harvey S. Wiener, in *College English,* February 1974. Copyright © 1974 by the National Council of Teachers of English. Reprinted by permission.

Charles Scribner's Sons: Selection from *I Know! A Riddle Book* by Jane Sarnoff and Reynolds Ruffins. Copyright © 1977 by Charles Scribner's Sons. Reprinted by permission of the publisher.

Preface

When the cry of back-to-basics hit full force in the mid-1970s, friend after friend stopped me on the street, telephoned, and scrawled hurried postscripts to letters: All these people were concerned parents who wanted to help their children advance as writers. What steps could a mother or father take to influence a son's or daughter's writing abilities?

I looked in the libraries and the bookshops. But, in spite of what educators had already begun to call the "writing crisis," I could not find a single volume to tell parents what to do to help their children develop competence as writers. I was not long before I knew that I had to write such a book.

The first edition of *Any Child Can Write* appeared in 1978. The Book-of-the-Month Club chose it as an alternate selection, and I discussed the book with Tom Brokaw on *The Today Show*. When the book went out of print a short while ago, letters and phone calls from parents all over America, especially those dedicated to home learning, helped me convince Bantam to produce a new edition.

As a parent and a teacher I want to share with other parents my ideas for a fruitful, enjoyable home program in writing. Such a program starts in the building of attitudes and moves through simple, varied, and practical experience with the written word. A mother or father can direct such a program with confidence and can help a youngster develop abilities somehow overlooked or not adequately attended to in school.

You are without doubt your child's teacher, the best kind in many ways, because you love the one you teach, share the joys and suffering of your child's attempts, and want desperately to assure his success.

My suggestions in this book take into account a parent's busy schedule and other constraints; but they also speak to the parent who is willing to give up some time to help his or her child from losing out on a chosen college or career because of a failure to master the basic, but essential, skills of writing.

There are things you can do—and you can have fun doing them.

In planning this book I am indebted to many people for their ideas about good writing and about how inexperienced writers learn best. Many of my suggestions are not original; I learned them from teachers, poets, counselors, tutors, and parents. My friend Professor Don M. Wolfe taught me most of what I know, and often our ideas are so alike they are one man's thoughts. To other friends and colleagues—Mina Shaughnessy at the City University of New York, who died long before her time; Greg Tobin, my editor at Bantam, who believed in the new edition right from the start; Curtis Kelly for getting the first edition off the ground; Professors Nora Eisenberg, Marian Arkin, Dan Georgakis, and George Groman at LaGuardia Community College; Don McQuade at the University of California at Berkeley; Elaine Maimon at Queens College; Charles Bazerman at Baruch College; Filmore Peltz, Noel Kriftcher, and Fred Cohen, distinguished high school principals; my agent and friend John W. Wright—I am indebted for ideas, advice, encouragement, and support. I am especially grateful to Bob Habich for his help on the first edition. Dee Shedd did a first-rate job in preparing the manuscript, and I thank her too. Mary Pride, author of *The*

Big Book of Home Learning, has been a loyal booster of *Any Child Can Write*.

But the people to whom I am most indebted for the book are the children whose writing demonstrates what young talent, when tapped, can produce. Accordingly I want to thank the following young writers: Sharon Adler, Kathy Apfel, Twyla Boardley, Pamela Bonavoglia, Karen Bracy, Judy Brewster, Helen Cohen, Angela D'Apica, Terry Dause, Mike Davis, Marie Della Porta, Patricia D'Esposito, Brian Donovan, Valeria Drafts, Sherri Dubner, Patricia Durante, Michael Eannelo, Karen Sue Evans, Ruth Feder, Alayne Finkelstein, Leo Finkelstein, Stacy Goldstein, Ellen Greneman, Leslie Gross, Harold Gruber, Katie Halper, Joe Havens, Eliezar Havivi, Janet Hutter, Lauren Hutter, Rose Jachter, Nancy Jones, Gary Kimball, Gina Kirsch, Hedy Klein, Sharon Klein, Vivian Krasner, Michelle Landburg, Robin Leach, Denish Leonard, Albert Leone, Mark Levine, Mindy Levine, Myra Leysorek, Sonia Markmann, Darrin McGowan, Theresa McGraw, Shelly Modlin, Caroline Narby, Scott Norkin, Frank O'Connor, Carol Orefice, Debbie Osher, Jeffrey T. Pope, Mona Rosenfeld, Etta Rybstein, Beth Ross, Tony Schott, Erica Sher, Andrew Siscaretti, Eddit Southern, Carl Sterns, Rosemary Tyson, Charles Walker, Donald Walters, Myra Weiser, Joseph Wiener, Melissa Wiener, Saul Wiener, Beth Ann Winters, Carol Zubatkin. To these and others I am grateful for showing conclusively that any child can write.

Introduction
THE SECOND "R"

Writing as Exploration

Writing is a magical realm of expression that allows your child to come to terms with the joys and pains of daily living. It is a way for your child to explore the inner self. A few words, a few sentences glow on the page like a little crayon drawing. It is an expression of personal vision, a perception of the world as your child sees it. It is also a permanent record of experience—words and sentences holding and keeping the essence of a moment in language.

Every day your child's life holds innumerable moments that bombard the senses through sight and sound and smell and taste and touch. Etched in your child's mind, either conscious or unconscious, these moments dwell in the brain, awaiting language to transform them into experiences that are intelligible and meaningful both to the child and to others.

It is this language of the senses that every child has at his or her fingertips. And it is this language that any child, with guidance, can transform into writing—to capture forever the special flashes of meaning a young life holds.

The key word here is *guidance,* and this is where you, as a parent, can play an important role. For if you have looked closely at your child's classroom learning, you will see that many schools fall short in guiding youngsters to develop essential writing skills.

What's Happening in School

Consider for a moment your child's grade school teacher as he leaves the classroom at the end of the day. On the chalkboard behind him he has written the homework assignment: "Read pages 25 to 45 in your social studies book and *write* the answers to the questions on page 46; *write* up the experiment on air pressure we did in class today; *write* sentences for your week's spelling words; *write* a book report on the biography you took from the library." If he's a conscientious teacher, he's gripping a worn leather briefcase that is already bulging with written work collected from thirty children that morning. At home the burden of his students' work haunts him. Reams of paper stand in ugly, reluctant piles on the desk or on the kitchen table. Under such circumstances, how can the teacher do an efficient job when it comes to the instruction and evaluation of writing? How can he build in your child a positive attitude toward written work if he himself, being overburdened, views it as a tedious, unrewarding chore?

He can't.

And that's where you come in. By setting up an atmosphere in your home that encourages creative written expression, you can give your sons and daughters an outlook on writing that will build confidence in their abilities to use language.

And that's where this book comes in: It will help you, who know the importance of written communication in today's world, help your children develop essential writing skills.

Some Basic Thoughts About Writing

Writing serves in a number of ways. First, writing lets your children show what they know; and, as such, it becomes a means by which a teacher judges your child's knowledge of a subject. When the instructor reads the answers to a history test or to a list of questions about science, she checks on the student's mastery of content. But, more often than not, she has decided that if students show that they know the answers, it really doesn't matter how successful the writing is. With time limitations and excessive student loads, rarely will a teacher comment in the margin about sentences or the quality of ideas on a page of social studies homework. If you look at the last few pages of written work returned to your child by her teacher, you won't find much in the way of suggestions for writing improvement.

Writing teachers think about two broad areas when they evaluate a child's work. First there is the world of ideas and the way a writer puts those ideas together. Often called "rhetoric" or "composition," this aspect of writing is the product of the way a mind works in dealing with thoughts. It involves invention, discovery, logic, organization of ideas, and style. Second, there is the area of correctness, often called "mechanics," "grammar," or "usage." This is the domain of more easily measured skills: A word is either right or wrong, a sentence is either complete or incomplete, an apostrophe is either required or not required.

Even in this arena, apparently guided by agreed-upon rules and conventions, lively academic debate fills the scholarly journals—should we use *that* or *which*, do we write *It was I* or *It was me*, must we use *who* or *whom*?

I like to use a comparison between effective writing and the human anatomy to illustrate these two broad areas. Rhetoric, the idea and organizing part, is like a person's body: the blood, muscle, bone, tendons, and nerves. Correctness, the right-or-wrong features of our language system, is like the skin, the outer layer, what we see straight off when we think of the human animal. This analogy is a good one, because it equates the writing process with a living being—but it is helpful only if we keep in mind that both the skin *and* the body make up the whole person. One without the other is incomplete.

Just as skin and body make the human being, so ideas and correctness make writing. Without the clear expression of ideas, the outer layer of correctness has no meaning. Nonsense correctly spelled and punctuated is still nonsense. Similarly, brilliant ideas that follow none of the principles of correct writing fall apart, a heap of fluids and organs without skin. Often, in fact, it is only through correct expression that a writer can make her ideas known in the first place. Of course, when I teach writing in the classroom, I focus first upon the internal organs, so to speak, the expression of ideas by means of effective language. I try to build up to a concern for "the outer layer," or correctness. So the level of sentence construction, the ideas at the heart of the writing, and the degree of error all go hand in hand. Clearly, writing to communicate demands that ideas, the language used to explore them, and the conventions of correctness all work together.

Of course we are concerned with demonstrating knowledge through written language. Every book, letter, memo, or report you read illustrates what the writer knows or understands. When a child writes about himself he's also, in a way, showing what he knows. But I am not concerned here with what the written word can tell about how many books on Russia your youngster has absorbed or how meticulously he took notes on the experiment with a gasoline can that demonstrates principles of air pressure. My interest is with the expression of *ideas,* the muscle and blood of writing.

With your help and guidance your children can use the resources of their own experiences to develop that magical ability to express an idea—to capture the essence of a moment.

Poor Writers: On the Question of Blame

It's no news to anybody reading this book that today's school children as a whole are poor writers. College teachers over the country, pointing to low scores on entrance exams and poor writing samples submitted by freshmen, are stunned at the writers' inability both to express ideas clearly and to use the conventions of correctness in conveying those ideas. Who, they wonder, is at fault? How can generations of youngsters pass through high schools, earn diplomas, and still not know how to write? Why is it that previous groups of girls and boys could write so well, and even master the complex rules of grammar (a demand rarely made on students today)?

What is the answer? Why are our children not learning how to write?

As with all simple questions there are too many complex factors to offer simple answers.

The schools, even with the best of intentions, contribute their share to the problem. Although, clearly, there are many dedicated teachers who approach rigorously their responsibilities to teach students how to write, the portrait I drew earlier of the overburdened elementary school teacher shows part of the problem in the grade schools. In some of those schools that do insist upon writing—there are enormous numbers of literary magazines, class news-papers, and yearbooks churned out each year—instructors often take what students create and rewrite, edit, and correct the material themselves, instead of teaching children how to make revisions on their own. Still other teachers, in stressing the free and creative spirit of the writer, will praise badly organized, poorly supported writing because of a tiny flash of insight from the writer. Others, sadly, have no good ideas to give children at all. One sixth-grade teacher confided to me a while back that he taught writing no more than twice a year. Twice a year! "It's frustrating. There's not enough time. And I really don't know what to do."

In the junior and senior high schools, where teachers see themselves as specialists and teach "English" only, there's not much attention to instruction in writing either. First, the curriculum is overloaded with literary appreciation. Those courses of study that include units for writing are not explicit and are weak in their demands. I might add, incidentally, that English instructors complain little about this: It is only in teaching literature, many feel, that their true mission lies. As important as it is to teach poetry and the Great Western Tradition, the scope and dimension of literature programs in the schools are often beyond the student's needs. Time spent in teaching symbolism, onomatopoeia, and blank verse might be better spent in teaching about topic sentences, supporting details, verb tense. I know I am striking, now, at the life's blood for many teachers. There is something about the personal satisfaction and prestige derived from teaching an appreciation of fiction that is impossible to dislodge from the English teacher's outlook. Unfortunately, that attitude does not accompany the teaching of writing skills.

When I first wrote those words in 1980, my daughter, Melissa—you'll read more about her and my other two children, Joseph and Saul, throughout this book—was eight years old, just moving through the lower grades of public school. I built my conclusions on many years of teaching experience in the schools. I had hoped in 1980 that by the time my own children reached high school age, significant changes in instruction would make them regularly practicing writers throughout the grades. Unfortunately, nothing of the sort has happened. Melissa admits and I confirm by observation that writing instruction is still in the subbasement of any building of knowledge constructed by the schools. Though a good writer—she is managing editor of the newspaper and has won prizes for her writing—she picked up much of what she learned at home and on her own. Joseph, an eighth grader now and an editor of his junior high school newspaper, cannot remember learning much about writing, occasional school composition assignments aside. Saul, now in fourth grade, rarely produces samples of sustained sentences and paragraphs that show that he's learned anything about writing in the classroom. I hear hopeful comments from my elementary and secondary school colleagues about how instruction in writing is changing for the better, but, as I observe the landscape, except for showcase schools here and there, progress is a lazy turtle inching its way across educational reform.

In college the situation is pretty much the same. Professors moan about the awful state of student writing; but having to teach freshman English instead of literature is, to many, a fate worse than death.

It is true that, in the last few years, college English departments have turned with imagination and energy to teaching composition. Throughout the country directors of writing programs are establishing writing as a discipline worthy of rigorous study and investigation. Intelligent approaches to college writing have mushroomed at the campuses of Beaver College, Yale University, Miami Dade Junior College, Ohio State University, the University of Iowa, and the various colleges of the City University of New York.

In spite of all this, however, the freshman writing course is still the stepchild of the English curriculum.

To overcome this sad situation, one might reasonably ask if a teacher's training ought not to include more study of techniques in teaching writing. But more than *what?* The astounding reality is that few teachers in grade school, junior high, senior high, or college have had *any* training in how to teach composition. How to teach reading; how to teach mathematics; how to evaluate tests; how to teach science—in all of these, yes, but no course in how to teach writing. Now, in response to public outcries, some interesting courses and programs in writing for future teachers of English are developing at schools such as the University of Michigan, SUNY Stony Brook, UCLA, University of Southern California, CCNY, and Columbia Teachers College, among others. Thoughtful books on teaching writing by Don Murray, Lucy McCormick Calkins, Peter Elbow, and James Britton in England are now readily available to help teachers develop comprehensive writing programs through the grades. However, I'm willing to bet that at the moment, your child's teacher probably has had *no* instruction in how to teach composition.

Teacher attitude and preparation offer one clue to your child's poor achievement in writing, but there are others. Human beings vary in abilities. Some children never develop the skills parents would like them to develop; or they cannot learn in the time frame the schools have established arbitrarily. This is *not* the same as saying each child cannot be brought to his or her own level of maximal achievement. Putting ideas into written language with ease, grace, and clarity is a skill that is not easily learned. In any consideration of achievement, there is also the question of talent. But writing is just like any other creative skill—painting, drawing, ice skating, swimming, diving. Some people astound the world with their natural abilities to do things others reach only after great struggle. The point is that if we make the struggle we often *can* achieve our goal despite our own limitations. We'll not all turn out like Picasso, Torvill and Dean, Janet Evans, and Greg Louganis; but if one of the skills they command interests us we can learn it, and we can feel pride in our achievement even if we fall short of greatness. It means practice, hard work, and dedication, but if it's important and enjoyable to us, and, especially, if we begin at a young age, almost anyone can learn to draw or skate or swim or dive.

Another reason today's children seem to have poorer writing skills than yesterday's children do stem, in part, from the advantages of the modern world. There is no doubt that television, movies, slides, tape recorders, video units, stereos, citizens band radios, transistors, and portable televisions are making the written word in some sense obsolete. Even letter writing, a form of communication we once could have said with absolute certainty that children would need throughout their adult lives, may now be replaced by the exchange of homemade cassettes or long-distance phone calls.

The irony of the seeming obsolescence of the written word in the wake of the media explosion is that written language continues to play a critical role in the way we communicate. People *write* programs to motivate computers; children at school must take notes on what they learn, no matter what vehicle is used to convey the information to them; and parents still, and shall forever, write letters. Despite their seeming affection for nonwritten, often nonverbal forms of communication, our children know what awaits them in a career if they lack writing skills. I've seen brilliant young students who are articulate, clever, and personable turn away from professions in law or business management because they believe they cannot write well enough. In many jobs, skill in writing and advancement through the ranks are correlated.

Will *your* children reject law, teaching, computer programming, management, public relations, government, civil service, editing, advertising, police science, research science, and countless other professions because they question their own skills with written language?

Sadly, many parents too fall easy prey to the media, which drain the family's time and which keep them away from the written word. In how many households do children never observe parents put pens or pencils to paper? Do you know that a family can keep a shopping list (such a basic writing exercise) without jotting down a single word? Just stick a peg in a wooden board, alongside the printed word for each staple, such as milk, butter, and eggs. How unfortunate.

On the other hand, some children are lucky enough to see mothers pursuing degrees and scribbling the notes for a sociology paper; or, perhaps, they may see their fathers behave like mine: Every Saturday afternoon my father sat in a green club chair working out the New York *Post* crossword puzzle, a tattered copy of *Roget's Thesaurus* at his side, and a yellow pencil locked between his thumb and forefinger.

There are innumerable writing experiences for a parent and child to share. They are waiting for you.

And so, this book. As you look at the ways to help your child, you'll be looking at yourself as a user of the written word too. So be warned, it's not easy. Yet, given the poverty of other resources from which your child learns to write, you, the parent, must get the ball rolling.

2

Notes, Signs, and Shopping Lists:

HOW CAN A PARENT HELP?

Setting Examples

Children learn by imitation. As soon as my daughter could crawl about freely, she would slip into my study during the early hours when I write, and watching me carefully as she played, she would demand her own pencil and papers. Long before her second birthday she would sit on the floor near my chair, scribbling on small white sheets that she begged from my desk pad. The sight of her father scratching away at his desk each day set the frame for Melissa's own writing activities. Her dexterity advanced so well that when we tried to teach her to eat with a fork, we used a writing implement as our referent. "Hold it like a pencil," we urged. Watching me type, she soon asked for her own typewriter. We bought her a red plastic children's type-writer, and it remained one of her favorite toys straight through her seventh or eighth year.

Many years back a cousin of mine had a short story published for the first time. His little boy was so excited to see the magazine bearing his father's story that with a feverish pace the child dashed off three little stories of his own!

Of course not every child has a professional writer for a parent. Still, there are countless opportunities for your child to watch you performing simple writing tasks every day. And there are few better ways to establish writing as a vital and enjoyable process than to watch Mommy or Daddy. These observed activities easily become joint endeavors as your child grows older and demands to participate.

In this chapter I want to explore some simple, everyday types of writing that you can set into motion at home. Even before we get to that, however, you need to collect the simple equipment required for your child's writing experiences.

The Tools of the Trade

It's not a big task to keep available the things your child will need for frequent writing activities. Most households already have many of the items I suggest. Gather them together and make them accessible to the child.

Here's what you'll need:

• *Writing paper.* Don't be fussy: Any type will do. It's a good idea to offer as many kinds as you can. Loose sheets of different sizes will acommodate your child's unpredict-able preferences at any given moment. Always try to pro-vide unlined paper as well as lined, and if the lines are narrowly spaced, do not *insist* that the writing fit between them. You should encourage, but not demand, writing within widely spaced lines. Variety is the key to paper supply: Your child may want to use two- by three-inch note sheets, plain white paper, lined yellow pages, backs of envelopes, index cards, the reverse side of ruined sheets, newspaper edges, napkins, personal notepaper, all with equal interest and pleasure. A book, a spiral-bound pad of pages, or a tablet will provide more permanence for your child's work. Spirals suit a youngster's sudden whim to rip out a damaged page.

• **Heavy-duty paper.** Provide index cards, oak tag sheets, cardboard from shirts, the backs of pads, cut-up shoe boxes or cartons. These make good homemade signs and resist tearing when they are hung from a wall or door.

• **Stationery.** Some notepaper of your child's own and some cards that can be stamped and posted will go a long way in establishing the value of letter-writing. If you're lucky, letter-writing practice during the early years (three and four years old) will save you phone bills later on!

• **Writing implements.** Pencils and crayons allow children a wide range of expression, according to their tastes and inclinations. Supply and encourage the user of erasers. Teach your child that all writers make mistakes often and that correcting errors has value (much more of this later on). During a trip through Europe we found colored pencils were a wonderful, durable set of writing tools. Making pictures and words in color held our child's interest on train rides where long, dull stretches of landscape and empty coach compartments offered no diversion; and an inexpensive sharpener fixes a broken point simply. Crayons, though more versatile in color possibilities, break easily. However, for many children, a crayon is easier to manipulate than a pencil. If your child is still developing dexterity, supply large thick crayons. I am at a loss to understand children's attraction to pens (perhaps they think it is "grown-up" to use pens!) but nothing thrills a four- and five-year-old more than writing in ink. As long as you watch your white linen tablecloth or orange velvet couch, pens are fine. If you encourage felt-tip pens—children love their variety of colors—buy only the water-soluble kind so that you can wash the pink and aqua off a ruffled blouse or the back of a thumb or an elbow.

• **Chalkboard and chalk.** Chalk and chalkboard in the child's room support writing activities, providing excellent opportunities for experimental writing exercises and for practice with newly learned words. A picture and a few words easily are erased to make way for another presentation. The feeling of the chalk in your child's hand, the different angle of the writing surface from the usual horizontal on the desk top to the vertical on a chalkboard easel or on a wall provide a learning alternative that will reinforce what your child practices on paper.

• **Word books.** A variety of alphabet and word books provides more than reading activities. Many books encourage a child to follow dotted or broken lines in order to write out the alphabet or to spell out words, to copy words printed in large letters alongside pictures, or even to write original responses to questions. (The Dr. Seuss-Roy McKie book, *My Book About Me,* is a notable example of this last group.) These are all fine, so long as they remain activities for enjoyment. Nothing will turn a child away from writing faster than "work" assigned to him in a word book by a parent. An older child (fourth grade and up) should have a dictionary, and the upper junior and senior high school youngster will need a thesaurus as well; these are two indispensable tools for any writer. Inexpensive pocket dictionaries work handily for the older child, but the small type and incomplete definitions often confuse grammar school youngsters. You might want to explore some of the titles listed in Appendix C; but, in any case, your child ought to have an illustrated children's dictionary. A good, hardbound adult dictionary should stand on a conspicuous shelf; and you, if for no reason other than to set an example, should refer to that book frequently. A good dictionary returns its investment many times over. Start building correct habits as soon as possible. The thesaurus, a word book that names synonyms, not definitions, helps adolescents and young adults expand their writing vocabulary. Children who suddenly realize its potential love the thesaurus—but it needs careful supervision.

In chapter 7, I will deal more fully with the dictionary and thesaurus as tools for your child's learning.

• **Miscellaneous.** Here are some useful items that allow your child to spell out words and sentences rather than to write them in his or her own handwriting.

• *typewriter.* For ten to fifteen dollars (some are more expensive), a child's plastic typewriter offers an exciting tool for the young writer. Typing letters in upper case, the children's typewriter allows another medium for written expression. If you have only an adult typewriter available, urge your son or daughter to use it under your supervision (most typewriters are sturdy enough to withstand some rough treatment). Type out a few simple words in a sentence or in a question; have your child copy it or respond to it.

• *label makers.* For about two dollars, a label maker allows a child to stamp out words and thoughts on plastic tape. Encourage frequent questions about spelling, however; once the letters are imprinted on the plastic there is no way to erase them.

• *alphabet stamps and stamp pads.* Using a rubber stamp for each letter and a well-inked pad, young children can spell out words and sentences. This provides a physical involvement different from writing. Rubber stamps help teach alphabet recognition. As you help your child decide on some simple things to write, ask her to select the letters, and name them together. The words stamped out on a sheet of paper will spell out your youngster's thoughts.

• *computer word processors.* A whole new world of writing adventure has opened up for young children lucky enough to have computers at home! I'm always amazed at how even five- or six-year-olds feel comfortable enough at a computer keyboard to learn the rudiments of word processing no matter what the hardware or software. Joseph was nine and Saul six when the IBM PC invaded my office, and before long they were showing me the ins and outs of the computer age. We use Volkswriter (Lifetree Software), a rather simple word-processing program with built-in auto tutorial that even computer-anxious reactionaries (give me back my pencil and yellow pad!) like me can learn easily. The two boys regularly create stories and poems on the computer, and it stimulates their interest in writing in ways I never could have imagined.

You also might want to look into one of the sign-making programs like Print Shop (Broderbund Software) and then watch out as signs and labels sprout like mushrooms all over your house. Later in this chapter we'll look at the special role of signs and labels in helping your child build skills and confidence in writing.

Now that you have supplies for your home writer's workshop, here are three simple writing activities you can nurture with ease at home.

"I've Got a Little List"

The shopping list (that instution challenged by the pegboard!) is one of the most accessible writing activities. Children of three or four who know their letters and sounds should be encouraged to add words to the list for the supermarket. For those still learning about the alphabet and the sounds letters make, preparing a shopping list offers painless reinforcement. At the grocery shelf, ask your child to read the word he wrote and to select the item—a can of beans, a bar of soap, or, better, a favorite treat, that brown bag of M&M's or sandwich cookies in cellophane.

In general, lists provide substantial writing practice for any age group. You and your child can prepare a guest list for the next birthday party; a list of toys to take on a visit to Grandma's; a list of favorite foods or best friends; a list of things to do on a special day; a list of clothing to buy for school—the ideas are inexhaustible. As your child grows older, the list can be adapted to his or her own interests and needs: a list of records to buy from the radio shop; a schedule of activities for after school; a list of expenses to keep track of weekly allowance or money earned in baby-sitting.

You may recall that Benjamin Franklin kept lists throughout his life. During his twenties, his project was to arrive at moral perfection, so he listed thirteen virtues that he believed necessary and desirable. He made a little book, giving a page for each of the virtues; and drawing red lines to make columns for each day of the week, he marked with a black spot every fault that he felt he committed in regard to a specific virtue. To people today this plan for moral perfection sounds strangely oversimplified, but list keeping does help bring some order to plans or schemes that we see as important. It works for children as well as for adults.

My view of a parent and three-, four-, or five-year-old working together on a list—the shopping list, for instance—is simple and stress-free. For a child who has not yet mastered the alphabet you, the parent, must write slowly, firmly, and clearly in large letters, saying the letters aloud, then pronouncing the word. Next, ask your child to say the word. If he shows interest, urge him to copy the word onto a separate sheet or directly alongside or below yours. Right now, you are trying to establish positive attitudes, so do not worry too much about undersized or oversized or incorrect or transposed or mixed upper- and lowercase letters. Praise your child's effort before you point out his error.

For a child who has command of the alphabet, a parent also might encourage list writing. A youngster without advanced skills often can write his name, can contribute at least that to the joint list-making venture, even if mother or father has to write all the other words. You might suggest titles that include your child's name, titles looking like these: "Hilary's Favorite Foods" or "Guest List for Matthew's Party" or "Clothes to Buy for Maria." In preparing the list you should ask your child to suggest items, which she should then try to write. If she has a sense of the sounds letters make, encourage her to say words slowly and to try to figure out the letter or combination of letters that make a sound. Give as much help as needed. After an incorrect guess you might say, "Good try! But here the letter *S*, not *C*, makes the sound you want." If your child cannot determine the letter, tell it to her. The goal is to get your child to print an immediate experience in her own writing. Once the word stands out in green or red or blue upon a page, it is your child's own, a word to read and to savor, a word for you to read and to praise.

For your next shopping excursion, let your child make a list of things you both need. Be patient; name the letters to spell the words or word parts your child cannot manage alone. After the two of you prepare the list, read the words together—first your child trying to read his own writing and then you rereading the list. Watch the way her eyes light up as you read your child's words!

Here is a list that my daughter Melissa—at five and a half—and her mother prepared one July afternoon before a vacation trip (the Pampers were for my son Joseph):

GOGGLes PAMPeRS FIX DADDYsWatch
BABYHARNeSSTHONGSFoRMelissa

Busy gathering things together, my wife did not supervise the writing, although she did help name the letters as
Melissa sat at the kitchen table and penciled in the words.
Barbara showed little concern, therefore, for the fact that
words ran together occasionally, or that the words were
not placed under one another as in a more conventional
list. The point is that Melissa wrote the items—many
things she wanted for the beach—in her own handwriting,
and she knew that the writing would lead to a concrete act.
During the shopping trip that followed, Barbara frequently asked "What's the next thing here? Read this for
me," in order further to reinforce the vitality of the writing
experience.

List making won't stop with the preschool years—especially if you convince your child that writing can be a
powerful means to deal with issues in your daily lives.
Case in point: Like many busy families, as the children
grew older we tried to divide up kitchen chores and responsibilities so that the youngsters would share in the
cleanup. "Saul, you set the table"; "Melissa, please clear";
"Joseph, load the dishwasher": Every night the assignment was made with names rotated so that no one felt
unduly burdened. The daily announcements worked for a

little while—and then the bickering began. "I did that last night!" "It's not fair—he always sets and that's the easiest job!" Why don't you make a schedule, Barbara suggested. The kids loved the idea. I'm amused that they didn't reach for a pencil or pen as I would have done instinctively, but instead dashed to my office downstairs, loaded Print Shop on the computer, and produced this list, which now hangs commandingly from a cookie-shaped magnet on our refrigerator.

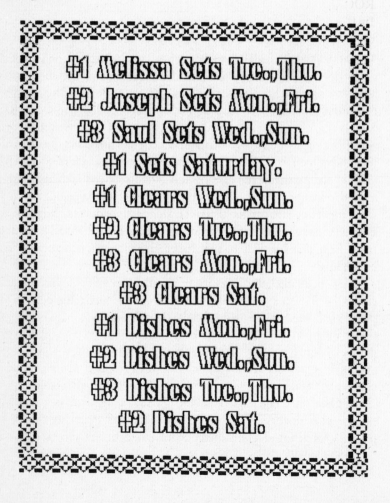

#1 Melissa Sets Tue., Thu.

#2 Joseph Sets Mon., Fri.

#3 Saul Sets Wed., Sun.

#1 Sets Saturday.

#1 Clears Wed., Sun.

#2 Clears Tue., Thu.

#3 Clears Mon., Fri.

#3 Clears Sat.

#1 Dishes Mon., Fri.

#2 Dishes Wed., Sun.

#3 Dishes Tue., Thu.

#2 Dishes Sat.

Keep Out!: A Sign for Room or Door

Another enjoyable and easy writing experience is making a room sign. After books, one of the early contacts the child makes with written language is the printed sign. Long before they read in any formal way, many children can recognize the word STOP in red on the metal octagon near a street corner. Signs such as EXIT, OUT, IN, and even more complex signs like ENTRANCE, CLOSED, MEN'S ROOM make up basic sight vocabulary for many children. In the supermarket, for example, letters scream out SALE or MILK or COOKIES, words that any child can learn to read after some exposure.

If you are eager to expand your child's writing experiences, draw upon the familiar world of signs that surround him. The sign that a child prepares for his room is an indelible mark of his own needs and experiences. Plastic door signs that say *David's Room* or *Jennifer's Room* are available at any five-and-ten, but why buy such a sign when your child can make it himself? A sheet of paper or cardboard (and perhaps some wood backing), a crayon or pencil, a bit of cellophane tape or a thumb tack—*voilà*—there's a sign-making shop right in your own home.

Aside from naming a room as their own, children can use signs to label objects throughout their rooms. *Window, closet, desk, bed* are words that your son or daughter can easily write and affix to a nearby object. Adding the pronoun *my* or your child's name to the sign establishes the object as part of your youngster's own territory. It is *my bed* or *Gloria Liu's closet*. It's no one else's.

Other signs can express your child's preferences for behavior in the room. My five-year-old niece wrote a No Smoking sign for her bedroom door because she hated the smell of the cigarettes her parents would forgetfully smoke in her room.

Your child might also represent an object, in a little drawing, to accompany the words on the sign. In this activity you can guide her in a solid language experience: Your child identifies some object or impression; writes it down on a sign with your help; affixes it somewhere at home; and has constant opportunity to read the words in her own handwriting.

With computer technology your child can make signs of many sizes and designs. Every celebration in our home finds a six- to eight-foot computer banner across the kitchen wall, such as Happy Thanksgiving. I still like this sign that Joseph and Saul made for my office door years back when Print Shop first came to live at our house.

At birthday time for our children one of our rituals is to hang hand-lettered and illustrated birthday messages to start our youngsters on their special day. As the children sleep at night we hang our notes and drawings with masking tape over their beds, on the bedroom door, the bathroom mirror, the place setting at the kitchen table. Melissa is almost eighteen now—she and her brothers are making the birthday messages for each other—and I know that she still loves to see Saul's crayoned robin or bluejay with his silly message "Tweet, tweet, Happy Birdsday." You don't outgrow a loving birthday note written by someone in the family.

Let's Leave a Note

Like a sign in your child's own writing, a handwritten note communicates a personal message. But the note is more detailed communication than a simple sign. In a note your child writes a message for a select audience, usually only one person. Because a note is such a simple form of writing and because it often brings about some action, it is an exciting activity for the youngster.

I am distinguishing a note from a letter because of length and formal elements. Of course, letters and notes often have exactly the same parts—salutation, content, closing, signature. I will take up letters later on; but for now I want to think of a note as a brief message to someone, a message with the specific purpose of giving instructions or information.

A chalkboard in your child's room can provide the field for an interchange of daily notes between you and your child. When Melissa started to show interest in words, my wife would slip into our daughter's room as she slept and would write a little note in yellow chalk: "Dear Melissa, I love you. Love Mommy." One morning we discovered that under those words Melissa had copied parts of the message to yield: "Dear Mommy, I love you. Love Melissa." Well in to Melissa's elementary school grades Barbara continued to write chalkboard notes. A line divided the board horizontally, the bottom half for our daughter's responses.

With a little thought you can establish note writing as a frequent activity at home. The exercise is short enough to engage the attention of young children as well as older ones. Under your supervision, your child can write the note himself, realizing immediate satisfaction from a task successfully performed.

If it is necessary to write a note to a teacher to excuse an absence, why not have your child prepare it? Your youngster can write this note easily, in a sentence or two, with your help:

Dear Mr. Stevens,

> *I was absent on Monday, May 3, because I had a virus.*

> > *Sincerely,*

Here, too, show painstaking patience: Spell letter combinations that your child might not know; help your child say sounds clearly so that she can determine the letters in a word, especially the consonants. You should sign the note under your child's signature; it will give your stamp of approval to your son's or daughter's efforts (as well as your legal approval to the absence), and the teacher will receive a joint project in writing.

You see the idea, of course—any child with some basic alphabet skills can write a brief note. Leave the classic note for the milkman: "No milk today." Leave a message for an older brother or sister: "We went shopping at Sears." Leave a message for a spouse returning from work or from an errand: "We are in the backyard." Instead of leaving a letter for posting in your mailbox, leave a note for the letter carrier: "Please ring bell for letter," and let your child hand over the mail.

As you'll see in more detail later on, the household that clearly links writing with self-expression can encourage children to deal with confused thoughts and feelings and to find acceptable outlets for anger and frustration. One of our guiding principles at home when anyone feels an uncontrollable rush of anger or annoyance is "Write it down!" We have our share of explosions and verbal battles, certainly; but when events push our children to fury's edge they know that doing combat with pencil and paper is a much more acceptable release of feelings than shouting matches or temper tantrums.

Chaim Ginott, the brilliant child psychologist, recommends that youngsters release emotional pressure in private by drawing a picture to express their feelings or by writing about their tumultuous emotions. We endorse this recommendation unhesitatingly with our children. Occasionally, the written piece forces its way into a more public arena. Melissa will write a long note, passionately reviewing her side of an issue that we've disagreed on, or apologizing for a fit of temper. And Saul, at five and a half, suffering a parental injustice that neither my wife nor I can recall now, stomped off to his room one morning, only to sail this missive down the steps:

Parents with imagination can take advantage of the easy success achieved in writing brief messages. Prepare a game to determine the guests' seating plan around the table at your son's or daughter's birthday party (for ages four and up). Seats should be numbered with words, *one, two, three,* and so on, or with numerals, 1, 2, 3 (or both); and, of course, your child will write the words or the numbers, each on a small card to tape on the chair backs. On separate papers (one for each guest) help your child write this message: "Please sit in chair one" (change the number in each note). Fold up the papers. At the party, each guest picks a folded message from a box, matches the word or number in the note with the sign on the seat, and sits down. Aside from the fun at the party, your child has performed a task in writing which, because of its repetitive nature and because of its ability to produce action, is a highly positive creative experience. This is exactly the kind of writing reinforcement you can provide in your home.

When written communication relate to some desired action and achieves some clear result, it asserts an important, valuable aspect of written language in your child's mind.

Writing and Reading, Hand in Hand

Experienced teachers call instruction in reading and writing "language experience" or "language arts" because the two areas, joined with speaking, round out the instructional process language. Although reading skills are beyond the intent of this book, these two areas, writing and reading, are closely related, especially in the initial learning stages. For example, to learn the alphabet, a child looks at the letters and also writes them. Part of being able to recognize a word comes from being able to write it and to read it back; for many people, including adults, the tactile aspect of writing is an indispensable feature of learning. When I teach reading, I try, wherever possible, to use the students' writings. When the context is part of their own lives, students' paragraphs are fertile grounds for building knowledge in reading.

What I'm saying is that practice in writing is a vital part of practice in reading. Underdeveloped readers can advance their skills through the writing process: A child captures an experience in words; he reads back the writing; someone questions comprehension and vocabulary within the framework of that writing activity. Certainly, the youngster needs to read at some time what others write. But in the early stages of language awareness the writing activity is an integral part of reading. When Johnny writes something at home and then reads it aloud you're helping him with two critical skills.

I have focused here on those simple, everyday activities that any parent, without the slightest formal training in how to teach writing, can use to encourage language growth at home. These writing exercises are fun, too, if you follow the approaches outlined here. After all, in building a favorable attitude toward writing, you want to ignore the pains.

3

Experience and Creative Expression

A View of Creative Expression

When Count Leo Tolstoy, the great Russian novelist, explained the meaning of art, he established a critical relation between the writer and the written effort. "To evoke in oneself a feeling one has once experienced," he says, "then by means of movement, lines, colors, sounds, or forms expressed in words, so to transmit that feeling that others experience the same feeling—this is the activity of art." It is no less an expression of the creative written process for a child than for any professional writer.

What does Tolstoy suggest? First, you can see the writer, the artist, as a person who experiences things—an event, a momentary flash of time, an action performed or observed, a thought—things that arouse a feeling in him. The writer stores that experience, that feeling within him, and, in order to solidify it in words, he makes it happen again within himself at some later time.

Well, which children do not feel emotional responses to thousands of moments each day, do not lock those feelings within themselves, feelings rooted in the experiences of daily living? Those responses, the experiences, and the emotions that accompany them are a vital dimension of human existence. Combined, they are the earth from which good writing can blossom forth. Surely, your child shares with Tolstoy the origins of creative written expression. Not every child will write a *War and Peace;* but the raw materials—events and feelings, actions and emotions, experiences and reactions—on these, professional artists have no monopoly. Of course, the quality of the experience and the perception of it vary from person to person. Also, those particular experiences someone selects for storing vary from person to person. Thus, five people may share a common moment, but the perception of it, the depth of emotion it arouses, the permanence of the impression upon the mind and body remain unique in each individual.

In Tolstoy's scheme, the artist remembers the experience of some feeling. Then, his purpose is to transmit that feeling to someone else "by means of movement, lines, colors, sounds, or forms expressed in words."

Do you see the continuum? An experience that registers some feeling in the mind makes its imprint by means of the senses. The sounds, the smells, the colors and actions, the sensations of taste and touch provide the passageways for the emotional experience a person stores as memory. To transmit that experience to someone else he uses language that *conveys* those senses. With Melissa's help. I can represent this scheme visually.

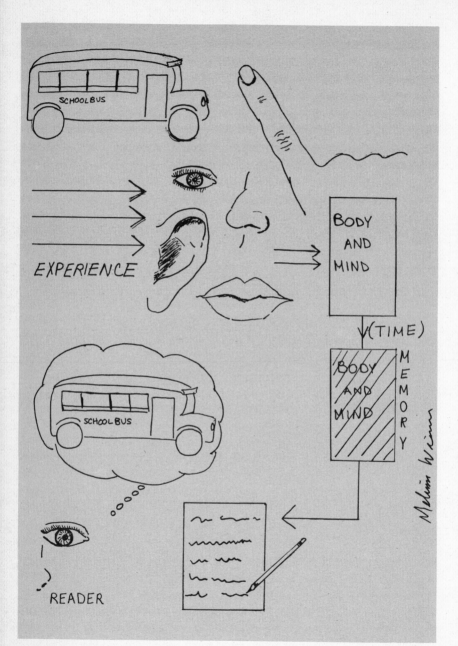

Your child might react to an experience on the school bus, an experience that evokes a feeling and impresses itself upon her mind. The paths the experience travels are the senses. Through the responses of eyes and nose, of hand and ears and mouth the moment registers. The experience takes on special qualities as it remains in storage. When your daughter translates this stored experience into written words, she conveys through language, as best she can, the same sensory responses that aroused her reaction in the first place.

In finding the right language to portray that experienced emotion, there are wide differences from person to person. There's no promise here that in developing as a writer your son or daughter will capture the artistic skills of a Willa Cather, a Thomas Wolfe, a Leo Tolstoy. There is a promise, though, that given his or her own strengths in confronting daily life and in the use of language, your child can grow and experience success.

Autobiography: A Child's Experience

Going through life, as most children do, with a normal set of sense organs—going through life, *alive*, really—assures a range of experiences and emotions that mark the mind and heart. By using words daily, children develop an endless reserve of language, poised to record feelings, thoughts, and events on paper. A child who looks at his mother rushing off to work in a whirl of red and blue and waving good-bye from the doorway; a child who hears the beep of a horn, the squawk of a jay, the scream of thunder; a child who feels sand burn her fingers, who presses a snowflake to her cheek; a child who smells trout frying or breathes in the scent of pine or the sea or fumes from a bus on a summer morning, that's your child. And that's a writer waiting to grow.

You can tell that the focus here on written expression suggests a different sense of "creative writing" from the usual one. Many people (especially teachers, for some reason) mean "imaginative" writing when they say "creative." Often in assigning imaginative writing, a teacher asks a child to record some pretend situation. I have read about "My Voyage with Columbus" or "What It's Like to Travel in Outer Space." It's not that I have complaints about imaginative writing (I'll describe some enjoyable activities of that sort later on) as *one* part of the developing writer's program. But to stress it at the expense of writing about personal experience is to turn away from the basic stuff of creativity.

A better synonym for creative writing is "autobiography." Those countless moments in an individual's life— brief, intense stretches of time—stud a child's day and glitter in the mind like diamonds long after the moments pass. By recalling those moments of experience through sensory language—specific, exact, sharply drawn—the young writer can practice the vital skills of writing. So, when I speak of creative writing, I shall mean "autobiographical," my basic philosophy being that you should mine the riches of experiences in every child's world, riches for the pen or pencil to transform into record.

The Parent Sets the Stage

The parents set the stage in the home for children to share their experiences comfortably, and without fear, ridicule, or criticism. This sharing begins with speaking. You need to encourage the youngster, without prying, to talk about moments he wishes to share. "What did you do at school today?" "What did you do outside?" "Who did you talk to on the bus?" Questions like these will start things off. Such talking sessions will provide a pressure valve for the complex events in your child's life as he grows older. In homes where children feel free to examine their experiences, deep, underlying questions and problems can surface in the course of easy conversation. Sadly, in many homes there is not even a possibility for interchange about daily experiences. I hope that you'll find time to read my book *Talk with Your Child* (1988). In it I lay out a home program of regular conversations between parents and children— conversation that builds essential language and reading skills.

If you've tried talking sessions with your youngsters, you know that you can sometimes draw a blank. You might get a one-word response: "Nothing" or "Nobody" or "No." Or, you might get a brief answer without much substance: "I had a fight with Johnny"; "We drew pictures"; "Lisa showed me a frog"; "Mrs. Harris showed us an experiment." What do you do then?

Draw out the details. Ask your child to flesh out the story in his or her own language. First show your interest, framing questions whose answers will draw out the experience and its emotions in your child's language. "A fight!" you might say. "Where did it happen? What about? You must tell me all about it!" or "Well, I can't remember when I saw a frog last! What did it look like? What sounds did it make?" Taking cues from your child's narrative, you can ask occasional questions. Show great concern for the details, especially those that demand your child's recall of the sensory experience; ask questions to elicit those details. You want to know about colors, about sounds that objects make, about movements and actions, smells and touch sensations, about the exact words people say. Ask when events took place—afternoon, morning, before lunch, at recess—because the question will help your child's inner eye to focus upon the moment awaiting language. Even the youngest child thrills in giving these details, and with a little encouragement will even act out responses. A child who hops about the room with glee when asked how a frog moves would earn my applause; and then I would ask, "How would you tell someone who couldn't see you just how it moves?" I'd hope to hear "He hops" or "He flip-flops" or "He bounces." What solid, sharp actions! If I heard "He moves" or "He walks," I'd reach out for more exact words. In later chapters, I'll talk about ways to develop precise language.

As soon as your child can speak about experiences, you'll want to begin this kind of creative questioning. At two or three or four years, your child begins to sharpen the powers of observation that are so critical to effective writing. An awareness of sensory detail is one of the essential skills you can help your child to develop. Later as a young man or young woman he or she will learn of other kinds of details—quotations from reliable people, statistics from reputable sources, case studies, paraphrases from books or magazines—and will adapt these new details easily to an already established pattern in development ideas.

Mothers and Fathers as Storytellers

If your child does not readily communicate the details of a particular moment, you yourself must turn storyteller. In this way you can take pressure off your child, who may feel suddenly intimidated by your request—no matter how gentle—for the story. Sometimes the emotions evoked by an experience arouse more pain when we recall it than it did when it happened. Back off. Tell your way story, alive in action and setting. "So you saw a fight, too! Well, I saw two men screaming at each other this afternoon, right in front of McDonald's. The rain had turned everything wet and sticky. Well, a man backed his Chevy into a new white Oldsmobile. Then a teenager in a plaid shirt leaped out of the Olds and slammed the door. 'Why don't you watch where you're going, you old goat!' he boomed. 'You little dummy,' the driver of the Chevy screamed from behind the steering wheel. 'Why did you park in front of the hydrant?' Fortunately, a police officer strode up to settle things before they got ugly!" As you speak, call up your own dramatic energies, changing voices to show how people talk, lacing the tale with whatever excitement, or sadness, or joy it might evoke. In this kind of telling, concrete details set an example for your child to share similar experiences. Name places and people (where you can) carefully. Use words that suggest clear actions. Name colors and sounds and use words for touch sensations. These stories establish a framework and act as models for your child. By supporting the value of your child's experience, you will help remove an impediment to writing I see every day in the classroom: "Nothing interesting ever happens to me" or "I have nothing to write about."

If you need a formula for the kind of atmosphere that leads to effective writing, it is: speak-listen-write. Remember: experience is the heart of creative expression.

4

Pictures, Words, and Sentences:
LAYING FOUNDATIONS

Words and the Young Artist

Your child's early attempts at conveying sensory impressions spread out as splashes of line and color on a page. In crayon, pencil, or ink youngsters portray a vision of reality unique to their perceptions and their talents. At first the scribbles and scrawls, the wide arcs, the concentrations of design propose a shapeless landscape of color and texture; then, bit by bit, the components fit together into some partially recognizable whole. There you see a bird with an oversized wing, a beak like a broomstick, one leg; here stands a house, next to a child who is twice as large as the building and spectacular for the arm shooting from her

36

neck. Next, in a sunburst of light and swirls of red, yellow, green, orange, and gold, a creature looks at you gloomily from crossed eyes. If your child has easy access to the tools of writers and artists, the scrawls will fill numerous pages, and you'll probably run out of space to hang these little gems. But in how many drawings—especially those created by your two- and three-year-olds—can you actually name the general intent of the artwork, to say nothing of its specific parts?

When, with a flourish, your young artists present their latest works, you have another opportunity to put into practice the principles I outlined earlier, the speak-listen-write approach to creative expression. Don't be one of those parents who, afraid of hurting the child's feelings, only praises and never ventures a "What is it?" Of course, the way in which you ask the question will determine the nature of the response. But asked without impatience and without a suggestion that your child is either wrong or untalented, a "What is it?" often unlocks a glorious stream of narrative, filled with colors and sounds and glimpses of action that only a child can see. Questions that show interest and urge a solid attention to details will help your child sustain the narration and increase the delight you can harvest from the moment. "Why is this boy bending over?" "Where's the driver of that bus?" "Why are there no leaves on that oak tree?" Listen carefully to the responses. Never chide your child for not portraying a person or an object in an expected way. Here in the explanation of a picture, your child is sharing an event that marked his consciousness. A youngster's pictures and stories offer snapshots of the child's vision and psychology. Trained counselors can learn a good deal about a child's personality—his problems, talents, fears, and successes—from the pictures that he draws. For you the pictures are yet another starting point for writing activities.

Pictures and Words: Making Connections

In these little talks about some drawing, you establish a critical connection between the picture and the word as means to convey experience. Probably you have begun to make captions on your child's artistic efforts with a word or two. Like sign making, activity, this helps to reinforce her reading skills. As you write the word *house* or *girl* or *bicycle* above or below the object, you help your youngster to build her sight vocabulary. You also establish the need for written language early in the communication process. At first, you go ahead and write the words (just one or two for each picture, no more), asking your child to letter just below yours. Later on, when your child knows the letters, encourage her to write the word as she speaks it, helping her with the sounds.

Ultimately your daughter or son will connect picture and word. You'll notice, after a while, that your child will add labels of her own. The degree of correctness for the three-, four-, and five-year-old is not of much concern here. Your first reaction to your child's own attempts at lettering a word should be to offer praise. Read the word or words your youngster writes. She'll love to hear your voice reading it. If you can't read the word, ask your child to read it for you. If the letters are way off target, after praising the effort say something like, "I see what you *tried* to write, but your letters are not quite right. Let me show you how to write that word." With your child's permission, print carefully on the picture (otherwise use a separate sheet of paper). Then ask your youngster to write the word from your model and to read it from her own writing.

But if the words that your child attempts, despite errors, convey their message clearly, hang the picture up without fussing over correctness. Remember, you're still building positive attitudes toward writing as a means of self-expression. Don't make your child self-conscious about errors at this stage. You're going to have to use your judgment here—when to make suggestions about correctness and when to say nothing. But, on the whole, for the preschool youngster your basic goal is to establish positive attitudes. Once your child knows that words convey meaningful aspects of experience, correctness has a real purpose.

Look at this marvelous birthday gift my son Joseph made for me several years back.

With perfect phoenetic skill, Joseph captured the sounds in each word he wrote. Despite the fidelity to spoken English, apparently Joseph's words do not all follow the conventions of our spelling system. *Tropakl* and *tangck* are marvelously inventive orthographics, aren't they? Still, you can bet that some first grade teacher would have her red pencil all over them in a flash! The advantage in being the parent of a young writer (as opposed to the teacher) is that you can adore the intent and ignore the mistakes as you will. In fact this was no time to call attention to misspellings. It was hugging time. After a lengthy display in our home art gallery—the kitchen refrigerator door—the scene hung in my office for a long time. I could tell how Joseph delighted in seeing his work beside me. By now, fear not, he knows how to spell *tropical fish in a tank*. Now he maintains a tropical fish collection in a twenty-gallon tank in his bedroom. That drawing signaled an early interest in the underwater landscape.

As I suggested earlier, a drawing and the words that expand and enrich its meaning can provide an outlet for your child's concerns. When we decided to sell our Long Island house, we greeted an endless stream of possible buyers. Our daughter, Melissa, then not yet in kindergarten, tried to represent the event in a drawing and words:

In talking with her about the picture, my wife and I learned that she had not really understood what selling a house meant. "Who will sleep in my bed when they buy the house? May I take my toys?" Melissa asked. We tried to clear up her misunderstandings, which might have smoldered unnecessarily. Of course, in the words she wrote we paid no attention to the errors (those vowel combinations plague children straight through the fifth and sixth grades). We praised Melissa's independent efforts, grateful to talk about a problem our daughter revealed through pictures and words.

Accent on Sentence Sense

As soon as you feel that your son or daughter has a reasonable sense of letters and sounds (this sense can begin as early as three, depending upon the exposure to language and alphabet skills), you want to encourage your child to use full sentence captions. Though the one- or two-word statement may have value as a label it is insufficient in establishing the range of information that a sentence can offer. A sentence names a subject, certainly; but it also tells what that subject is doing or what is being done to that subject. It communicates a series of details that expand and alter a basic idea.

The earlier you can help your child establish a "sentence sense," the fewer the problems in complete expression later on. One of the major writing errors that start early and persist well into college themes is the production of incomplete sentences. Though later chapters will explore correctness more fully, I want to spend a little time here in considering sentence sense. I don't think children in school receive enough attention in this area of their writing development.

Research into language patterns over the last few years indicates (believe it or not) that when people speak, they usually do speak complete and complex sentences. This idea challenges old notions that spoken language often lacks correct grammatical form. The very young child, of course, communicates in words and clusters of words that frequently lack the formal elements of correct sentences. But once a youngster feels comfortable with spoken language, you'll be impressed with his ability to form what we call "grammatical" sentences, sentences generally complete in their construction. One of my colleagues tells her students that they are incredible sentence machines, that they know grammar much better than they think they do. This knowledge can help you establish an approach at home: Don't assume that your child cannot construct complete sentences, because all evidence suggests that he can.

You are not trying to teach him what he already knows. But you will attempt to offer practice in *writing* complete sentences so that your child extends his speaking skill to the page and develops a sixth sense for *written* grammatical language. Despite a child's ability to speak grammatical sentences, writing complete ideas with correct punctuation can turn into a game of chance, and the sentence becomes something permanent, which the immature writer shudders to change.

Of course, in daily speech both children and adults frequently use incomplete sentences:

> "Hi, Margarita!"
> "Hi, Beverly. Where's your brother?"
> "Sick in bed."
> "Why?"
> "Oh, nothing terrible. Just a bad cold."
> "Too bad."
> "Yeah. No football practice."

In the dialogue above, one can argue that there is only one complete sentence: "Where's your brother?" Part of the very nature of spoken communication—its speed, its demand for immediate response, its request for action, its dependency upon questions—insists upon fragmentary utterances. Certainly, there's nothing *wrong* with speaking in fragments as part of everyday conversation.

The interesting thing, however, is that not many fragments on children's papers resemble those you might hear in daily speech. The fragment I see most often is one in which the writer has lopped off an incomplete unit from a complete one. He's cut off a dog's tail and is telling everyone that it's a dog too. Some people contend that a child's writing contains many incomplete ideas because he is used to hearing speech fragments, but I've not seen enough proof of that to convince me.

When children begin to read, they will be exposed to incomplete sentences in written language. The signs that surround them—*Exit, No Smoking, Sale*—though clear enough to convey information, are not complete sentences. In their attempts to catch the eye quickly and to sear an idea or a product into the mind, newspaper and magazine ads scream out "Newest, fastest way to order"; "Value event"; "Right now . . . Movie Flights to Florida Only on Airline X." This stylistic use of fragments undoubtedly makes an impression on inexperienced writers. Certainly newspaper headlines and magazine ad copy read like the kinds of incomplete sentences I have seen on children's papers.

In spite of their abundant use in our spoken and written language, fragments do not earn respect as examples of correct and mature writing. One of the certain ways for your high-school- or college-aged son or daughter to fail an English course is to write essays that contain sentence fragments! Teaching students how and why to avoid sentence fragments and how to correct them are a teacher's constant chore in the classroom.

Parents should encourage children to speak about their own pictures and, through questioning, invite them to express whole thoughts in full-sentence responses. When a child's statement does not name a person or an object; when it does not tell what that person or object is doing, ask for more information. I know that questions by their very nature invite incomplete responses; and I know it's perfectly legitimate to speak in fragments—everyone does it and gets along fine in communicating ideas. I suggest, however, that we prod our children to speak complete sentences. This is not to tell them they're doing something *wrong*, but to provide them with speech models that they can use later in writing. For this reason, good teachers, knowing the value of the complete sentence, insist on oral responses that express complete thoughts: I don't think that enough teachers pursue this goal vigorously. Also, a good part of their students' lack of attention often stems from the teacher's poor questioning techniques. Too often teachers ask questions whose answer can be only *yes* or *no*. When teachers do this, they prevent children from making sustained responses.

Avoiding Bits and Pieces

In grade schools, on bulletin boards, in hallways, in rooms, in scrapbooks made by children, and on notebook pages, you often can see incomplete statements accompanying illustrations. I once saw a beautiful series of Bible pictures that were drawn and colored by children. Each picture included a few words about the illustration and when hung alongside one another they told the story of Joseph and the coat of many colors. The drawback was that some of those captions were sentence fragments. For example, the words above a picture of wonderful brown camels laden with packs and accompanying men in red, green, and yellow robes read: "Going across the desert." That's not a full sentence! There is no subject. It doesn't tell who is making the journey. Nor do we have the words *are* or *were* to accompany *going*, words required to make the sentence grammatically correct. I could determine the missing details by looking at the picture, but the necessary information to structure the sentence correctly should appear in the caption. Furthermore, from the lower grades on, students are taught that all sentences start with a capital and end with a period. By putting a capital letter *G* on the word *going* and a period after *desert,* the teacher reinforces the student's incorrect belief that this fragment is a compelte sentence.

Now you may argue that a statement accompanying a child's picture is a title and as such does not need a complete sentence. If so, then the title should have capital letters for the beginning of each major word: "Going Across the Desert."

Certainly, it is important to learn to write titles for pictures, paragraphs, and, later on, stories and essays. It's a good starting point, as I have illustrated, for young writers. However, in our attempts to develop skills, title writing often does more harm than good. By its fragmentary nature, a title does not encourage sentence completeness as a key element in clear writing. Inexperienced writers often use titles unwisely. Instead of using the title as an invitation to read on, a young writer will often depend on it as a part of the composition itself. For example, in a piece called "My Saddest Morning," a child may begin his first paragraph, "It all happened one day last June." Instead of establishing the point of the essay in the writing itself, the young writer refers immediately to the title.

I am suggesting that you move your child away from those one- or two-word titles. When he or she begins writing words to accompany pictures, encourage the preparation of a complete statement. You can look at a picture such as the "House for Sale" illustration on page 40 and say, "Whose house is this that's for sale?"

"Ours."

"See if you can speak a sentence that tells what your picture is trying to show."

You may very well get: *Our house is for sale* or *This is our house for sale* or *We are selling our house*. If you do, with your child's permission, write the sentence directly on the drawing. Say the words as you print them; then encourage your child to say the words. Better still, help her write the sentence herself. If you do not get a sentence response at all, *you* offer the sentence.

Another way to help children develop skills in speaking and writing full sentences is to remind them to use words from your question in a response. When you say, "What is this a picture of?" about an illustration and the response is "A house," you can say, "Come on, Beverly. This time use a whole sentence. Use some of my words if you want to. Let's try again. What is this a picture of?" You might hear, "This is a picture of a house." No matter how impatiently the child offers that complete thought, praise it, and get it on paper!

I worked this way with my daughter, Melissa, on her little stick drawing of a park (she was barely three and a half for this one).

When I asked her what the picture was, she answered, "A park." (The picture really did become clearer when she pointed out the seesaw on the left, the child on the slide next to it, the big girl and little girl on the swings, the ball, and the sandbox.) Using the kinds of questions I have mentioned I managed to get the complete sentence: "This is a park." With my help over the rough spots, Melissa wrote the sentence herself. She printed in all capitals, so I didn't mention that a capital letter should open a sentence. But I did call attention to the period at the end. All through her elementary school years she loved making that dot at the end of a sentence!

Imagine my delight in seeing this independent effort of Melissa's before her fourth birthday. For days, she questioned me about her imminent annual visit to the doctor because it included, as she recalled from her last birthday checkup, a fingerprick for blood testing. I comforted her as best I could but, as usual, she needed to work this one out for herself. On the morning of the visit I found her at her desk with this before her:

At first I thought she had jumbled some letters together. But she explained: "I took my baby to the doctor and she was sad. The doctor wrote on his pad 'Do not be sad' and gave it to her. So she felt better."

The point I made earlier, that creative effort can provide a pressure valve for a child, a means of confronting and working out pressures, fears, and doubts, certainly holds true in this drawing and its supporting language (notice the line under each eye in the figure on the left—tears!). Although the words run together without space between them, they spell out a sentence. Correct vowels do *not* appear, except in one case. This happens because the vowel, alone or in combination, offers such a wide variety of sound possibilities that it is troublesome to a child. In some words the vowel has no sound at all but serves merely as a bridge between other letters.

Despite its problems, this picture and sentence stand as an independent effort by a three-year-old. I want to point out what I see as its strongest features: First, the letters representing consonants are all correct: *d, n, t, b, s, d*. Next, the words offer a full sentence. Without regular exposure to sentence sense, Melissa might have penciled *happy* over the left picture and *sad* over the right. However, she revealed the fullness of the experience she was attempting to convey in the sentence she wrote. Here, in a nutshell, are all the possibilities for an entire narrative. If I wanted to help Melissa expand the picture and sentence into a paragraph, this production would offer lively results.

But the most remarkable quality of this creation is that it suggests that Melissa at almost four can use written language to communicate experience. Here the sentence works along with the picture, acting as a commentary on it. No simple labeling of parts in a drawing, the written statement through language goes beyond the limits of visual representation. As you work with your young writers, you want to make them aware of the power of words and sentences to capture time, thought, and emotion.

Scissors, Paste, and Sentences

Whenever you can, try to encourage your sons and daughters to write sentences that tell the ideas behind the pictures they have made. I have talked about drawings because they often grow from a child's spontaneous doodling. More formal attempts, such as finger painting, watercolors, and cut-and-paste creations, are also good starting points for written language, especially for a child who draws reluctantly or too self-consciously.

Every child enjoys cutting pictures out of newspapers and magazines and then pasting these cutouts on sturdy paper to make collages. Encourage this activity. "Why don't you cut out the prettiest room you can find?" or "Cut out as many pictures of red things as you can" or "Go through the magazine and cut out the things you find that start with the *b* sound." After your child completes his artistic effort, listen for a sentence response to your "What is it?" question and try to get your youngster's verbal statement on paper. He can pencil the letters himself, or you can do it. The point here is talking about the picture. Help your child construct a full sentence underneath his work: "This is a large happy room" or "These things are all red" or "All these things start with *b*." You can relate this activity to holidays, seasons or months of the year, parties or celebrations, special events at home or at school.

As your child grows older, the possibilities for relating visual and written communication expand. Pamela, one of my students, submitted an exciting photo essay to me. She cut pictures out of magazines and mounted each one in an order she had determined. She placed the photos in a sturdy binder and wrote a title on the cover: "Life in Harlem's Ghetto." Each picture captured a moment of Harlem, its humor, anguish, ugliness, and delight. The assignment required only the visual component. Later on I intended to ask the students to write about their pictures.

But Pamela needed immediately to clarify the meaning of the picture. On the back of each photograph she wrote an explanation. For a picture of buildings blanketed in smoke and showing tangled hoses stretching like tentacles from fire trucks she wrote: "Buildings are so ruined and just get burned down." In another photograph a boy of twelve or thirteen with a wide gash in his forehead stood beside a police officer, who gripped the boy's plaid jacket. The caption way "Some rob, steal, and kill to make it." The last picture in the sequence shows a man in a leather jacket on a rainy night. He sits like a heap of junk in a wire refuse pail on a nameless Harlem street corner. Pamela's caption reads "Loneliness, problems, depression, lost, 'I can't seem to find the way out.' "

I recommend the photo essay as a wonderful activity for parent and child on a rainy afternoon. It's the kind of creative play that, once begun, can hold a boy's or girl's interest for a while. First talk about some overriding theme for the project—"violence in the city," "spring is here," "Christmas is a happy time"—and then suggest that your child write one sentence expressing the main idea of each picture. If you have an old tin box of family pictures, or if you encourage your youngsters to use cameras to take their own photographs or slides, this creation will be great fun.

Seeing the Skill Advance

Once you help your child rely upon full sentences to convey information, you will, no doubt, observe some interesting things. First your youngster will want to squeeze more and more verbal information into one sentence. If she does, you can suggest using two or three sentences rather than stringing together ideas with "ands." Here, five-year-old Melissa prints two thoughts in separate sentences.

THIS IS A SWimming Lesson.
I WAS AFRAID TO GO
UNDER FOR PENNIES.

Lots of activity fills this picture: two children standing (Melissa on the right, she insists, because *she's* wearing the bikini); a lifeguard in the middle, one child in a facedown float. Our question-and-answer session led to the first sentence; it tells the basic idea of the drawing. The second sentence is rather complex and describes the most important detail, from Melissa's point of view. She eagerly wrote

the sentences you see (I helped with spelling and working
out sounds); but she quickly lost interest and rushed off to
play. Had she remained, I would have helped her turn
other parts of the picture into sentences that build a narrative. Later on you'll see how a similar drawing can set
the ground plan for a more sustained writing effort.

Five-year-old Katie Halper presented this charming
sketch to her mother, Nora, who talked with her daughter
about it at length. As Katie dictated, Mom wrote the story
of the picture on separate paper.

Look at the happy friends. Anna leans on me and smiles. I smile too. She's like a little sister.

It's interesting to note that a child who learns to use sentences early and to rely upon sentences as the key means of conveying information soon tends to subordinate pictures to verbal expression, rather than the other way around. Earlier, I showed how a child tries to convey his messages through pictures, and how you can help build sentences from the pictorial elements. Now look at parts of a little book made by five-year-old Matthew. He tells his story in sentences but draws only one page of illustration. First he writes, "Matthew and Rachel can run." On the next page he states, "Matthew can run faster than Rachel." The next two facing pages look like this:

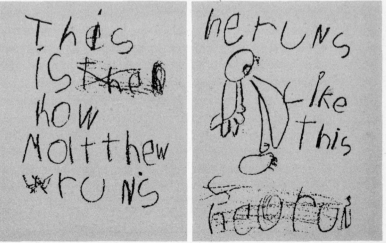

Matthew's drawing supplements his writing. We cannot tell just what special features of his running the picture tries to show, but clearly he sees the picture as a way to demonstrate some action or event for which he does not have words. As you talk about your child's picture, you can help your youngster move from a *drawn* description of a story to a *verbal* description in writing.

Your child will learn to use words to create written snapshots of actions, events, and details.

5

The Senses at Play:
IMAGES AS BUILDING BLOCKS

Sense Words Up Front

I'd like to tell you how you can help your child develop sensory language in order to create word pictures.

You'll need the following definitions: *Sense words* or *sensory language* or *sensory detail* mean words that convey sense impressions: sound, smell, sight (color and action), touch, and taste. Words like *boom* or *whisper*, *musty* or *piney*, *squirm* or *leap*, *orange* or *violet*, *hard* or *wet*, *sweet* or *salty* appeal to the reader's senses. For some of the senses it's a simple matter to find word equivalents for real sensations. Perhaps sound is the easiest to capture because our language has many words for naming sounds—not only words like *shout* and *explode* and *cough* (words for sounds) but also words that make the sounds they name, like *woosh* and *buzz* and *bark* and *click*. Words for color and action similarly fill the language, as do words for touch sensations, though to a lesser degree. Words that name smells are less abundant, and those for taste sensations are the least available.

When I speak of *concreteness*, I mean the degree to which a word names, specifically, the thing it represents.

It's clear among those three word choices which is most specific: plant, flower, rose. *Plant* names a large and very general group. *Flower* narrows the group by excluding vegetables, nonflowering shrubs, many trees, vines, weeds, and so on. But *rose* is the most exact of the words, the most "concrete," the word that has the sharpest visual quality. Write *flower* and readers need to make their own choices—one person sees a daisy, one a chrysanthemum, another a tulip. Good writers want readers to form exact visual connections, to see things precisely in the way the writers see them. They do not want to allow readers their own selections. After all, it's the *writer's* experience and vision that must be conveyed.

When a writer expands upon a single word to heighten its specificity, I call that *concrete sensory detail*. By using highly specific sensory language a writer can intensify the picture-taking quality of words. Look at the levels of concreteness in these three attempts at word pictures:

1	2	3
a rose	a yellow rose	a dry yellow rose drooping in a crystal vase

In 1, the writer has avoided the word *flower* or some other general word to limit the visual impression somewhat, but the word *rose*, nonetheless, lacks detail. The reader has an incomplete picture. In 2, the picture expands with a single appeal to the sense of sight: *Yellow* identifies one color only. (After reading 1, how many of you saw a *red* rose?) Yet in 3 the most complete word picture appears: *dry* names a sensation of touch; *drooping* puts forth a clear, specific sight impression; *crystal vase* sets a location, and the word *crystal* offers an appeal to sight, even touch, if you consider the bumps and lines that mark the surface of such a container.

Through the power of concrete sensory detail the *image* asserts itself. An image is a picture in words, a language snapshot alive in sensory appeal. A successful image creates a clear and exact scene in the mind, leaving no doubt about the author's intent. Smells, sounds, and sensations of touch and taste are just as essential as the visual dimension when advancing specific details of an *image*. It's possible to take the concrete word picture in 3 and expand it into an image of even more concreteness:

> In a shadow on the dresser sat a dry yellow rose, drooping in a crystal vase.

A writer who is aiming to capture the essence of a place or an event could expand that sentence to a few sentences, a paragraph, or to several pages, each line striving for sharp images. For example:

> He stood at the edge of her bedroom, the scent of her everywhere, lonely and troubled. He knew her by the smell: a whiff of lemon soap; and then in a winter draft from the window above the bed, perfume, chill and sharp, all the scents from the bottles on the silver tray mixing, suddenly, then vanishing. "Carol?" He coughed, its echo stealing off swiftly. As he stepped into the room a thick, sweet taste coated his tongue, something determined, yet frail and fading. And there, there in a shadow on the dresser sat a dry yellow rose, drooping in a crystal vase.

Joseph Conrad, a master of sensory detail and one of the best English novelists, shows how imagery is basic to a writer's purpose; in the preface to *The Nigger of the Nar-*

cissus (1897) he writes: "My task which I am trying to achieve is, by the power of the written word to make you hear, to make you feel—it is before all, to make you *see.* That—and no more, and it is everything." In its intent to present something exactly as the writer perceives it, the image rich in concrete sensory detail is everything indeed.

Children are awake to the sensory world; they respond to it, they store images of it long before learning the language to recall it from memory. When naming things for your toddler, right from the start, you must try to find the exact word for an object; *le seul mot juste* as Balzac would say. When reaching out and touching a *leaf,* your child should hear that word along with *flower* or *plant.* Your child should hear your say *robin* or *sparrow* as well as *bird* when he or she hears and sees the flap of wings outside the window. As you help your youngster of five or six to write the word for an object in a picture, search for the most precise expression: *elm, bakery, Park Road, skirt* all name more specifically than *tree, building, street,* or *clothing.* In writing there is a magic to naming—especially proper names—that involves the reader instantly: *Cricklewood Drive, Kings Highway, Hout's Department Store, Grand Central Station* weave a spell that *street, highway, department store,* and *train station* cannot.

Four Writing Games and Variations

After early writing activities like the ones I discussed in previous chapters, you should encourage the use of specific language by using some of the following games at home. Children of seven, eight, and older can play these games.

• **The "What's the Best Word?" Game.** The purpose of this activity is to pick a word that most *exactly* names an object—a real object or the picture of one in a magazine. For example, you might say, "Okay, Maria, let's play a word game. I'll point to something in your room and say two words. You tell which word names exactly what the thing is. Ready? *Furniture. Desk.*" Ask her to explain the choice, though it might be a while before she can communicate to you the notion of "general" or "specific." Help your child see that a word such as *furniture* can mean many different things and that *desk* names much more precisely what the object is. Here are some other word groups that move from the general to the specific. Expand the group to three as your childs skills advance.

	I	II	III
1.	fruit	apple	
2.	toy	top	
3.	room	kitchen	
4.	cereal	oatmeal	
5.	book	dictionary	
6.	food	vegetable	carrot
7.	liquid	drink	milk
8.	vehicle	automobile	jeep
9.	meat	beef	hamburger
10.	medicine	pill	aspirin

This is not an easy game, but it's worth your efforts. Even though writing is not involved at this point, your child begins to learn that written language should strive to be as exact as possible. When your child wants to write, scramble the groups, adding where you can, and ask your youngster to copy the words in order, starting with the most general and going to the most exact:

food
↓
vegetable
↓
carrot

Ask your child to draw the most specific item to reinforce the precision of the wor1 you're stressing. For *food*, there are too many possibilitie ; for *vegetable* a choice, too; only *carrot* gives the specific clue to the reader. If you have time to make a separate index card for each word, ask your child to arrange the cards consecutively, putting the most specific item last.

An easier variation of this game is to make a list of some general objects (such as *furniture, flower, tree, candy, book, drink, jewelry, toy*) and as you read them one at a time, ask your child to write a specific example or two for each. Show how to do the first one to avoid confusion, and help sound out and spell the words.

Writing each general object on a separate card allows you or some other person (perhaps another child) to play along. Read one item and have your child write a more specific word; then your youngster will read the general word and you write down the example.

• **The "Name the Action" Game.** Words for actions also name with varying degrees of exactness. You want to help your child see how some words capture actions more exactly than others. This is partly a vocabulary-building activity; but children of all ages have at their command language that names action. Words such as *walk* and *move* can be replaced by much clearer verbs: *Run, hop, hurry, trip,* are just a few. I put the verb *to be* in all its forms—*is, was, were, are, am*—first on a list of culprits that offer especially weak pictures. These words are essential to any vocabulary, but powerful writing never overuses them. Some others on the list are *go, get, have, begin, seems, appears*—for every one of these a word with a more clearly named action will improve the visual connection.

Use your child's innate ability with action language to set up some "Name the Action" games. This one is fun for groups of children: On separate slips of paper write the words for precise actions: *skip, dance, hop, wiggle, jump, drag, crawl, tumble,* and others. Fold the papers and put them in a shoe box or hat. A child chooses a slip from the box and reads the word silently. You can help out in a whisper, if necessary. The child then moves across the room and tries to perform the action the word suggests as the other children try to guess the word and write it down. This game works very well even with much older children where the vocabulary is more difficult: *amble, stroll, zip, zigzag, slink, steal.* With this game you also can teach your child that some words mean the same thing on the surface but have different qualities. For example, *flee, race,* and *hurry* all mean *to run,* yet each one brings to mind a special idea. *Flee* suggests escape; *race* makes one think of a sport; and *hurry* implies the need to meet a deadline.

• **The "Build an Image" Game.** This game develops your child's skill at expanding an image by adding details. Start with simple words that add to the sensory appeal of an object, then move to building sentences of highly concrete detail.

Examine one word at a time, helping your child build images in several stages, beginning with the name of an object. You can do it in three columns:

1.	2.	3.
Word	**Add a Color**	**Add a Touch Word**
sweater	green sweater	green woolen sweater
table	brown table	hard brown table
sink		
rug		
apple		

If necessary, help your child add the words in columns 2 and 3. Of course, you can vary the column headings for different kinds of sensory details:

Word	Add a Smell or Touch	Add a Sound or Color
apple	cold apple	cold crunchy apple

Your child shouldn't pile up descriptive words in front of the object; two or three are enough. Later on, introduce a model such as this one, but encourage the use of descriptive words before and after the object:

Word	Add Color or Other Sight Word	Add a Touch Word	Add a Sound or Smell or Action in a Group of Words
pencil	yellow pencil	smooth yellow pencil	smooth yellow pencil *racing across a page*
sparrow	brown sparrow	cold brown sparrow	cold brown sparrow *peeping on the roof*
orange	wrinkled orange	dry wrinkled orange	dry wrinkled orange *with a bitter smell*

Above, the words in italics add sensory details to the image; but the details do not cluster in front of the object being described. In the first two groups, the added details start with a word ending in *ing*. In the third group, *with* is a position word that shows relationships (called a *preposition* in grammatical terms) and opens the describing group. If you show them examples, eight- or nine-year-olds should have little trouble following instructions like these: "Now, before you put anything in this last column, try to add the information by beginning with a word that ends in *ing*, for example, *laughing*, *dancing*, or *peeping*." Or, "Let's add the details by beginning with a word, such as *with*, *on*, *by*, *near*, or *in*." Make sure that you provide details to fit the object if your child has any question about it—not all words lend themselves to these kinds of describing elements.

After your child has done five or six examples, have him select one and illustrate it on a separate page, writing the description above or below the picture he makes.

Examples are important here. Whenever your youngster practices writing, try to show what someone else wrote about the same thing. That will let your child see how easy or difficult the task is. I've included numerous models in this book, which you can show your children. These examples have been written by young writers like your sons and daughters.

The image games I just described are muscle builders, ways for parents to help inexperienced writers practice turning their observations into language.

Now I want to move toward writing complete sentences that are rich in sensory detail.

• **The "Sentence Building" Game.** Help your child build a sentence from images in the third column in any of the image-building games I recommend earlier. Here is an excellent opportunity to compare fragments of sentences to whole sentences. Make a fourth column to allow your child to build a full sentence.

I	II	III	IV
Word	Add a Smell or Touch	Add a Sound or Color	Make a Sentence
apple	cold apple	cold crunchy apple	I bit a cold crunchy apple.

or:

table	brown table	hard brown table	I touched the hard brown table.

or

The hard brown table stood in the kitchen.

or:

sparrow	brown sparrow	cold brown sparrow	I heard a cold brown sparrow peeping on the roof.

or

A cold brown sparrow peeping on the roof flew suddenly away.

In these examples point out the difference between the complete sentence and the gramatically incomplete image in columns I, II, and III. Talk about the capital letter at the beginning and the period at the end of the complete sentence. Show that by expanding the image into a sentence, the writer has more opportunity to add sensory language. In the second sentence about the sparrow, the word *flew* adds visual dimension. Words like *fluttered, flapped,* or *screeched* would contribute the element of sound if added to the sentence.

In this way, you can aid your youngster of four or five to connect sense words with objects and actions in his or her own world. Plan some activity that will relate language to art. Pick a word that suggests a sensory response; a color such as *red, blue,* or *orange;* a touch word such as *soft* or *rough;* a taste word such as *sweet* or *salty;* an action or sound word such as *fast, noisy,* or *quiet.* Make a list of things that represent color, sound, action, smell, taste, and touch sensations in your child's experience. Ask your son or daughter what the word brings to mind. "What color is it?" or "How does it move?" or "What does it smell like?" so that each written item arouses a sensory picture. At first suggest five or six items, then more. (Older children can write their own lists; younger ones will need your help.)

Red

> a sweet, cold apple
> Joseph's frozen cheeks on a March morning
> my new velvet pants
> the numbers that flash on Daddy's clock
> the strawberry jam I spread on crunchy whole
>   wheat toast

Notice in the example that each item offers details beyond the basic sense word *red,* which *does not* appear in any image. If your youngster wants to use the basic word in an image, fine, but encourage him to find substitutes for the word: an older child might use *scarlet, maroon, ruby,* or *wine.*

After your child has produced a list of good sensory details, help her prepare a homemade book. Few games excite a youngster as much as making her own book with a cover bearing the title and her name as author. Using this list, supervise the creation of a book about red, called *My Book of Red Things* or simply *Red Things*. For each item on the list, your child will draw or cut and paste a representation of the image. At the top or bottom of each page your child should write a full sentence, such as: *Red is a sweet, cold apple.* Help develop a sentence for each picture. You can see what a valuable game this is for a very young writer who might have had trouble putting words for images on paper. Using the list as a guide and your sentence as model, your child can create her own sentences by copying the information you helped her prepare. She can staple the pages together and give her book as a gift to Mommy, Daddy, Grandma, or Grandpa.

Some children who enjoy rhyming can write little jingles of images built from sense words. Here are some rhymes from eight- and nine-year-olds:

What is Yellow?

Yellow is the sun shining bright
Yellow is an electric light
Yellow is the lemon peel
Yellow is how bright I feel

What is Orange?

Orange is a pumpkin bright
Orange is a flame that glows at night
Orange is the color of the burning sun
Orange is the fruit that's good for everyone

Notice how each line in the rhyme is a complete sentence. (I'll say more about poetry later.)

Other sentence-building games start with a complete sentence that has very little sensory concreteness. You and your child expand the sentences in stages by adding details:

> The dog ran.

**Add
color and
or/touch**

1. A furry brown dog ran away.

**Add
sound**

2. A furry brown dog ran away, barking noisily.

**Name a
place**

3. A furry brown dog, barking noisily, ran away down Allen Street.

Some child might suggest changing the word *ran* into a sound word in order to follow instructions. Encourage it. Writers always change words and move their positions. Notice, in sentence 3, the words *barking noisily* stand in front of the word *ran*, whereas in sentence 2 they come after the word *away*. Children can see that writers often shift sentence elements around and play with words, moving them for their sense or sound or for special effects they might achieve. Thus, sentence 3 could also have been written:

> Down Allen Street a furry brown dog ran away, barking noisily.
> Barking noisily, a furry brown dog ran away down Allen Street.
> Down Allen Street, barking noisily, a furry brown dog ran away.

The last two show higher degrees of complexity, sentences you'd most often find in the writing of children in their teens. Be aware of the fluid elements in a sentence, and encourage your child's experimentation with sentence parts before those teenage years. I'll talk more about shifting and expanding sentence parts in chapter 7, when I discuss sentence construction and correctness.

I'd like to suggest another expansion game here. In the "Sentence Staircase" the writer climbs down by adding or changing details to a base sentence. This is an excellent follow-up to what you've been doing with sense images because it offers a little more challenge. Start with a simple idea and have your child add details according to the instructions alongside each step.

Sentence Staircase

A child played.

Describe the Child	A child *with brown eyes* played.
Tell When	A child with brown eyes played *one crisp winter morning.*
Name a Sound	*Giggling,* a child with brown eyes played one crisp winter morning.
Tell Where	Giggling *in front of his house,* a child with brown eyes played one crisp winter morning.
Use Other Specific Words	Giggling in front of his house, a *boy* with brown eyes *jumped up and down* one crisp winter morning.

You can help shift the parts around in the final sentence:

Giggling, a boy with brown eyes jumped up and down in front of his house one crisp winter morning.

In front of his house, a giggling boy with brown eyes jumped up and down one crisp winter morning.

In any case, the final sentence demonstrates the writer's sensory awareness. Aside from the sound word *giggling*, which was specifically requested, he shows action *(jumped up and down)*, touch *(cold)*, and color *(brown* eyes). He has replaced more general words like *child* and *played* with more specific language.

Here are some simple sentences you might want to use in your "Sentence Staircase" game.

> A man worked.
> The book fell.
> A tree moved.
> The car drove away.
> A cloud passed by.
> A woman danced.
> A girl ran.
> The baby cried.
> The radio played.
> She pulled him.

You can also have fun with imagery in sentences about people or objects around the house. In each sentence your son or daughter should appeal to at least *two* senses with as much concreteness as possible. First, you write one about your son or daughter:

> Melissa squirms on the velvet chair in the living room and coughs into her small pink hand.

Give your child the paper on which you have written your sentence and ask her to read it aloud. Then ask her to write one about you. Here are some examples:

> *In the den Daddy snores on the couch while the fire in the fireplace crackles and turns his face red.*

The refrigerator hums noisily as I touch its cool silver handle.

Mara licks her black paw and then purrs at me with her green eyes in slits.

These are some good subjects to write about in a single sentence:

a book
the telephone
a doll
a child's shirt or dress
a closet door
a brother, mother, father, or sister
a neighbor
a pet
the sink
a piece of candy

Two Longer Efforts

For a longer exercise in using sensory detail help your child practice writing riddles. The riddle should give details of the object without naming it, so that someone else can guess what the object is.

How to Write a Sense Riddle
1. Show how the thing moves or how people move when they use the thing.

2. Name colors that help us see the thing.

3. Tell the sounds it makes.

4. Tell what we would feel if we touched it.

5. Name a smell that might help us know more about it.

6. Do not name the object!

Here are two riddles as examples, the second one written by an older writer:

> This thing is silver and shiny. It has a black piece of plastic near the top. You must push it down. It feels hot when you put something in it. It makes a popping noise. It smells of bread. What is it?

> This smooth white rectangle sputters up Polo Road every evening, with the clink of bells and squealing children down the street. One youngster steps up to the rectangular object, holds out a silver coin, and a man in a white hat swings open a door with a thump. Curls of smoke wind out and the odor of chocolate and strawberry and coldness fills the air.

In the first riddle about a toaster a conscientious parent could help her child change her use of the pronoun *it*, which is repetitious. You might say, "Look at sentences 2 and 4. Can you move some words from the end of each sentence to the beginning? Help your child create sentences like these:

- When you put something in it, it feels hot.
- Near the top it has a black piece of plastic.

Here your attention to clear expression works along with your concern about effective sentences.

Comparisons for Solid Imagery

As speakers, children make comparisons instinctively—it's this movie as opposed to that one, this book instead of that, this restaurant being as good as that one. Language relies upon comparison; it allows people to see one object in terms of another, helps them suggest resemblances for clarity and for impact, and sometimes infuses one object with the other's liveliness.

A *figure* is a comparison that helps to produce an image. *Figurative language* is language that compares things: a writer brings together two different objects and produces a meaning or an effect that paints a fresh, vivid picture.

Our everyday expressions are highly figurative. "He's building castles in the air" compares a dreamer to an engineer or a bricklayer. The comparison is improbable. Yet when you think of the disaster a castle in the air would be, you see how insubstantial is the dreamer's life—the comparison works! Slang terms like "She bugs me" or "He's a drip" set up comparisons that seem implausible but nonetheless make sense. Through overuse, comparisons become trite; they lose their ability to bring a picture instantly to the mind.

Children have a remarkable gift for figure. Their language shimmers with comparisons: "Billy ratted on me"; "Hey! Cut it out! I'm not your punching bag!"; "She looks like an old witch"; "Quit your bellyachin'!" "The fur is smooth as velvet"; "My milk is cold as ice."

In great literature and poetry, the good figure opens windows of thought through sensory detail. If you work with your child to develop techniques of comparison, you'll be pleased at the visual impressions he can create.

Any child can produce a comparison using *like* or *as* (called a *simile*). Write out some unfinished sentences, like those below, and have your youngster put in a word, or words, to complete the figure. Don't be surprised if some of your child's responses seem trite. Children haven't enough experience to recognize overused words and phrases. I suspect you'll be delighted at some of your child's precise uses of imagery. Below are responses you might hear from young children:

- She hopped like *a sleepy frog.*
- The bus shook from side to side like *a yellow horse.*

- The kitchen was quiet as *night*.
- My brother makes as much noise as *a hundred popping balloons*.
- The oaks moved like *tall angry men*.

In several of these, the use of sensory language heightens the visual quality of the comparison and therefore the image. You can see color and hear sound; you can see descriptions of emotion and settings. The use of comparison and the use of sense words combine to make a vivid picture.

Let your youngsters try to complete these comparisons:

- The wind blew like _____.
- The car started up like _____.
- She ran like _____.
- When it snows (rains) on our street it's like _____.
- He ate like_____.

When writers treat nonliving or nonhuman objects as if they had human qualities, they use a figurative technique called *personification*. Here an object is compared to a living thing. The writer is not saying, "This *is like* this," but instead, "This *behaves like* a person." (Notice the word *person* in *personify* and *personification*?) So we have:

The wind *muttered* through the quiet oaks.
A yellow floorboard *moaned* at my shoes.
The morning sun *scattered* gold dust on the grass.

In all these tasks a nonhuman object *(wind, floorboard, sun)* performs some task usually thought of as reserved for humans *(muttered, moaned, scattered gold)*. Personification adds intense visual quality to an image.

Ask your youngster of nine or ten (or older) to look at or to listen to the following ideas about familiar objects. (Change the proper names to suit things and places in your home or city.)

- The refrigerator *made noise*.
- The light *went on*.
- Our door *opened*.
- A sparrow *flew* by.
- The maple tree *moved*.
- Our Chevy *starts* slowly in the morning.
- Fido *sits* as I open his can of dinner.
- The wind *is* on the desert.
- The crayon *fell* to the floor.
- The television *came on*.

Then say, "Pretend that each of those things moves or talks or acts like a person. Try to change the italicized words to words that show the object acting like a person. I'll do the first one." Next to each sentence in the list write a new setencce that changes the meaning by using personification:

> The refrigerator *made noise*.   The refrigerator *hummed*.
> The maple tree *moved*.   The maple tree *scratched at the window*.

Ask your child to do one or two examples herself. The new sentence should be easy to write because the youngster will use many of the same words as before. Offer help where it's needed, especially in the new elements, but let your child speak the whole new image before she writes it down.

You also can help your youngster of seven or eight to develop the skill to personify by asking him to pretend he is the object. Make it a game, and have your children write (or you help them write) the name of an object on a slip of paper. Then, ask them all to select one of the slips from a box, each child pretending to be the object named. With crayons your child then draws the object being portrayed, and writes three or four sentences to show what the object does or says as if the object were a person. Remind your children about sense words. Here is an example:

> I am Carrie's brown wooden door.
> I squeal when she pushes me.
> I cry when she slams me.
> I shake her hand with my cold silver knob.

Walk around, admiring the pictures in the making and giving all the help you can. Offer comments like: "That's a good sentence, Carrie ["I am Carrie's door."] Why don't you put in a color? And tell us what the door is made of." After the children finish, have them show their drawings and read their sentences aloud.

Another example of figurative language is the *metaphor:* the comparison that makes two seemingly unlike things equal.

> His eyes, little brown berries, darted everywhere.

In the sentence above the berries *are* the eyes, though clearly the comparison is suggested. *Metaphors* say that each term really *is* the other thing. If I wrote:

> His eyes, like little brown berries, darted everywhere

the word *like* would *compare* the two objects, eyes and berries. In a *metaphor* the comparison is only *implied.* Metaphors add a fresh, visual quality to written language by drawing together two seemingly unrelated items.

Your children enjoy these kinds of comparisons, and you can encourage your children to practice with metaphorical language. Think about the success, a long while back, of the song from the show *You're a Good Man, Charlie Brown,* "Happiness Is . . ." and the Peanuts book by Charles M. Schulz, also called *Happiness Is.* In both cases an abstract word—*happiness*—helped the writer imply comparisons between that word and some real object or event by means of sensory language.

Writing images for an abstract word is fun for children as young as eight years old. Here are some examples:

> *Happiness* is going to the doctor and not having to get a shot.
> *Excited* is going to a slumber party for the first time.
> *Disgusted* is my sister breaking my toy.
> *Scared* is seeing shadows in the night.

In each of those examples a child has defined a word in terms of an observed event, implying a comparison between the abstract word and some concrete experience. The sentences above, however, lack sensory language. The children who wrote them should be urged to use color, sounds, actions, and sensations of touch and smell in their metaphors. "Which toy does your sister break, Leslie? how does she break it? What sound do you hear when it breaks?" Here's a sentence developed from those questions:

> *Disgusted* is my sister crunching my tin soldier under her shoe.

This child already has improved the image's sensory appeal. I would say, "Wonderful! I love that word *crunch!* Now, tell your sister's name, add a color, and maybe some information about where it all happened." See how the writer went on to build a clear and original image by expanding the sensory appeal:

> *Disgusted* is my sister Ivy crunching my tin soldier under her shoe on the gray kitchen floor.

Building image definitions is an easy and enjoyable activity for a child at any age. Look at these by twelve- and thirteen-year-olds:

Fear is sitting in the creaking dentist's chair, seeing only the top of Dr. Rifkin's bald head as his trembling hand tries to zero in on a cavity.

Hope is a blind beggar in a tattered coat who hears a tin coin tinkle in his rusted cup.

Happiness is a small boy, his hands burrowed into the flannel warmth of his pockets, as he presses his nose on the window of a bakery shop.

Life is the questioning blue eyes of my infant cousin, Richard, opening for the first time in amazement to greet a changing world of life and death.

Life is a brown-haired dachshund, spinning frantically in search of his short tail.

Life is a flock of ducks flying in a wedge in the sky and trying to dodge frightful buckshot from the guns of anxious hunters.

Life is a rosebush growing in my garden, full of thorns but fragrant and lovely.

Life is two young children sneakily squatting on the carpeted steps, watching with anticipation the assorted gifts placed beneath the glimmering Christmas tree.

Although there is room for making the details even more concrete in these sentences (Where is the beggar? What's the name of the bakery shop?), they allow the reader to visualize instantly because of their use of sensory language.

When your child has practiced making a comparison between an object and a person, you can encourage him to give that object human qualities using several figurative expressions. A five-year-old can finish sentences like the following ones, which you have prepared in order to teach comparisons.

The refrigerator is an old man.

It _____ and _____ all night.
When it opens _____.
When it closes _____.

(Possible response):
The refrigerator is an old man.

It *coughs* and *trembles* all night.
When it opens it *breathes out cold air from its mouth.*
When it closes it *growls.*

Encourage your youngster to supply his own complete sentences and then to personify the object of the sentences.

As parents you can provide the machinery and technique for your child so that he can tap the well of senses and experiences stored in his memory. The games and suggestions in this chapter should arouse your child's language awareness and experience and should provide methods of honing writing skills.

Correctness, Part 1:

AN OUTLOOK FOR YOUNG WRITERS AT HOME

The Writing Process

Any successful written product—a story, poem, letter, or an essay, for example—is rooted in a carefully executed (though often varying and unpredictable) process. Inexperienced writers seem unaware of this process: In their rush to finish the job they skip steps, take shortcuts, struggle too soon with editing. One of the most valuable ideas that you can help your youngster learn is that writers perform a series of related and overlapping tasks in exploring, defining, and shaping a topic. No rigid sequence underlies the writing process; but a finished work always represents an effort that has passed through a number of stages.

The writing process begins with a kind of preparation called *prewriting*. What is *prewriting*? Simply, all the activities that writers perform to stimulate ideas and details before sustained writing begins. In order to limit a subject and uncover possible ideas about it, writers first shape their thoughts informally. Prewriting includes three activities.

• **thinking and talking about an idea** Help your child advance her thinking for any piece of writing that she wants to produce. Serve as an idea sounding board. Use brainstorming, the technique developed by business executives to assure productive conversation and collaboration in solving problems. In brainstorming—literally, a storm in the brain—you speak freely on an issue, raising lots and lots of questions, and then try to answer them. No idea is ever considered off the mark or inappropriate. Nobody edits comments; you say whatever comes into your mind about the topic.

What should your child be thinking about before she begins to write? The subject certainly: What are its possible features? alternatives? special dimensions? Here is the point at which to nurture inspiration and invention, those imaginative leaps that set an idea in motion. Even with young children, help review the notion of *audience*. Who will read the writing—you, Grandma, or other immediate family members? your child only? a friend? a teacher? a distant cousin? Knowing the audience always helps a writer direct thought and language appropriately. Advanced thinking and conversation and the questions that good listeners and friendly critics like you can ask about a subject will help your child generate enthusiasm, identify thoughts and feelings, find new information, or discover lack of focus or confusion.

• **reading other writing or examining pictures or other media** Exploring what others have done on an interesting subject is an excellent starting point for writers of any age. Consider library resources: Perhaps a word and/or picture book, a photograph, an encyclopedia entry, or a movie will help shake loose an idea. With your child read limericks before writing them; read a book about trucks before drawing a picture and writing a sentence about a cherry picker you've seen in the neighborhood; read a myth before inventing one.

• **doing writing warm-ups** Putting pencil to paper in informal warm-up exercises helps stimulate ideas, especially for children of nine or older. Try *free association:* Write a subject on top of a page and ask your child to put down everything that comes to mind about the subject. Or use *timed writing;* for a set period—five minutes, say—your child writes nonstop on a subject, even if he must write *I can't think of what to write.* The point here is to let a flood of words fill up the page without editing anything. Or, help your child make a *subject tree.* A subject tree helps you move visually from one level of thought to another as you consider various aspects of the topic. Starting with a key word, you draw lines from one word to another; the final product looks like a tree with branches reaching out toward possibilities for focused writing. Any one branch can serve as a starting point for developing other ideas. The young writer who developed the subject tree on tightrope walkers might write about the dangers of tightrope walking, the various circus acts that rely on tightrope walking, the necessary equipment to perform the task, or the kinds of tightrope walking beyond the circus tent. Note how each idea is a limb from the topic trunk and how further specifics branch off from the limbs.

Thus, when a writer begins constructing the sentences, and paragraphs that ultimately will be his "work," he is building on considerable prior activity, both in his mind and on paper. You'd be surprised at how few children struggling to write—indeed, how few adolescents and adults as well—follow the steps I've listed. All too often

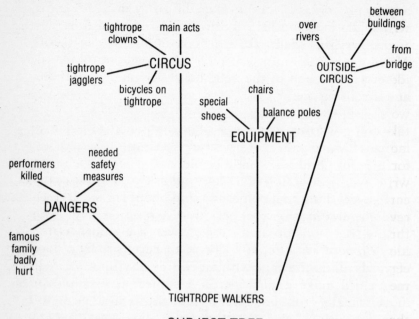

SUBJECT TREE

beginners try to write a paragraph, say, long before it's ready to be written. As a result, what they produce as a final copy is undeveloped, poorly crafted, and weakly reasoned. Prewriting activities are really thinking on paper, five-finger exercises for limbering up. You play with words, phrases, and ideas, following where they take you, without worrying about order or completeness. You see where your own impulses, thoughts, and interests lead you. Then, you can write a draft that ultimately will move you down the road to a final product.

I used the word *draft* and I want to define it here. A draft is a work in progress. It is another step on the journey to a finished product. Writers produce several versions of a work, changing each one by refocusing ideas, adding or subtracting words, and altering sentence structure, style, and language. I cannot stress enough the idea of drafting and its essential role in helping children succeed as writers.

Let me give you an idea of how I work when I write. After prewriting, I write continuous sentences to get my ideas down straight, and depending on the particular task at hand, I either race across the page or sweat over every word. Unfortunately, there are no rules for how long it takes to get down something that a writer will find satisfactory. The recursive nature of writing takes me back and forth from sentences I'm creating to those I've already written. I put down new words and change or add to earlier ones. At one point I look back at my pages and revise, sometimes lightly, sometimes extensively. Often I go through several drafts, in each case making choices of ideas, syntax, vocabulary, diction, style, other choices, too, certainly—an often frustrating set of options. What pleases me finally rarely looks much like my first attempt.

When I sense that I'm nearing the end of my work, I then turn my attention to correctness. Let's look at the concept of correctness now and how it affects your youngster.

The Fever of Correctness

Correctness and error are issues of extraordinary complexity, not only for their roots in social stigma and mobility but also for their fuzziness as terms about writing. You already know about the interplay between idea and expression, between what a writer means to say and how the writer actually says it. We identify mature sentence construction with correctness, yet an immature sentence might have no mistakes and still be an example of poor writing. In other cases correctness seems easy to judge. *Coming* spelled with two *m*'s is wrong. The two sentences

I ate peanuts. They tasted salty.

written in either of these ways are wrong:

> I ate peanuts they tasted salty.
> I ate peanuts, they tasted salty.

The first is wrong because no punctuation separates the sentences; the second is wrong because a comma does not separate the sentences adequately. The sentence "One of the boys are sleepy" is incorrect because the word *one* is the subject, and since it is singular, it requires a singular verb *is*. (One of the boys *is* sleepy). But even among those mistakes it's possible to rate different levels. Some mistakes seem more important than others, especially as young children learn to master the writer's craft. Some errors we wisely overlook at specific stages of development.

Somewhat related, the age variable imposes conditions too: I worry less about *coming* spelled with two *m*'s in a seven-year-old's writing than I do when the word appears spelled incorrectly in a paper of an eighteen-year-old. Even there, complexities abound. Many college students are writing in a systematic way for the first time, never having had formal instruction in writing. Under usual circumstances, a young woman of eighteen should know how to keep sentences apart correctly and how to spell *coming*. But if, for whatever reason, she has not practiced writing until then, how can someone judge fairly her degree of achievement? Nevertheless, a strict language code says that a misspelled word is still a misspelled word and sentences run together without suitable punctuation are wrong. So quick or easy judgments are again confounded.

All these muddled thoughts about error burn youngsters with a fever of correctness and arouse hysteria in them or intolerance for mistakes. I have seen a child pushed to tears by the tiniest blemish on a page—a misplaced stroke of pen, a word crossed out, an eraser smear. Children writing at their desks in a classroom crumple fresh sheets of paper endlessly. I hear angry crackling, mumbling under the breath, little feet stomping down the aisle to the basket. This preoccupation with unblemished effort murders a child's creative instincts.

But no wonder youngsters have this attitude. Several classroom practices encourage it. Children have learned that erasers are tools of defeat, that crossing out on a page admits stupidity and unforgivable error. On spelling tests, the teacher will judge only the child's *first* written response—changes, erasures, crossings-out disqualify the word from correctness. Some educators see this rule as a protection for the writer who, when changing answers, often changes from right to wrong. Yet many youngsters view the prohibition as a conspiracy against their attempts.

The irony is that a teacher removes *his* mistakes with a quick smudge on the chalkboard, which is a kind of open territory where errors can be snuffed out with a gray felt eraser, a few fingers, or the sleeve of a dress or a shirt. I have watched children trying to create words or sentences on the chalkboard. They surround themselves in clouds of chalk dust, the eraser smearing its way across the slate with frenzy. Letters must be just so, words spelled exactly. Amid all this effort a child tries to crystallize an idea so that it makes sense in a sentence or two. More unhappy are those unlucky students who must copy answers from their own pages onto the chalkboard. They suffer the glares of seventy onlooking eyes, everyone waiting to attack the first mistake. The tension of correctness and neatness often adds serious pressure to performing at the chalkboard.

How Do Writers Write?

Writers are rarely neat. When they create, they are unconcerned with being "correct." The very act of creation sends a pencil or pen all over the place, a thought there in the margin in a hurried scrawl, line after line slashed with gray impatience, a sentence intended for the bottom of the page written *before* earlier sentences which are not yet written. Writers doodle; they jot down notes and even irrelevant reminders on their pages; they misspell with religious fervor; they draw long, snaking arrows from words far down a page so that they know to move those words to other places. In generating early drafts, writers who use word processors often avoid looking at the screen when words are flowing. Stopping to correct a misspelled word or to puzzle out sentence structure can dam the flood of ideas.

The landscape of a page that records creative activity is a battlefield of statements—the scarred, the scratched, and the murdered exist along with those chosen to survive. Professional writers, surely, crumple up and destroy sheets of paper at different stages of invention, but no absolute concern for neatness or correctness (in the sense that children perceive it) motivates their actions.

I am not saying that writers do not need to follow the conventions of correct writing when they offer their work for someone else to read. Errors in spelling, grammar, syntax, and logic have no place on the final draft. Someone else reading a writer's creation mounts from the start an uncertain stallion, expecting a smooth ride. Error is a burr beneath the saddle; depending on the rider's tolerance, a throw or two from the horse may end the journey. When this happens, the writer has failed.

The efficient writer scours a draft for error *before* preparing the final copy. If he types the final manuscript himself, he'll work more quickly from error-free pages. But if he submits the rough copy for someone else to prepare, he must proofread the retyped draft meticulously, because a typist will copy word by word what appears on the original copy. Errors carried from the old copy to the new one can be caught at this stage.

Many young writers focus their energies prematurely on the final stage of their manuscript. To these novices it's not a matter of getting ideas down, exploring them, and working them through as much as it is putting something down that's neat and correct. This attitude robs the young writer of a key stage in the writing process, the pencil and paper laboratory where experiments and failures should be welcomed.

In your goal to help your child build positive attitudes toward writing, you must defang this monster of correctness. And to help you see what writers go through, here's part of the rough draft manuscript for an earlier section of this book. Look at page 88 to see how it turned out finally.

Ben Jonson's offhand comment about the way his contemporary Shakespeare worked—"in his writing (whatsoever he penned) he never blotted out a line"—may apply to pure genius. But, even if Jonson is right, few others (and you can look at rough drafts by Keats, T. S. Eliot, Virginia Woolf, and other great writers to prove it) work without blotches and smears on their pages.

Teach children an easy approach to correctness. When your youngster looks up in terror from a page and whines, "I made a mistake!" look at his work and say, "Good! Isn't it lucky that you found it! Why don't you cross it out and go right on?" or "That's why we have erasers! Fix it now if you want to. But why don't you keep going until you finish, and then I'll help you fix all the mistakes later on." In this way you make error a noncriminal offense by refusing to condemn it at the stage where it has little importance. At the same time you establish the value of making corrections *after* the flow of ideas develops into a page of written language.

Here are some more tips:

• *Encourage "rough writing" wherever possible.* To allow thinking and doodling time, word seeking, play, and

[margin note: two lines seem right, address items.]

the word *like* tells ~~outright~~ that two things ~~are being laid~~ would side by side for comparison will be compared. In a *metaphor* the comparison is implied. only ~~📍~~ Metaphors too add a fresh, visual

quality to language by putting together

~~One of the effective ways~~ To encourage (your child to) practice in this ~~method of comparing~~ type of comparison thing about the success a ~~program~~ while back of the song "Happiness from the show *You're a Good Man Charlie Brown*

is ..." and the book *Peanuts* by Carl Shultz, *check name!*

also called *Happiness is.* In both of these cases ~~the writer selected~~ allowed the writer to imply an abstract word --happiness-- ~~and implied~~ comparisons ~~metaphorically. The writer used sensory~~ between that word and some real object or event

[margin: Writing images for an abstract word]

by means of sensory language. ~~Help your child write images for~~ is fun for children of eight or older, ~~a word like happiness or some other~~ abstract ~~term.~~ Here are some examples:

exploration, the sloppier the page the better. Encourage alterations, cross-outs, and fearlessness about misspelling. When I taught in elementary and junior high school, I always insisted that my students prepare a sloppy copy and that they submit it along with any revisions.

• **Encourage rewrites.** Writing demands *rewriting*—the older the child, the more intermediate drafts you can encourage (two is about right) before any thoughts of final copy. Help your child understand that the rewrite is not a punishment or an indication of personal failure, but a way of making the final copy clear, easy to read, and free from error.

• **Consult, consult, consult.** Encourage your child to see you as a friendly writing coach. Be available to listen to words, phrases, and sentences. Provide comments on your youngster's developing ideas. Make suggestions. Talk about writing.

• **Supervise rewrites and correction of errors.** Train your child to *correct* errors, not always to be on the lookout to avoid them, before attitudes formed by school experience develop. Praise your child's efforts even if they are "wrong"; and *then* talk about mistakes. The four-year-old who sounds out the word *barn* to write on top of her picture may write *bran* instead. What do you say? "Well, Ellen, you're trying to write *barn* and you've got all the letters rights. Good for you! But you didn't put them down in the right order. Shall I help you fix it or do you want to try yourself?" Once you work through the error, make no fuss; encourage your child to cross out or to erase the incorrect word. If necessary, print the word correctly on the page (with the child's assent), and ask your youngster to copy it. When you first see the error, avoid clucking or an impatient "That's not right!" unless you want that lovely barn with its tilted red silo torn into shreds by an injured child. Furthermore, be prepared for resistance. Despite gentle treatment of mistakes, a child often will say, "I want it *wrong!*" Then you say, "That's all right. It's yours. But if you want someone else to understand and like your writing, you should do it right. It's easy, look. . . ."

Your early responses to error generally will focus on spelling until your child is eight or nine and begins writing original sentences and little stories in school. However, a parent can build sentence sense and help develop more sustained efforts at a much earlier age. After that you'll be responding to other more advanced kinds of mistakes, and will need a general understanding of the principles of the language. (See Appendix B.)

Reacting to Error

The painful correction of error after error, especially when accompanied by a parent's impatience, disgust, or anger, squashes the seeds of writing that lie dormant within your son or daughter. It's a delicate and subtle skill to be able to ignore some mistakes while pointing out other more serious ones. In general, don't worry about commas on a young child's paper. For the child of ten or eleven, the use of commas in some easy, familiar places should be no strain: in dates, between city and state in an address, after the salutation in a friendly letter, and so on. Later on, I'll give some very general guidelines about the writing skills your child should grasp at different ages.

Many good texts are available that will help you learn more about correctness in writing. Read your child's own language arts book from school or pick up a writing handbook at a bookstore. (You might be interested in *The McGraw-Hill College Handbook* which my colleague Richard Manus and I wrote for college freshmen.) A language arts textbook at your child's level can teach you and give you a guide to what his age group should be learning.

Don't convey your own limitations, fears, and frustrations about writing through excessive treatment of error. That would obviate any hopes you had of your child's developing good attitudes toward writing. Praise effort at all times with pleasure and excitement; listen without distraction to a youngster who speaks aloud original written sentences, and encourage this kind of reading frequently; fuss over the finished product—hang it in the kitchen on the cupboard, send a copy to Grandma, leave it at Mom's or Dad's place at the breakfast table. As your youngster grows older, continue your positive responses to his writing, but show more and more attention to correctness—never so much that it supersedes your interest in the way your child develops an idea and supports a point.

Your Code of Ethics: Writing for School

Just what is the role of the mother or father in seeing that written school assignments are done well? How much should a parent help a child write for his teacher?

The responses vary as widely as the problems faced by young writers themselves. Many believe it is dishonest for a child to receive major help in preparing schoolwork. After all, a piece of writing is something created by an individual, and as an expression of his or her mind at work, it is inviolate. In any large-scale tutoring effort in which the parent plays a major part in organizing and correcting a paper for school, an instructor's grade cannot be an honest evaluation of a child's work. Some parents will not help their seventh or eighth grader prepare a report for school, but will type the paper, making corrections as the typing proceeds. Others will examine a paper before it's submitted and will correct any serious errors. Still others comb the pages for all spelling mistakes, correcting them before their youngster submits the work, perhaps even demanding a rewrite. But some will question all these attempts on ethical grounds. If it's not completely the child's work, what's the point in presenting it to the teacher as such? Following this line of thought, many feel that a parent must ignore her child's writing for school. Others will examine papers *after* the teacher returns the writing in order to help their child understand the teacher's corrections and comments.

Still others believe that providing assistance to writers as their ideas form and develop is a much sounder way to advance skills than to try to help in the correction or revision of a paper already graded by teacher. They think it's best to influence the expression of ideas, and to explore in sentence and paragraph form as a child develops drafts before preparing the final copy. Certainly, some argue, a parent should encourage her child to talk about the writing assignments a teacher gives, so that the work moves along the right track. Then again, shouldn't a parent help a child plan a school assignment, even outline it as it grows in complexity from term to term? Can mothers and fathers really permit a paper loaded with errors to go before the teacher's red pen if there is a chance to correct the mistakes first, to spare the youngster wounded feelings and a sense of defeat?

Given these contradictions, what does a parent do? It's hard not to compromise excessively, but truth sits on both sides of this rocky issue. As in any attempts to solve problems edging on dilemma or predicament, the key is judgment, your judgment as a parent and a fair-minded human being who understands your child.

A teacher will not generally expect young children in kindergarten and the first and second grades to prepare extensive written work of an original nature at home, though some simple homework and copying activities may take a child's time after school. That leaves lots of room for you to help your child develop writing skills and attitudes in ways this book suggests, and with a clear conscience! But, as children grow older, as demands on their writing performances grow more and more serious through the grades, you do need to know where to draw the line in offering help on something the teacher will score.

When it comes to aiding your youngster with classroom work *in general* (I'll look at your role in a specific project when I examine the report in chapter 15), go to see your child's teacher if you have doubts about what's fair. Ask him how much assistance you should give your son or daughter when your child writes assignments for school. Because attitudes and responses to this issue vary widely, you'll want to clear your position with the instructor. If he says that you should not help the child organize ideas, for example, don't do it for classroom work. One of the good things about encouraging frequent written activities at home is that you can explore problems writers have without having to worry about overstepping some hard-to-define border. This is not to say that I believe it's all right for you to rewrite or to correct slavishly papers children write at home just because no teacher will judge them. Your child is still your major concern; it's his or her written work, not yours. Still, for writing at home, you can make your advice more direct, and you can be less concerned about violating the code that work submitted for a teacher's evaluation must be the child's own.

As you try to define your position in your sons' and daughters' writing assignments, I advise you in the way I advise inexperienced teachers starting careers as English instructors. Teachers of writing are guides and counselors—I used the word *coach* before—who help writers find the most successful means of expressing their ideas. The best way to achieve that goal is through questioning without putting words in a child's mouth: "What do you mean by this?" "Which ideas do you want to put first?" "What details can you use to support your point?" "Do you see the three spelling mistakes that I see on this page?"

In the list on next page I've tried to summarize some do's and don'ts as you work with your children on writing for school. Don't be concerned that I'm recommending some ideas I've not yet explored in this book. I'll talk about things like word choice and sentence growth later on.

Again, a child's age, your judgment, and the teacher's demands are the final arbiters. Look this over with special care if your writer is in the third grade or higher.

Tips and Pointers:
How Parents Can Help with Writing for School

STAGE	DO'S	DON'T'S
PRE-WRITING	**1.** Encourage your child to explain the assignment as she understands it. Ask questions so that you're *sure* she understands it.	**1.** Don't interpret the assignment. Don't tell her what the teacher wants. Ask questions so that your child can figure it out for herself.
	2. Encourage your child to think about the topic before writing anything. Encourage your child to talk with you before writing. Do brainstorming. Ask questions to make sure that she can offer details to support any ideas. Visit the library to stimulate creative thinking on a subject.	**2.** Don't respond to questions like, "What should I write about?" without making a wise range of suggestions from which your child can choose without feeling obliged to follow your ideas.
	3. Encourage your child to record unedited thoughts on paper. Make lists or subject trees; use timed writing and free association.	**3.** Don't add details for your child. Ask questions: What color? What size? and so on.
ROUGH COPY	**1.** Remind your youngster of how writers write. Show the page of "rough writing" from this book (p. 82) or better still, a page of your own writing before you turn it into something you'd want to show someone.	**1.** Don't worry yourself or your child about neatness or correctness.

STAGE	DO'S	DON'T'S
	2. Ignore mistakes. Encourage cross-outs. Encourage skipped lines for information to be added later.	**2.** Don't push too hard. If your child draws a blank, turn to other things. Come back to the writing after a glass of milk or a game.
	3. Spell out words only if your child asks you. Write them down for your child to copy. Better, help her sound out the words.	**3.** Don't let spelling get in the way of the writing effort. Let youngsters *guess* at spelling until later on.
	4. Keep an eye on errors so that you can direct your child's learning about some of them later on.	
READING THE ROUGH COPY	**1.** Ask your child to read the work aloud. Praise it!	**1.** Don't interrupt the reading no matter how many suggestions you can make for improvement.
	2. Ask questions: "What color was the house?" "What sound did the door make?" "Would you like to use those words to give a better picture?"	**2.** Don't correct the errors.
	3. Show sensitivity to word choice in general. "You've said, 'The shoe *crunched* the glass on the pavement!' What a wonderful sound word!" or "You wrote, 'My sister *walked* to the door.' Why don't you try to find a word that shows a better picture of how she moved?"	**3.** Don't add any details.
	4. Explain the use of the caret (∧) to insert omitted words. Draw arrows out to the margins, if necessary. Encourage sentence revision; your child should add words, delete words, and shift sentences.	**4.** Don't show any disappointment about poor writing or about errors.

STAGE	DO'S	DON'T'S
	5. When you see a glaring mistake, help your child find it and correct it herself. After you're both satisfied with the ideas expressed, say, "Oh, oh, I see a place in the first three lines where a sentence should end. Can you find it?" Or, "You have six spelling mistakes. See if you can find them." You'll want to use proofreading techniques here (see the next section in this chapter). You might suggest that your youngster use a different color pencil so that corrections will stand out clearly.	**5.** Don't make any reference to neatness or sloppiness.
	6. Encourage sentence diversity. Say, "Why don't you put together two sentences toward the end? You can use *and* or *because* or *since* to join them together." Or, "You've used *and* so many times to join sentences. Can you put them together in another way?"	**6.** Don't expect correctness in areas that your child does not understand or has not yet learned. Again, it's your judgment: If the first few letters of a difficult word tell you what your child means, you may want to ignore the error completely. However, don't allow an attitude of carelessness or indifference to the writing process to develop.
	7. Given the age and attention span of your child, with especially thorny topics or especially hard-to-read rough copies, suggest another draft written from the first.	

STAGE	DO'S	DON'T'S
COPYING OVER: THE FINAL DRAFT	**1.** Encourage your child to the prepare a careful final copy. Talk about how the page should look. Consider the teacher's requirements. Where does the name go? the date? the title? May your child write on both sides of a page? What margins does the teacher require? Offer hints about good handwriting. Periods at ends of sentences should be clear and firm with enough space between the period and the next word. Capital letters should be clearly capitals. With cursive writing, dot the *i* directly over the letter and not between the *i* and *e*. Discourage circles as dots for *i*'s.	**1.** Don't type or write the paper over for your child no matter how "sloppy" she claims her handwriting is.
	2. Answer questions about spelling. Spell out the toughest words, writing them down on a separate sheet for your youngster to look at and to copy over. Encourage her use of a dictionary in this final draft stage. Look up words together.	**2.** Don't hang over your child as she copies her paper over. Answer questions if she has any— but this is her effort so don't make her nervous. Welcome questions. You can decide whether or not to answer them after they are asked!
	3. Listen as your child reads the paper aloud. Ask her if words sound smooth together, if sentences make sense to her.	**3.** Don't be embarrassed if your child asks you to spell a word and you cannot. That's what dictionaries are for! A youngster who sees her mother or father reach for a dictionary develops good habits.

STAGE	DO'S	DON'T'S

4. See that your child proofreads carefully. Do careful proofreading at two points: first, *before* your child copies over a draft to make it final and, second, *after* she has prepared the final draft. Using what you know of previous kinds of errors your child makes can help focus the proofreading activity: "Carla, last time you misspelled *disappoint* and *already*. Let's see if you've spelled those words correctly this time" or "Last time you had trouble with sentence endings. Let's check the paper over so that you put in all the periods where they belong."

4. Don't be ashamed if you can't help figure out problems that both you and your child perceive. Reach for a book if you can, or ask your child's teacher about a particular sentence (a note attached to the writing when handed in will be fine).

5. Given your child's age, no teacher should expect an absolutely correct paper, especially not for the very young, so don't be overly zealous. Your child should apply what she has already learned and what you feel she should know.

6. Don't be reluctant to refuse to help in places when you believe it might be ethically unsound. Say gently but firmly, "Beverly, I don't think Mrs. Wilson would want me to help you with that one. After all, it's your work and you'll get the grade for it. But let's see how you can find out the answer yourself."

STAGE	DO'S	DON'T'S
THE GRADED PAPER RETURNED	**1.** Read the teacher's comments together. Make sure that you child understands what's said.	**1.** Don't complain about the grade or the effort. The attitude must be, "Let's see what the teacher says so that you can do better next time."
	2. Talk about discouragement. Explain how in writing people learn by trying and by making mistakes. Tell about how professional writers often have their work severely criticized and refused for publication.	**2.** Don't challenge the teacher's judgment. It's all right to disagree, but remember that many responses to writing are subjective. The question is, do the instructor's comments explain her evaluation of the paper? Has she made her standards for evaluation clear before hand?
	3. See that your child works carefully on correcting errors even if the teacher does not require it—and this comes before any revision (see 5, below). Suggest a different color pen or pencil as your youngster makes corrections according to the teacher's comments or symbols in the margin.	**3.** Don't tell you child how to correct errors the teacher points out. Help her find out how to make corrections on her own.
	4. Help your child keep a record of her usual errors. This effort is especially valuable: first, by giving practice not to repeat error; and, second, if your child consults her errors before she writes the next paper, she can signal herself about mistakes she often makes.	
	5. Insist that your child copy misspelled words—correctly spelled—onto a list of individual spelling errors (see pages 302 to 303). If the mistakes fall	

STAGE	DO'S	DON'T'S

into patterns (that is, *plurals, -ie* mistakes, *suffixes,* and so on), help your child group the errors on index cards or on small sheets. When you can identify patterns, the task of learning about correct spelling is not overwhelming. Make sure that your young writer consults the list before each writing assignment.

6. Many instructors (especially in junior and senior high) will ask for a revision—that is, they expect students to rewrite papers based upon suggestions for their improvement. Encourage revision along the lines the teacher suggests *after your child understands and corrects the errors.* Otherwise, in revision, youngsters may avoid the words or structures that caused the problems and thereby lose the opportunity to learn how to correct mistakes.

Proofreading, Hedge Against Mistake

Proofreading is the single most valuable hedge I know against error. A shocking number of mistakes on a page often may be traced to careless proofreading.

What is *proofreading?* It's a term borrowed from publishers who ask people to read over material set into type (called *proofs*) so that the errors made in printing from manuscripts are corrected. Using conventional symbols and following a publisher's style, a proofreader writes his marks on the printed proofs after comparing them to the original manuscript; the printer then resets lines or pages of type to correspond to the alterations. When I use the term *proofreading*, I mean it as a process of looking for errors at various stages of writing. As you saw, I suggest that you encourage young writers to look for errors at two stages. First, children should read over rough copies before preparing final drafts. In the rough manuscript they will consider broad areas for improvement: word choice and mature sentence structure, as well as spelling, word use, and sentence completeness. Second, they should proofread after the final copy—in which major errors should no longer appear. Here writers find mistakes that slipped past them when they read over their rough copies or mistakes that crept in while they were preparing the final manuscript.

Teachers repeatedly overlook the difficulties children have in performing this task. Frequently I've heard them scold children, "You haven't read this over!" Proofreading is a hard job. To be effective, a writer must do it in a manner quite opposite to the way he ordinarily reads; that is, in proofreading, his eyes must look at only one word at a time, not roam over groups of words in an attempt to take in ideas quickly. Even a first grader who is barely able to read is led on, pursuing the meaning of the paragraph, as she moves to the end of a sentence. Though she may read each word separately, she is not seeing the word exactly as it appears. She is seeing parts of the word, or maybe she unconsciously is substituting a completely different word that helps her make sense out of the sentence. Familiarity further confounds an inexperienced writer who proofreads; for when reading what she herself wrote, the writer often sees words on a page that are in her head but not really written down. Often I've heard youngsters read words that do not appear in one of their sentences. For example, a child who wrote, "She eat by herself," read over and over again, "She *can* eat by herself." I kept saying, "What?" and she kept reading the word *can*. It was only when I asked her to touch the word *can* that she saw with great surprise that no such word existed in her sentence!

It's possible to help a child learn how to read for errors—this is a valuable skill that you should encourage. I like to explain the difficulties in proofreading by asking youngsters to read this:

```
ASK NOT WHAT
YOUR COUNTRY CAN
CAN DO FOR YOU,
BUT WHAT YOU
YOU CAN DO
FOR YOUR COUNTRY.
```

It's usually a while before they realize that *can* and *you* have been repeated. Why do they miss those errors? People tend to see what they *expect* to see in familiar sentences, instead of what is actually there. Next, they read quickly (having been trained to do so); and with sentences they know, people read especially fast. John Kennedy's statement, though certainly familiar, is much *less* well known to a child than his own writing, so imagine how easy it is to overlook mistakes there.

Here are some techniques that will help your child proofread more accurately:

- Read aloud. Listen for words or sentences that sound strange, funny, or "don't sound right."
- Read *slowly*. Read one word at a time. If you use a pencil to touch each word as you read it, you'll slow yourself down.

- Use a ruler or a blank sheet of paper to cover all the writing below the line you are looking at. In that way your eye is not drawn too swiftly onward.
- For younger children and for those with a number of serious careless errors you might want to follow a suggestion I learned from one of my colleagues. Use an index card with a piece—about half an inch long and as high as a ruled line—cut out of the left corner, like this:

Place the card over the line with part of the first word showing in the space you have cut out. Have your child read only what appears in that space, as he moves the card across the line.
- If you've written more than a sentence, read your writing from the last sentence to the first one. For an older child this technique helps her separate ideas, and keeps her from unconsciously filling in missing details from previous sentences.
- Correct errors in spelling, capitals, and punctuation directly on the first draft. If a word has been left out, put a caret in the sentence where the omission occurs and write the word above. If there isn't enough room, draw a line from the caret out into the margin and write the word. If there are too many corrections on the page, do the final draft again.

Spotlight on Writing in the Grades

Philosophies and approaches vary so widely from grade to grade, city to city, state to state, that it would be impossible to offer any accurate representation of specific writing programs in the schools.

You might ask whether or not there is a sequence of skills that all schools should follow in establishing a series of writing courses. There is, certainly, a sequence in word and sentence recognition usually followed in most *reading* programs. But in writing, children need to put down ideas and responses based on experience. Good instruction helps young writers build vocabulary and exposes them to a variety of sentence patterns; however, no one can predict exactly which needs come when, which errors show up at what time, which errors go away during what year. Further, writing is a holistic process; that is, a writer at any age needs all the skills to convey whatever ideas he or she wants to put in writing at that moment. I think it's impossible to say what skills any writer needs at what age or grade level. In every grade I taught (including college freshmen), I had to explain about sentence endings, about the rule for forming plurals of words that end in *y*, and about capital letters for geographical areas.

Even when accompanied by a strongly worded statements that children develop as writers at different stages, that regional language patterns make varying demands on skills development, that home language patterns affect writing needs, and that no absolute standards of competence may be established for children in particular grades or at particular ages, providing a sequence of skills for parents and teachers is bound to create nervousness about the child's progress. When parents see lists of competencies arranged by age or grade they assume that *all* children should have learned the skills by a certain age. That's nonsense. Writing in the home luckily avoids the need for looking at set achievement levels. At home, you can help the child write according to his interests and abilities. And you don't have to worry about suiting an arbitrary sequence. If it's too hard, all you have to do is stop.

Despite these objections to providing a sequence, I think you should have a *very* general sense about the skills some programs help children develop at what points in their writing careers. This information can guide you in knowing what *not* to press on your child, and what to encourage at home and when to encourage it. I want to give you this material in the broadest possible terms so as to avoid as much as I can the "Is my child normal?" or the "What's wrong with our school district?" questions. I hope you will keep in mind, too, that there's a great deal of required repetition and that skills on one level must be reinforced on other levels. Also, writing skills must be part of a total language-arts program. Skills in reading, speaking, performing all support the writing area. If you want more specific information, get exact writing goals year by year from your children's teachers or language arts specialists (you're perfectly right to insist that the school have a plan for writing-skills instruction; and your child's teacher should be able to tell you her goals for writing improvement for the class).

As I have already indicated, advancement in writing relates to a complex development of skills, especially in reading and speaking. Children in early stages of reading-skills development cannot be expected to write words independently and fluently if they do not read, use, and recognize them. There is no accurate way to predict by a child's chronological age the stage at which he should be as a user of the language.

In the next chapter we will look at some special word problems children have and at some techniques for expanding facility with words. We'll consider the role of the children's dictionary, and examine some games you can use in the home to build up the child's ability to write good sentences.

A General View of Writing Goals in the Schools

WRITING EXERCISES AND
RELATED COMPOSING SKILLS

LANGUAGE SKILLS

FOR THE EARLY GRADES
(KINDERGARTEN, FIRST, SECOND, THIRD)

Words as labels

Sense words

Simple sentence

Two or three simple sentences
(to describe an event, a picture,
and so on)

Copy work (sentences, words,
invitations, messages)

Some independent writing

Dictation: copying a brief story
as the teacher reads it

Dictation: children speak a
sentence or two as a teacher
writes it

Some word processing and
composing practice on the
computer

Stories using spelling words

Poems

Titles for pictures

Class
Effort

Lists for class shop-
      ping excursion
Instructions to
follow
Daily plan or log

Drafting

The *sentence* as a unit that tells
or asks

Headings on papers

Capitalization (for beginning
sentences; for names of people;
the word I; names of cities,
states, countries; names of
schools and other familiar
buildings like supermarkets or
banks; names of holidays,
months, and days of the week;
main words in titles of stories;
salutation and closing in letters)

Sentence sense: recognizing a
complete thought

Punctuation: periods and
question marks at ends of
sentences; periods after initials
and simple abbreviations (Mrs.,
days and months); apostrophes
to show letters omitted in
contractions; commas in dates
and in key places in friendly
letters

Plurals: s and *es* endings;
exceptional plurals as they arise
(*children, pianos*)

Word use: correct forms of words
(*brought* not *brung, ran* not
runned, and so on); seeing
differences between words that
sound alike (*it's, its; here, hear*);
avoiding slang (*ain't, his'n,* and
so on) simple pronoun use

FOR THE EARLY GRADES
(KINDERGARTEN, FIRST, SECOND, THIRD)

Prewriting ("Warmup")
strategies: brainstorming,
reporters' questions, timed
writing, subject trees, and so on

Vocabulary: practice with new
words; changing shape of words
with new endings

FOR THE INTERMEDIATE GRADES
(FOURTH, FIFTH, SIXTH)

Paragraphs: effective opening
and closing sentences; good use
of supporting detail, especially
sensory; correcting sentence
ideas with transitions

Writing descriptions

Writing stories of real events
that show clear sequence

Writing fanciful, make-believe
stories

Original letters to relatives,
friends, pen pals

Poems and rhymes

Short plays for acting out

Gathering data

Brief reports on books

Brief reports requiring an
encyclopedia

List-writing

Taking notes

Diary or journals (individual or
in-class projects)

Fables

Minutes of meetings

Sentence sense: combining
sentence elements; writing
longer, more complex sentences;
relating properly more than one
idea in a single sentence; seeing
and writing whole sentences;
keeping sentences apart; varying
sentence openings; how subjects
and verbs work together; how
verbs show tense

Dictionary use: for spelling,
pronouncing, finding meanings

Capitalization: of names,
peoples, abbreviations, outline
topics, titles of people and
books, in first word of
quotations, in addressing
envelopes, for the deity,
geographical regions

Punctuation: quotation marks
for someone's exact words,
apostrophes to show possession;
commas (for pauses as opposed
to stops in sentence endings) in
series, in quotations, to separate
elements in sentences; to set off
yes and *no*, to set off the name of
someone addressed in a sentence

Vocabulary: how to build words
from parts; selecting clear,
specific words; using vidid
words; using new vocabulary in
writing

FOR THE INTERMEDIATE GRADES
(FOURTH, FIFTH, SIXTH)

Articles for newspapers

Brief business letters

Magazine ads

Television commercials

Original cartoon strips

Original film strip captions

Filling out forms

Summarizing materials read

Regular practice with computer word processing

Regular prewriting and drafting

Plurals: patterns of plural formation (*y* to *i, f* to *v,* some special foreign words)

Grammar: basic grammatical language, explanation of key terms; functions of basic sentence elements

Word use: more on correct verb forms (*choose, freeze, swim,* and so on); comparing with and without *more* or *most;* no double negatives; using correct pronouns; more look- and soundalikes (*loose, lose; quit, quiet, quite,* and so on), uses of slang

FOR THE PRE-HIGH-SCHOOL GRADES
(SEVENTH, EIGHTH, NINTH)

Paragraphs: narration and description practiced frequently; other paragraph forms introduced and practiced: comparison, use of illustrations, simple listings, cause and effect, definition. Paragraphs expanded now in length; details support a clearly stated topic; effective use of transitions

Experiential writing: personal experience revealed through concrete sensory language

Interpreting data from charts and writing down findings

Using secondary sources: books, newspapers, testimony from knowledgeable people

Sentence sense: keeping sentences apart, joining sentence elements; avoiding fragments; experimenting with more and more sentence patterns; varying sentence length; types of tenses; special subject-verb problems

Capitalization: all uses; distinguishing places that exclude capitals (words for animals, flowers, sports, seasons, directions)

Punctuation: the semicolon and colon; commas after opening sentence element and for parenthetical parts of sentences; parentheses

FOR THE PRE-HIGH-SCHOOL GRADES
(SEVENTH, EIGHTH, NINTH)

Imaginative writing: dreams, wishes, make-believes

Writing dialogues

Writing up interviews

Essays: longer compositions that argue and analyze

Book reports

Character analysis

Original fiction: stories, poems, vignettes, plays, TV scripts

Writing answers on subjective-type exams

Basic techniques of research: bibliography; using sources properly

Writing about literature: why a poem or story is good; how it achieves a certain purpose

Business letters: of inquiry, application, complaint

Making out job applications

Dictionary Use: for history of word, etymology, parts of speech

Vocabulary: more prefixes and suffixes; thesaurus use to expand word resources; using new vocabulary in writing; continued practice with selecting exact, vivid words

Plurals: all uses

Grammar: more grammatical terminology; recognizing and identifying grammatical elements; using grammatical knowledge to create sentence patterns

Word use: more on tricky verbs; *should have* and *should of; between* and *among;* more look- and soundalikes; sensitivity to word choice depending on situation; correct pronouns

FOR HIGH SCHOOL AND BEYOND

Paragraphs: review and practice of previous skills; introduction of new forms: division, classification

Details: review and practice of sensory language and other kinds of supporting details

Sentence sense: continued review based upon error and need

Dictionary: different kinds and how and when to use them

Capitalization: all uses and abuses understood

FOR HIGH SCHOOL AND BEYOND

Longer compositions: how to write introductions and conclusions; how to correct parts of paragraphs; how to hold together paragraphs in a long composition; how to select appropriate forms (narration, comparison) to suit the subject of the written exercise

Using deduction and induction

Arguing convincingly

Analyzing clearly

Responding to books in written essays and reports

Basic research techniques: gathering data, writing footnotes and bibliography

Writing research papers with documentation

Writing outlines

Preparing résumés

Writing expanded autobiographies

Understanding when to use personal reactions or objective data

Writing essay tests

Writing business letters

Original fiction: all types

Advanced computer word processing for ease of composing

Punctuation: review all; dash, hyphen, brackets; special uses for apostrophes; italics and underlining as compared with quotation marks; commas in all correct places

Vocabulary: continued review and expansion. Wide use of relational words (*on the other hand, consequently,* and so on); ease and familiarity with abstract language; expanded repertoire of word choices

Word use: practice with and elimination of sticking errors and fine points of usages

Grammar: Full exposure to a grammar system; ability to recognize grammatical elements—to identify and to write them; application of grammatical principles to structuring sentences and to determining correct punctuation.

7

Correctness, Part 2:
WORD GAMES AND WORD AND SENTENCE CRAFT

When more than 60 percent of California's top high school graduates failed a nationally used writing test a number of years back, the professor who reported the statistics felt that poor previous instruction not lack of intelligence created the problem. He gave three reasons for the failure. Students, he said, lacked skills in correctness of expression, in the ability to organize their writing, and in the ability to choose the right word to complete a thought.

Organization means putting together words and sentences that show clear and logical relations to one another and providing solid support for ideas. Teaching this skill always creates difficulties because problems in organization vary with each activity. Solutions for one kind of writing do not necessarily work for other kinds. To learn this skill, one must practice different types of writing on various subjects, must read with an eye to the way writers organize ideas, and must practice different kinds of organizational strategies. This is something that children as well as adults *can* learn.

By correctness of expression, I assume, the professor means good grammar, spelling, and orderliness of ideas. When I read the phrase "correct word choice to complete a sentence," I immediately think of vocabulary and ways writers put their words into whole thoughts. How can a parent help expand a child's word resources and her options for using those words in quality sentences? Here as in other areas of writing skills, you can use the home environment to prepare youngsters for later demands on their writing.

Building Vocabulary

Professor Mina Shaughnessy, a researcher in the most acute problems of inexperienced writers, and author of *Errors and Expectations: A Guide for the Teacher of Basic Writing* (New York: Oxford University Press, 1977), gathered sample after sample of poor *college* writing by young adults.

Her findings suggest some of the concerns that parents should keep in mind when working with children. In addition to extensive problems in spelling, she shows that these writers lack a variety of words for naming objects specifically. In most of the students' writing that she examined she points to great confusion in the use of word endings and beginnings as they change their function in sentences.

Experts agree that a child's vocabulary relates to the nature of his experiences and to the language he hears and uses to explore those experiences. Children have an innate love for words—witness your child's delight as you read aloud the improbable rhymes in Dr. Seuss books or as your child invents nonsense words. Never lose sight of the pleasure and fun of saying, using, and playing with words in every moment of shared experience with your youngster. A parent accompanied by a four-year-old who watches snatches of activity in a supermarket can direct and influence her child's vocabulary by observing and discussing the words that apply to the supermarket scene. A child may hear and use: *unloading, supplies, stack, crate, special, discount, coupon, container, margarine, aisle, sawdust, manager, refrigeration,* and countless other words that may be new to him or only vaguely familiar. In a natural way you should talk about objects and events, and encourage questions and observations. Here's my book *Talk with Your Child* coming in handy again! You'll find many ideas there for expanding your child's oral vocabulary as a prelude to advancing reading and writing skills.

After an exciting experience, you can aid vocabulary growth by guiding your child's use of words to describe that experience. A three-year-old rushing in and announcing, "It's snowing," has opened a door for word study. You might say, "Snow? Terrific! Let's see how many words you can use to tell about snow." Parent and child can enjoy this together and make up a list of many words, such as:

icy	dancing	lazy	like white paint drops
cold	white	flaky	playful
fluttering	swirling	wet	like falling sugar
soft	blowing	tickly	fluffy
frozen	shivery	powdery	slippery

All the vocabulary-building books and exercises and all the attempts to commit long lists of words to memory pale beside the invaluable connection of language and experience. A parent acts as a child's word resources dictionary by naming, constantly, the items that are part of a new or a familiar experience. A visit to the doctor yields: *examination, throat culture, patient, prescription, stethoscope, injection, blood pressure, vaccine, inoculation.* A child who helps with cooking hears and uses: *simmer, steam, blanch, blend, pot, pan, carving knife, dice, beat, mold, cinnamon, yeast, broil, bake.* A youngster who likes to wash the car with Mother or Father considers: *filthy, sudsy, scrub, hubcaps, grid, hood, taillights, headlights, windshield.* A talk about a picture in a magazine uncorks a flow of language. A bedtime story, a program on television or radio, a good movie, are ample sources of new words too. The question, "What does that mean?" from a boy or girl of any age who is reading a book or watching television is an invitation for a conscientious parent to help with vocabulary. Explain the unknown word, give an example, and offer other words that mean the same or nearly the same thing.

Often I will "plant" a word, using one my child might not know, and then I'll wait for her question about its meaning. Even with simple words, such as *pot* and *pan,* I suggest that you make the meanings distinct so that the difference between such familiar objects stays clear in your child's mind. Selecting the most specific word from among several and attempting to find more specific words for general ones also help children focus upon the *exact* meanings of words. Helping your child name opposites to words also fixes meanings in mind, though this is often difficult because not all words have true opposites and because in many cases there exist several opposites with subtle differences of meanings. However, opposites to words like *day, black, sweet, weak, boy, cold, sad, light, woman,* and *enemy* are simple to find, and children love and learn from the game.

Concrete language comes strongly into play here in this discussion of vocabulary growth. A while ago my wife overheard an instructive interchange between a child and an adult as they waited to see a performance of *Snow White* at the Westerly Parkway Junior High School. One mother, accompanying her young daughter and a group of the daughter's friends, tried engaging each in conversation. To one little girl with brown hair and smooth skin, she said, "Those are really cute shoes you're wearing." The child shook her long brown hair and said, "Uh-uh. They're not cute." "Oh yes they are, Mary," her friend's mother replied. "They're very cute." "Nope. They're *attractive*." The woman laughed. "Well, I still think they're pretty neat."

Here the child brought a precise word from her own storehouse of vocabulary, one much more valuable in suggesting the grounds for judgment than *nice* or *neat* upon which the older woman insisted. *Attractive* is not as precise as *new leather shoes* or *brown suede shoes*, but it improves time-weary choices such as *neat* or *nice. Cute* and *neat* and *good, interesting, nice, swell*, and *bad* are vague words, and are as poor for describing as the words *thing, item*, or *object* are for naming, and as *went, walked, was, appeared*, and *seemed* are for showing action.

When you have the chance to explore words with your children, try to select words that suggest qualities as precisely as possible.

"Well, Nicholas, how did you like the book Aunt Clara gave you?"

"It was good."

"Good? What do you mean?"

"It was good. You know. It was good."

"Do you mean funny?"

"Oh yes. It was funny. It was even silly."

As soon as a child taps her vocabulary for a precise word, help her explore the wide variety of words that can replace the vague one even more specifically. Make lists of precise words according to the child's interest and age.

Instead of *good* (for a book)		Instead of *nice* (for a person)	
funny	fanciful	friendly	happy
exciting	realistic	helpful	funny
silly	tender	gentle	peppy
unusual	challenging	warm	relaxed
scary	suspenseful	inspiring	lively
dramatic	humorous	good-natured	thoughtful
heartwarming	tense	kind	cooperative
truthful	romantic	generous	fun-loving
adventurous	lively	cheerful	adventurous
imaginative	frightening	loving	strong

Instead of *went* or *walked*	
rushed	hustled
drifted	limped
scurried	scampered
strolled	galloped
skipped	marched
hopped	eased
sailed	slipped
flew	rolled
jumped	paraded
stormed	hobbled

All these activities encourage children to explore options and help avoid the overuse of "standard" words—old reliables that are so much a part of the inexperienced writer's grab bag. In a subtle way, you are discouraging the common imprecise favorites: *thing, idea, way; give, make, get, be, put, walk, have, cause; a lot, interesting, important, big, much, many, good.*

The following games and those that appear in chapter 5 will help you develop your own resourceful approaches as you strive to expand your child's vocabulary. If you arrange to share exciting experiences—better still, if you and your child train yourselves to see excitement in even the most ordinary experiences—the language that grows out of such occasions builds and reinforces a valuable word supply. Your own sensitivity sets the pace for your youngster's lifelong attitude toward language.

Word as Chameleons

Part of a solid word-building program is to explore how words change their forms and meanings. Novice writers sometimes see words as unchangeable terms and use them incorrectly. For example, a writer with such a vision will say, "The *describe* of this person is hard to believe" or "The *fastly* car won the race."

Yet even a simple shopping-trip excursion with a sensitive parent can inspire a boy or girl to look at the chameleon-like nature of words. You visit the *bakery* and see the *baker baking;* as *shoppers* you go to the *shop* to do *shopping;* see *drivers drive* into a *driveway.* By saying the words, talking about meanings, and enjoying the fun of hearing changes in word sounds you and your child become aware of our language's immense flexibility.

Help your child develop lists of words that demonstrate their versatility. For the word *play,* the two of you might write down as many words that use *play* as possible:

Play

plays
player
played
playing
playful
playfulness

playtime
double play
play-off
playpen
a play

By offering your son or daughter a group of unfinished sentences, you can ask him or her to fill in the blanks with words from the list you just prepared. This will show you if he or she understands the vocabulary.

1. The children were _____. (*playing, playful*)
2. He _____ all afternoon. (*played*)
3. The pitcher helped in a _____. (*double play, play-off*)
4. The kitten was _____. (*playful, playing*)
5. At school I like _____. (*playing, playtime*)

Another way to help a youngster see how words change is to start with a base word and to ask your child to create words from it, words that suit the blank space in a sentence. Help out with the tough ones!

Sleep

1. I feel _____. (*sleepy*)
2. Two puppies were _____ on a rug. (*sleeping*)
3. She spoke _____. (*sleepily*)

This discussion of word changes brings me to a consideration of word parts. Experts are divided on just how much the study of prefixes, suffixes, and roots (or stems) helps a child expand vocabulary. Many believe that it is only *after* people know the definition of a word that knowledge of its parts comes into play and that one doesn't learn much about the meaning of a word from unpuzzling its pieces. When coming upon an unknown word, not many people take it apart to discover its meaning. *Expose* comes from *ex*

(meaning *from*) and *pos* (meaning *put* or *place*), but applying the definition *put from* doesn't help a reader who is
trying to understand the meaning of *expose* when she finds
it in a book. Once she knows it means *lay open* or *make
accessible* or *make known*, the reader can see a connection
between the definition for the Latin prefix *ex-* and the Latin
verb root -*pos*.

A older child, however, can rely upon predictable elements, such as frequently used prefixes and suffixes to
expand vocabulary. Sometimes this reliance is instinctive:
re- as a prefix is often fixed in the mind as *again* and
requires no conscious analysis. I think the schools stress
this method of language acquisition too much—teachers
often require children to commit lists of words to memory.

Yet, sometimes taking apart a word *can* help a child to
discover its meaning. For insistance the words *irresistible*
and *uncomplicated* can be broken down into small pieces
(into *ir-re-sist-ible* and into *un-com-pli-cat-ed*) each with a
meaning or a particular role in the correct use of the word.
Once your child has thought about the pieces and has put
them all together, he gains insight into the meanings of the
words. A young writer who knows the word *appropriate*
and understands prefixes and suffixes could change it to a
negative word that named a quality: *inappropriateness*.

Just how do you assist your child in learning about
prefixes, suffixes, and roots? First, you'd better understand
them yourself. A *prefix* is a sequence of letters attached to
the beginning of a word, a *suffix* is a sequence of letters
attached to the *end* of a word, and both influence its meaning. A *root* or *stem* is a group of letters that make up a base
word or part of a base word. Roots often come from Latin
and Greek and have special meanings. Letters can be
added at the beginning and at the end of the root.

Next, you'll want to help your child see how many
words depend upon the use of similar prefixes and suffixes.
Youngsters already have a number of these words at their
fingertips, and you can help bring the words together to

stress their relations to one another. I think you should take your cues from the kind of reading instruction your child receives—word parts are usually taught as word-attack skills for reading. In any case, don't be *too* ambitious in your attempts. You can help children prepare their own groups such as these:

"re-" words	"un-" words	"-y" words	"spect" words
*re*play	*un*happy	happ*y*	re*spect*
*re*write	*un*developed	funn*y*	*spect*acle
*re*ceive	*un*laced	fluff*y*	*spect*ator
*re*act	*un*dressed	furr*y*	in*spect*
*re*claim	*un*cooked	ic*y*	

Because your child generated the words from his own experience, he'll enjoy analyzing them with you. After you have talked about the meaning of each word your child suggests, ask, "What does the *re* do in each word?" "What does the *y* at the ends of those words do?" You establish a personal context for your child's study of language by looking at words that are already part of your youngster's own word bank. In this approach, you are saying, "These are *your* words, so let's see how they work for you."

Once your child recognizes the pattern of meaning in the word groups, you can add new words to that group. "You've got it now," you might say. "*Re* means *again*. What do you think the words *reclaim* and *reexamine* mean?"

In working with prefixes, suffixes, and roots you must make your child aware of the problems, inconsistencies, and frequent, unreliability of word-part clues. For example, a child who knows that *re* means *again* could peer forever at the word *reiterate* and never divine its meaning if *iterate* were a mystery. *Try* has no connection at all with the *y* suffix despite its last letter; *reason* and *really* have no relation to the *re-* prefix.

Knowing what word parts mean does not *always* bring about clear understanding. Failing to make sense of a

Prefix	Its Other Spellings	Its Meanings	Master Words	Root	Its Other Spellings	Its Meaning
1. de-	....	Down or Away	DETAIN	Tenere	Tain, Ten, Tin	To Have or Hold
2. inter-	....	Between	INTERMITTENT	Mittere	Mitt, Miss, Mis, Mit	To Send
3. pre-	....	Before	PRECEPT	Capere	Cept, Cap, Capt, Ceiv, Ceit, Cip	To Take or Seize
4. ob-	Oc- Of- Op-	To, Toward, Against	OFFER	Ferre	Fer, Lat, Lay	To Bear or Carry
5. in-	Il- Im- Ir-	Into	INSIST	Stare	Sist, Sta	To Stand, Endure, or Persist
6. mono-	....	One or Alone	MONOGRAPH	Graphein	Graph	To Write
7. epi-	....	Over, Upon or Beside	EPILOGUE	Legein	Log, Ology	Speech or Science
8. ad-	A- Ac- Ag- Al- An- Ap- Ar- As- Al-	To or Towards	ASPECT	Specere	Spect, Spec, Spi, Spy	To Look
9. un-	....	Not				
Com-	Co- Col- Con- Cor-	With or Together	UNCOMPLICATED	Plicare	Plic, Play, Plex, Ploy, Ply	To Fold, Bend, Twist, Interweave
10. non-	....	Not	NONEXTENDED	Tendere	Tend, Tens, Tent	To Stretch
ex-	E- Ef-	Out or Formerly				
11. re-	....	Back or Again				
pro-	....	Forward or In Favor of	REPRODUCTION	Ducere	Duct, Duc, Duit, Duk	To Lead, Make, Shape or Fashion
12. in-	Il- Im- Ir-	Not				
dis-	Di- Dif-	Apart From	INDISPOSED	Ponere	Pos, Pound, Pon, Post	To Put or Place
13. over-	....	Above				
sub-	Suc- Suf- Sug- Sup- Sur- Sus-	Under	OVERSUFFICIENT	Facere	Fic, Fac, Fact, Fash, Feat	To Make or Do
14. mis-	....	Wrong or Wrongly				
trans-	Tra- Tran-	Across or Beyond	MISTRANSCRIBE	Scribere	Scribe, Scrip, Scriv	To Write

word with discernible parts, a child easily could lose heart, and could question his own abilities. Teach your youngster that studying prefixes, suffixes, and roots provides a valuable means of building vocabulary, but it is only *one* part of a larger pattern of growth and development.

Before we leave this subject, let me call your attention to an excellent scheme for vocabulary training developed by James I. Brown and pointed out to me by Mina Shaughnessy. Professor Brown provides a table of fourteen master words made up by twenty prefixes and fourteen roots. What is so astonishing about these words is that, knowing the meanings of the prefixes and suffixes that make them up, one has access to an enormous number of words. I urge you to have a good look at this table.

Guesswork in the Limelight

I want to tie up the basic goal of improving writing skills with a general consideration of how to deal with questions about new words. I think it's very important for you to resist telling your child the meaning of an unfamiliar word straight off. At the early stages of vocabulary growth, you will sometimes provide definitions immediately, but as soon as you can, begin to free your child from depending on you as a source of definitions. Suggest the patterns that you follow when *you* stumble on words you don't know.

Most people first use informed guessing as a means of unpuzzling a new word. Don't you try to figure out the meaning from the sentence in which the word appears? Most times you can come up with a definition that's accurate enough to let you guess the meaning; later on, perhaps, you'll check your guess in a dictionary. Children need to practice this guesswork whenever they can.

Suppose your daughter asks you to define a word—for example, *irritated*. You can rely upon your child's love of games and puzzles to urge her to use clues in sentences to figure out definitions. "I know what that means, Amanda. But let's see if *you* can guess what it means when I use it in a sentence. Listen carefully to the hints before you say anything. 'The woman left the party because smoke *irritated* her eyes.' What do you think it means?"

This strategy won't always work. You may have to try other sentences that have more obvious clues. But once your child gets the meaning, it's one she's put together from your clues *into her own language,* and you have helped her to use vocabulary that is already part of her repertoire.

Go on talking about the same word, and suggest sentences in which the word can be used: "Good, Mandy. That's right. It means *bothered.* Suppose I said, 'Mother was *irritated* because I forgot to buy eggs for tomorrow's breakfast.' What would that mean?" You might say, "What are some things that *irritate* you?" or "What does your brother look like when he's *irritated?*" Finally, ask your youngster to write the word down and to construct her own sentence using the word. A picture cut from a magazine or newspaper or an original that your child has drawn can illustrate the new word for visual reinforcement.

A dictionary plays a critical role in expanding vocabulary and serves writers in many ways. Often, it provides new meanings for already familiar words. Other times a writer seeks a dictionary when he drafts a sentence using a word that strikes him pleasantly or harshly, and he is not sure it means what he wants it to mean in the sense he has used it. Or he may be groping for a word, his sentence flow dammed up by uncertainty: Is it *healthful* or *healthy,* *meritorious* or *meretricious, ingenious* or *ingenuous?*

The writer may be unable to think of the exact word he wants; yet he can look it up because he knows its opposite. Perhaps he uses a word whose meaning fits the sense he has, yet he dislikes the sound of it or it's not precise enough in this instance. So he turns to a *thesaurus* (a book of synonyms). But he'll come back to his dictionary to look up the meaning of the synonym, which he might not know too well. A writer will use a dictionary to check the spelling of words as he finishes his manuscript before sending it to the typist.

And, of course, the dictionary is a book for reading, whenever the author wishes to take time out from the preparation of his manuscript.

I want to show you how to help your child learn to use a dictionary in a productive way. Teach your child that a dictionary is a resource for expanding word power, a means for learning new ideas, and a way to spend time enjoyably. Set a good example by using the dictionary yourself. How often do your sons and daughters see you with it in your hands, checking the meaning of a cookbook term, a word from the news, or a word you have heard in conversation? Unless your youngster recognizes it as a tool that people use in real situations, a dictionary becomes a text left in the classroom.

School instruction in dictionary use is, by nature, an artificial process. Typically, the teacher demonstrates the feature of a dictionary entry. By the third and fourth grade children are already learning about alphabetizing, guide words, diacritical marks for punctuation, entry words, even something about multiple definitions of words. The teacher must also help a child use a dictionary selectively: Information is so abundant that children must learn to *ignore* extraneous material when seeking the one or two details related to their search. To help develop these skills, a teacher will provide a list of new words or prefixes, and will require children to practice using a dictionary. Except to check on the spelling of a word he is writing in a story or composition, a child often does not use a dictionary in school to suit his own specific and immediate needs. However, the home environment can foster that use, and one of your primary goals should be to guide your child to use a dictionary creatively. I suggest that you buy children's editions, suitable for your child's age group at different stages of his or her development.

Those alphabet books that you have been buying since your son or daughter's first or second year are kinds of primitive dictionaries. Picture dictionaries provide a number of words for each letter; the illustrations usually portray a word's meaning in visual terms. Sometimes the book will have picture explanation of a word's meaning and a sentence to demonstrate that meaning. Look at this sample from *The American Heritage First Dictionary* (Boston: Houghton Mifflin, 1986).

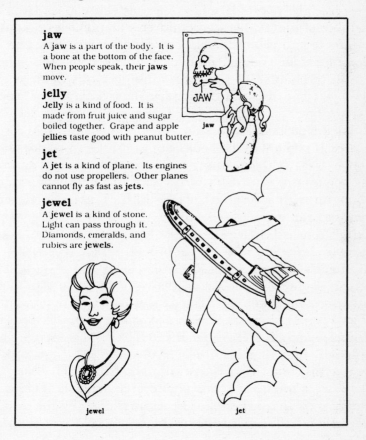

jaw
A jaw is a part of the body. It is a bone at the bottom of the face. When people speak, their jaws move.

jelly
Jelly is a kind of food. It is made from fruit juice and sugar boiled together. Grape and apple jellies taste good with peanut butter.

jet
A jet is a kind of plane. Its engines do not use propellers. Other planes cannot fly as fast as jets.

jewel
A jewel is a kind of stone. Light can pass through it. Diamonds, emeralds, and rubies are jewels.

jaw

jewel

jet

Because of its limited number of entries (*The American Heritage First Dictionary* offers only eighty-seven for the letter *A*, for example), picture dictionaries can focus your child's attention on the variety and delight of words, and your youngster will certainly pick up specific information and even will learn some new definitions. But picture dictionaries are not complete enough to be used as a tool to discover the meaning of unknown words. However, a picture dictionary helps your child establish the important habit of using word books as a source of information about language.

For eight-year-olds and over, you can choose from a number of more advanced children's dictionaries that are complete and clear enough for young writers. Buy one of these for your youngster's bookshelf and help him or her use it. In chapter 13 I suggest a number of specific ways that you can use the dictionary in a program of word expansion.

As a wordbook, a thesaurus is an important tool for a writer. It is the writer's book of options. If a word does not convey exactly the meaning or does not sound right among its neighboring words, a writer can check a thesaurus to come up with several other possibilities. Even an eleven-year-old can grow intoxicated with delight at the endless supply of word choices that exist for unspecific words such as *good*, *nice*, or *walk*. A simplified pocket thesaurus in dictionary form is a wordbook that's easy for a youngster to use. A child who looks up the word *happy* finds almost fifty different synonyms! The danger is that a young writer might run into trouble if he uses just *any* of those words to replace *happy*. For example, if you look up the word *happy*, you will find that both *delighted* and *blissful* are rough synonyms, but they are as different from each other as they are similar, and are not interchangeable. One can easily spot an inexperienced thesaurus user by the excess of million-dollar words he or she uses in place of simpler and more direct ones. On the whole, with guidance a child can learn to use a thesaurus to his or her advantage as a valuable sourcebook for the vast array of words in the language and their frequent interrelationships.

To an eleven-year-old, you can say, "Let's look up *happy* in the thesaurus and see how many words we can list." Your child will copy the synonyms onto a page and will ask about meanings and pronunciations for unusual words. You then will ask him to check a children's dictionary, then an adult one, in order to reinforce the interdependence of thesaurus and dictionary. Words supplied by the former are worthless unless the writer knows what they mean. After the list is complete, ask your youngster to write a sentence for some of the words or ask for an imaginative story of five or six of the words presented by the thesaurus entry. These kinds of language games use wordbooks to build writing skills.

Spelling Skills and Word Hot Spots

To the unprofessional eye, weakness in spelling imme-diately brands a writer as incompetent. Often the reader of a poorly spelled letter, memo, or job application makes an unfavorable judgment about the writer's intellectual abil-ity. This is unfortunate because poor spellers can be as intelligent or as unintelligent as good spellers, and compe-tent spelling does not assure skill in sentence structure. However, a page full of spelling errors jars the reader and often is disorienting. See how long you, as a reader, will put up with this piece written by a college freshman with no experience as a writer:

> Wmen's liberation is good in one way, but not in an-other way. Wemen should be paid the same amount of money as a men, in some field, for example. If wemen

have the knowlegde to become nurse, doctor or any other field, wemen should be paid the same amount of salary. If she doesn't have the knowlegde for that particular field, then she should not be paid the same salary. I think that wemen should have the same rights as a man. Because if a lady doctor is examining a patient, if she doesn't have the knowlegde, the patient eighter will become very ill or die. There are some job's in which wemen cann't work at, for example, sanatation department, plumer's ETC.

This eighteen-year-old author's bad spelling shocks you, no doubt, and leads you to the erroneous conclusion that he is severely limited intellectually. Yet it's easy to understand why you reached that judgment. Of all the writing-related skills children learn in school, they probably suffer most from spelling. You know the cycle in one form or another. First the teacher gives a pretest on twenty words for the week; during the rest of the week the children examine the twenty words, write each one several times and write sentences for each word; Friday is test day, when the teacher reads a word, uses it in a sentence, then asks the children to write the word down on paper and spell it correctly the first time. You know this pattern very well because you probably lived through it as a child and because you replace the teacher when your child studies at home.

I have a few insights to offer. First, you ought to know the seventy-five to a hundred words that are most frequently misspelled by children from the third grade through college. Look at pages 302 to 303 where I've reprinted such a list; it should help you be on guard for those words in your child's writing. They are the demons, the spelling headaches that plague most beginning writers and some accomplished ones.

Knowing problem words in advance helps you and your child keep a watchful eye for them. I believe one of the problems in teaching spelling is that letters in books look different from hand-printed letters. See the difference, here, between the *a* and *g:*

dragon *dragon*

Usually differences are not so obvious, but a youngster should learn the word in the medium in which he'll write it. When cursive writing begins, the differences among the three types of writing are more pronounced:

dragon *dragon* ***dragon***

Of course, a child must also see the word he's learning in type as well as in handwritten print so that he'll recognize it when he reads it. I always find it peculiar that spelling is tied more to reading as a skill than it is to writing. I rarely see a textbook that shows words in a child's handwriting. It seems to me that the mental picture that a child makes of the word ought to begin in the way he will *write* the word on a page. For older children and adults with spelling problems the teaching of diffeent words should be attempted through handwritten or hand-printed examples.

We should capitalize on the child's ability to create mental images. Therefore, I'd like to suggest another means of examining words. I have made a list wherein each word has a hot spot—a combination of letters that become confused in a writer's mind. What is interesting about these letter combinations is that they confuse *many* people. If you call attention to the hot spot in a memorable way (often with humor) you can help your youngster resist the problems these words present. Ask your child to look at five or ten words at a time, then to write them in clear firm letters. Underline, circle, or draw a box around the troublesome letters (in my list the hot spots are printed in italics); then play a game in which you and your child determine how to remember the hot spot, writing down the advice alongside the word. Here are some examples for the eight- or nine-year-old:

afr*aid*	Give *aid* after the *r*.
*amon*g	No *u* in this word—just *on*!
be*lie*ve	Never be*lie*ve a *lie*!
co*m*ing	Only one *m* in this word.
di*n*ing	Only two *n*'s in this word.
fri*end*	*I* am your fri*end* to the *end*.
ho*p*ing	I *hope* you remember only one *p*!
pleas*ant*	Do you see the *ant* in pleas*ant*?
sent*e*nce	Three *e*'s! No other vowel!
s*ur*prise	Say "Sir," but write *sur*. What a surprise!

You and your child will come up with countless others: "Look at *pa* in se*pa*rate"; "Rely on two *e*'s in sinc*ere*ly"; "No *e* in truly," are examples. These little memory tricks will go much further than rules or lists in helping your child with difficult spelling.

If your youngster returns from school with many words marked "incorrect" on a spelling test or in a piece of writing, you must be supportive yet firm. It's easy for a child to develop a sense of hopelessness about spelling—poor spelling often resists instruction. But spelling *can* improve if the writer is determined. As a parent you must encourage the kind of attitude that says, "Spelling improvement is possible."

How do you help the child build skills? First, develop a record-keeping system for misspelled words. Suggest that your child write words on index cards, and store them in a "Spelling Box," a homemade shoe-box affair; or you can suggest a list or chart format. Any of these is an excellent procedure for a child to use for study. Follow the steps you took when looking at spelling demons with your youngster (see pages 302 to 303). Here is a typical chart that focuses on individual mistakes:

My Spelling List
by Clair Anderson

Word	Hot Spot	Word with Hot Spot Underlined	Way to Remember
all right	two l's, two words	all right	Think of *all wrong*
across	only one c	across	a + cross
it's	apostrophe s	it's	it's = it is

Encourage your children to write their own sentences or little stories using the words that appear on these private lists.

Professor Shaughnessy suggests that writers group their mistaken words so that errors demonstrate a pattern. Using such a procedure, you may find that ten or twelve errors on a child's page will reduce themselves to four or five types of mistakes.

If your child asks you how to spell a word, spell it slowly and carefully, watching as your boy or girl writes it down. After your youngster finishes writing say, "Now let's put all those words you had trouble with on your own spelling chart so that you'll know them for next time." Even a four- or five-year-old who loves to write little stories will respond to a game of hunting out words and writing them down on a list. Of course you must exercise judgment about which words to bother with: A preschooler who struggles with a four-syllable word doesn't have to learn that word at this time.

As your youngster grows older, you will be inclined to advise, "Use the dictionary," when he asks you how to spell a word. I want to caution you about how frustrating this response can be to a poor speller. First, stopping to look up a word during the process of writing derails a writer from the track her thoughts are taking. If she must break her thought to look up a word in a dictionary, she might never come back to exactly what she wanted to say. When they use dictionaries, writers usually check spelling selectively, having been trained by practice to know just where to question the letters in a word. However, I have watched inexperienced young writers with dictionaries on their laps at story-writing time: They will stop at every third word to check their spelling. This is a terrible procedure, but teachers rarely point out its shortcomings.

Countless times I've heard "If I can't spell it, how can I look it up?" That *is* an intelligent question. It is also a good reminder of how little we have done to show children how to use a dictionary in such a situation. What do you answer?

Your conversation should run something like this: "Okay, here's a word that might cause you some problems in spelling: *crime*. Suppose you wanted to use a dictionary to check it. You've got to look under several possible spellings. The sound of the word might tell you to look it up in these ways:

cryme
kryme
creim
krime
krhyme
crime
crhyme

If you can't spell the word, you might have to check them all before you found *crime*."

With such a discussion you give your child some good tips about how dictionaries help spellers.

In fact, you should offer your child other kinds of advice about how to spell, advice that helps in the long-range acquisition of skills. Remind your sons and daughters about these steps toward better spelling:

- Listen carefully as someone says the word.
- Say the word yourself as you look at it.
- See if you can find the hot spot.
- Run your finger over the letters, saying each letter as you "write over" it with your finger.
- Close your eyes and try to see the word.
- Now write it down.
- Look at each letter. Check the word you have written against the word you were looking at. Did you include all the letters? Did you put the letters in the right order?
- Write the word again. Write a short sentence that uses the word.
- If you missed the spelling, put the word on your own spelling list.

Such procedures will help your child establish a learning program.

I've not encouraged working with spelling rules for several reasons: First, though the rules seem to work in teaching a child about word families, they do not seem to help him avoid misspelling a word he usually misspells. Second, very few rules stay with problem spellers for enough time to be practical. How many spelling rules can *you* remember today? (*Maybe i* before *e* except after *c*—and I bet you still have trouble applying it!) Teaching rules to young children assumes that a child can see and use the relations among word parts. Most poor spellers have trouble seeing word-part relations, so they cannot use the rules when trying to spell a word. The best way to use rules is to ask a child to state one in his own language each time he has spotted a pattern of misspelling among several words.

Sentences to Play With

If misused or misspelled individual words knock a reader off the horse, a trail of weak sentences on a page can similarly make the trip a pleasant or a nasty one. A paragraph of sentences that all start the same way, have about the same length, and follow pretty much the same pattern make a boring ride, a journey across a changeless landscape. In paragraphs were relations between ideas never focus, and where thoughts tangle, fragment, and run together, the journey becomes intolerable, and ordinary readers refuse to go further—they stop reading.

The manner of structuring sentences, of putting words together in ways that are clear, varied, and directly related to the expressed ideas is called *syntax*. The arrangement of words in a sentence is difficult for many writers. Immature college writers can astonish a reader, for example, in that their spoken language is often rich in varied structure—they put words together in complex, highly related forms—but their written language shows remarkable inexperience with the syntactic options. That's from lack of practice. Since effective writing is often measured by the writer's use of mature structures, you will want to increase your child's experimentation with sentence patterns. What I mean by mature sentence structure will grow clearer when you look at some samples, but at this point, just keep in mind that there's nothing *basically* mature or immature about the syntax of a given sentence. The reason should be clear: The structure a writer chooses must be the *best* possible one to put forth meaning intended. Sometimes a simple sentence of four or five words reveals the writer's intention better than a more complicated pattern. Other times, because of the play of ideas and the crosscurrents of related meanings, writers join elements that might better stay apart.

See what your reaction is to the structure of the sentences the writer uses to advance her meaning here:

> I held my friend Carol's new baby, Jim. I enjoyed the
> experience very much. We rested on a worn red easy chair
> in the warmth of the living room. I fed Jim his nighttime

bottle. He was too tired to drink. The television screen cast flickering shadows on the ceiling and walls. Jim strained to watch the screen. He licked the nipple with a tiny pink tongue. His head rested in the curve of my elbow. He gurgled with contentment. He fell asleep. I carried him into his room gently.

This writing is choppy, even childish. The sentences are needlessly repetitive and resist interrelating ideas for clearer meanings. The vocabulary makes good sensory appeal, but the writer's sentence patterns work against her effective use of language. Below the paragraph has been revised:

> When I held my friend Carol's new baby, Jim, I enjoyed the experience very much. Resting on a worn, red easy chair in the warmth of the living room, I fed him his nighttime bottle, which he was too tired to drink. As the television screen cast flickering shadows on the ceiling and walls, Jim strained to watch it. He licked the nipple with a tiny pink tongue, his head resting in the curve of my elbow. Then he fell asleep, gurgling with contentment. Gently I carried him into his room.

In this sample you can see a greater maturity of expression, because the writer interrelates the narrative events through the use of sentence structure. The first sentence makes a logical connection between the event and the writer's appreciation of it. The second sentence suggests simultaneous action (resting *and* feeding); in the first paragraph you read those as separate actions. Further, the second sentence uses the word *which* to relate the baby's tiredness and his inability to drink the bottle. Notice how in sentence three the writer shows a clearer relation between the flickering television and the baby's straining: One action depends upon the other. In the fourth and fifth sentences actions again depend on one another.

You can see the tongue licking *as* Jim rests in the writer's arm; and you can see the baby falling asleep while he gurgles at the same time. In the last sentence the use of the word *gently* creates a new emphasis and then provides a new sentence pattern, one not used before in the paragraph.

It's easy to see that in the second paragraph the writer expresses her thoughts more maturely in sentence patterns that state her ideas clearly and that keep more to her purpose in writing.

Although numerous studies have found that instruction in grammar has little bearing on writing growth, teachers continue to teach grammar as if it *did* influence writing skills. Others support the kind of plan followed by men like John Milton and Benjamin Franklin: Sentences that have been written by masters become models that developing writers copy for style and structure. Some relatively recent research suggests a new approach, which its originators call "sentence combining." Here a child, following directions, replaces one sentence element with an element from another sentence to create a tighter structure. By working with language supplied to him, a child shifts, replaces, and alters words and word groups. The assumption is that once he creates a sentence of complex syntax, he can then re-create that structure in his own language. Results from experimentation with school children by sentence-combining expert Professor Frank O'Hare bear out that assumption and demonstrate that such sentence-combining practice is not dependent upon a formal knowledge of grammar.

Look at this combining procedure, which is often called *embedding* because the writer inserts (embeds) an idea from one sentence into the sentence that comes before it, changing forms of words as necessary. These practices of combining sentences are called *transformations;* and the grammar system that describes the way the language operates through embedding is often called *transforma-*

tional grammar. It's really simple. In each of these groups, notice how the sentence (or sentences) in 3 results from combining features of 1 and 2.

1. The child cried.
2. The child was hungry.
3. The child who was hungry cried.

1. The old man tapped his cane.
2. The old man hobbled down Oak Lane.
3a. The old man hobbling down Oak Lane tapped his cane.
3b. Hobbling down Oak Lane, the old man tapped his cane.

I don't intend to suggest that you become *teachers* of this sentence-combining activity. That would be too time-consuming for the average parent and would require too much training. You'd need to invent countless sentence examples in groups that could be combined effectively into a final sentence that made sense. Further, you'd have to be able to write clues for your child so that the combining elements provide practice with various syntactic forms. Professor O'Hare's exercise for a group of twelve-year-olds would look like this:

A. The slave cried out for mercy. (ing)
   The slave threw himself at the sultan's feet.
   The slave had been caught in the harem. (WHO)

B. Crying out for mercy, the slave, who had been caught in the harem, threw himself at the sultan's feet.

Notice how the *ing* and the *WHO* in parentheses direct a youngster to perform special operations in combining the sentences. That example, like most of the others Professor O'Hare uses, is lively and well thought out, obviously requiring more time to construct than any parent (no matter how willing) would reasonably be able to give.

However, you can adapt a number of these sentence-combining ideas into games young children can play with great fun at home. In the first place, I suggest that you provide examples for youngsters to use their *own* language as they perform certain embedding activities. Next, you can offer a sample that shows the kind of new sentence that might be created. You will not come anywhere near a complete examination of possible sentence combinations, but I will indicate the kinds of activities you might set up so the child can practice sentence patterns.

Establish two columns for combining. Then ask your child to embed an item from column B into a sentence in column A, so that the result makes sense.

A	B
The car broke down.	who lives in Texas
My cousin owns a horse.	that I love
Carrie's book dropped with a clatter.	which fell from her desk

Once your youngster writes a sentence like this one:

My cousin who lives in Texas owns a horse.

you then provide a similar activity in which your child fills in blanks in a sentence:

My aunt who _____ writes _____.

I call this the Jigsaw Sentence—it is a puzzle with some pieces in place and others waiting for your child to create. Its advantage is that a child can use in a new syntax words that are based in his own concrete experiences. A child is writing about a real aunt, thus using his acquired combining skill to provide information relevant to his own life. After inventing pieces for the Jigsaw Sentence, a child then can follow these instructions: "Write a sentence about your sister and use *who* the way you did in the Jigsaw Sentence."

In my word-combing chart you'll find examples that you may copy with your own words and set into columns for your child to combine into a sentence. Remember, each item represents a type of combining. To be effective, you'll need to make up several examples for each, so that your boy or girl has sufficient practice. I'd say eight- or nine-year-olds could manage these games nicely—from the combining of elements in the two columns, through the Jigsaw Sentence, to a youngster's original statement.

A. Main Sentence	B. Word Groups for Combining	C. New Sentence	D. Suggested Jigsaw
We ran through Sunset Park.	because we were late (Similar words to start word groups for combining in this way are *although, since, after, so, that, when, whenever, if, how.*)	Because we were late we ran through Sunset Park We ran through Sunset Park because we were late.	Because ___ ___ ___, we looked ___ ___.

A. Main Sentence	B. Word Groups for Combining	C. New Sentence	D. Suggested Jigsaw
The sparrow shivered.	sitting on the roof (Similar words— almost any that end in *ng* work in this instance—to start word groups for combining in this way are *dancing, laughing, running, playing, singing, and so on.*)	Sitting on the roof, the sparrow shivered. The sparrow sitting on the roof shivered.	Dancing ____ _____ _____, the child _____ _____ _____.
Johnny made a snowball.	dressed in a warm red sweater (Similar words— almost any that end in -*ed* work here—are *placed, locked, poured, and so on.*)	Johnny, dressed in a warm red sweater, made a snowball. Dressed in a warm red sweater, Johnny made a snowball.	Placed _____ _____ _____, the doll _____ _____ _____.

A. Main Sentence	B. Word Groups for Combining	C. New Sentence	D. Suggested Jigsaw
		(Point out the humor— and the incorrect expression— if the combining element . goes in the wrong place: Johnny made a snowball *dressed in a warm red sweater.*)	
Flora baked cookies.	a good cook (Any word group that describes the person or thing named in the main sentence works here.)	Flora, a good cook, baked cookies. A good cook, Flora baked cookies.	Mommy, ___ _____, bought ___ _____.

Those four examples will help you and your child practice sentence combining techniques. Though they do not show a youngster how certain elements substitute for others, these sentence games encourage manipulation of sentence parts, which all writers need to practice.

I want to repeat that preparing games like these will take considerable time. Even if you don't have the time, it's enough to know about sentence-combining possibilities. A child who presents for your approval a paragraph that looks like the story of Jim on pages 134 and 135 will learn from your comments, such as: "There are excellent pictures here—I can see everything so clearly. But why don't you try to combine some of your sentences? Let's see. Can you put the first two together using *when?* Can you change *rested* to *resting* and then put sentences three and four together? What other combinations can you make?"

Though I've talked quite a bit about how to structure sentences correctly and maturely, you've no doubt noticed that I've not mentioned much about the incorrect sentences children write. I talked about sentence fragments in chapter 4, but I've deliberately excluded lengthy discussions about sentences that run together, about sentences whose verbs and subjects don't work correctly, and about sentences whose pieces do not fit together sensibly. Children make so many different kinds of sentence errors that it is the trained teacher's job to be able to react to those individual problems. A discussion of grammatical concepts here would take me too far from my purpose, which is not so much to make you competent in pointing out and dealing with language problems as much as it is to give you ideas for developing positive attitudes toward writing, and to help you guide your child in enjoyable writing activities at home.

For those of you who want more information about specific areas of correctness, I have provided an overview of language instruction in Appendix B. It will help you deal effectively with writing errors. I have not written a grammar course, only a sampling of some typical kinds of mistakes inexperienced writers make with sentences, and I follow it with suggestions for correcting those errors.

8

Snapshots of Special Places

■ ━━━━━━ ■

From the earliest moments of awareness infants respond to
their physical environments. As children grow, the intensity of those impressions strengthens through familiarity
and repetition (and sometimes through some single yet
dramatic event). The places in which youngster lives, eats,
plays, and dreams all make an indelible impression upon
the film of memory. It is to these powerful images that you
can turn for creative activities in writing. Description is a
key skill, one that your child will need to demonstrate
frequently, so nurture that skill as best you can in the
home.

The Senses, Front and Center

Which room will you and your child choose to explore
through word pictures? The choice is limitless really:
There's the bedroom, which defines more than any other
your child's world—dolls, trucks, and stuffed dogs lining a

143

wall, bits of rocks, crayons, cutouts strewing a desk; there's the bright yellow kitchen, the thud and click of its cabinets, the whirring of the refrigerator and its cold breath, the scent of apples and raisins from the oven where a pie crust lifts and browns; there's the park, not far off, and its creaky swings, its maze of gray metal bars for climbing, the crunch of dry leaves under sneakers; there's the doctor's office, such a mysterious, often scary place, crackling white paper stretched across an examination table, balls of cotton in round blue jars, that glass cabinet with bottles and boxes and silver tools; there's the grocery store or the street corner or the library or a church or an empty lot; there's the beach or the riverside, a living room, a friend's room, the bathroom, a ballpark, a gym, or a bakery. If you've been sharing experiences with your child, been talking and writing in the language of sensory awareness, you'll be impressed with all the possibilities for describing a place.

This is an exercise children of any age can practice with your guidance and assistance—even a child who writes haltingly and who must copy your attempts to put his words into written language or who must ask for words to be spelled with great frequency. It's the rare child who cannot observe a place, name an object, show its color or an action it performs, name a sound it makes or a smell it has or a sensation of touch it conveys. You've been practicing those skills with your child all along, so that when you write about some special place together, much of it is crossing familiar ground.

Begin by asking your child to describe the room in which he or she is sitting at that moment. With such an activity you have the place in constant focus and you can help your youngster construct sentences or even write them yourself as he or she dictates. Encourage your child's efforts by saying, "Very good! How about adding a color?" or "Let's put in a word to show how the thing felt when you touched it."

For a first writing assignment I often ask a class to describe their classroom as they write. Here is an example by a thirteen-year-old:

> On this October morning I hear the excited murmur of my classmates as Mr. Wiener introduces our theme topic. At once the teacher writes down the requirements of the theme. The milky, white chalk glides across the dusty blackboard. Once in a while the chalk creates a shrill screech, forcing me to tremble and quiver as I feel goose bumps. A gentle, lazy breeze flutters through the room, filling it with a feeling of sluggishness and an air of freshness. Jeff's fingers run quickly through his dark brown hair; a serious expression sits upon his face. Steven bites nervously on the cap of his pen as thoughts leap through his mind. As the teacher plods around the classroom, I hear his black shoes squeaking and shuffling along the floor. A faint tapping rushes from the back of the room sounding much like Indian war drums. I feel the iciness of the desk's iron legs as my feet lean toward them. The smell of the vinyl book cover floods my nose. Suddenly the bell rings: a quiet classroom turns into a hullabaloo. And so, another English period has become part of the past.

An easy way to encourage a youngster to record sense impressions is to play the following little game before your child actually begins writing his description. On a large sheet of paper, upon the chalkboard, on separate index cards, or on pages, help your child develop a table of sense images which later can be expanded and improved upon in a descriptive paragraph. First the writer indicates the place and time during which he or she makes the observations, then in each column, lists sense words and words groups evoked by the place at that time:

Sense Table

Place: my bedroom
Where: Kings Highway
When: Saturday morning

What I Saw	What I Heard	What I Touched	What I Smelled or Tasted
red and white blanket	the oil burner rumbling downstairs	soft blanket	coffee
pink walls	my bed squeaking	cold pillow and	sweet whole-wheat toast
black and white picture of the Country Mouse	Mom's footsteps	wall near my bed	
Barbie doll on the white desk			
yellow sun shining through the shades			

From those collected impressions the writer builds a description of the place:

It is Saturday morning in my bedroom on Kings Highway. A black and white picture of the Country Mouse is on the pink wall near the door. I see a red and white blanket on my bed. It feels soft. My pillow is very cold and so is the wall beside me. I see my Barbie doll sleeping over there on the white desk. She does not mind the yellow sun shining through the shades. I can hear the oil burner rumbling downstairs and my bed squeaking when I move. I hear Mom's footsteps in the kitchen. She is making breakfast for us. I smell coffee and sweet wholewheat toast. I don't like coffee, but the toast smells delicious!

You'll notice in this simple description how the writer relies upon the table of senses she prepared. The words "I see," "I can hear," "I smell" help provide starting points for full-sentence images. Encourage simple and direct statements; urge your child to write sustained sensory images. Even if all the sentences in these early efforts begin "I see" or "I hear," applaud them. Notice, too, how this writer combined sense impressions of different types and how she connected the ideas in her writing with words like *beside me, near the door, over there, downstairs.*

I have listed some goals for this writing exercise. It's an excellent idea to discuss this list with your child before writing begins. I've found that the clearer the expectations and aims for an activity, the better a youngster performs. With such a list at hand, your responses to your child's writing can be specific, more than just empty praise. I present these "goals" in question form as suggestions for effective writing:

What to Aim For: Tips for Strong Descriptions of Place

1. Do you name the place you are describing and tell where it is?
2. Do you tell the time of year or the day or time of day you are looking at the place?
3. Do you name several colors?
4. Do you name some sounds or actions?
5. Do you tell what things you touched and how they felt?
6. Do you tell what you smelled or tasted?
7. Do you connect the ideas together with words like *beside, near, over there, downstairs?*

These suggestions, coupled with the sense table, provide a stimulus for descriptive writing and later provide a guide for improving the first attempt. "What a lively description you have. But why don't you find a word to name the sound of Mommy's footsteps? Do they *creak, scrape,* or *thump* on the floor?" With clear aims and techniques, such as the sense table and list of goals, you can overcome one of your young writer's biggest fears, that of not knowing what to write about.

Wherever possible, show your child an example of what you mean. You can read the samples from this book to your daughter or son. You might write something yourself! Nothing illustrates better than an example: A child who reads another child's creation has a realistic model at which to aim his or her own level of achievement. Of course, the goals of an activity are always clearer when weighed against a completed project.

Along with our attempt to help children heighten and expand the level of sensory diction in their writing, talk about building, combining, expanding, and altering sentences. In the paragraph on page 145, the writer uses a simple structure: She begins many sentences with "I." You might say, "In sentence three why don't you try to change the sentence around so you don't begin with *I*?" (On my bed I see the red and white blanket.) "Now combine three and four using *which*." (On my bed I see a red and white blanket, which feels soft.)

Opinions in Focus

For the developing writer, sustained description rooted in sensory language can grow overwhelming. The more acute the writer's sensory awareness, the easier it is to collect details. A weakness often found in an inexperienced writer's attempts at description is that he or she presents a flood of images that have lost their focus when removed from the time and place of their origin and set on paper.

The youngster looks around and records whatever sensory impressions strike him. A single place can stimulate hundreds of responses and merely recording those responses fills page after page. Your goal is to make the description easier to manage by helping your child select key details that relate to each other beyond their mere common existence in a given place. What I am saying is that you must help your young writer learn which details *not* to include as much as you need to show her which ones are necessary to the description.

Before your child records sensory images she should identify some overall impression that has about the room she wants to describe. When she looks at a kitchen is it *messy, cheerful,* or *noisy?* When she responds to the doctor's examination room is it a place that's *scary, tense,* or *pleasant?* Is the bakery a *busy* place? Is the synagogue *quiet* or *loving* or *active?* Is the classroom *tense* or *relaxed?* Is the train station *bustling* or *empty?* By encouraging the expression of some attitude, opinion, judgment, or point of view about this place, you contribute to your child's developing skills as a descriptive writer and as a writer in general. You're helping to focus the description, and, in a larger sense, you are helping to train your child about details carefully.

I want to consider briefly the notion of objectivity. You may ask about the form of descriptive writing in which writers remove themselves from their subject matter, with the purpose of providing a complete, nonsubjective collection of detail. Scientific or reportorial writers fancy themselves wholly objective; their goal is to collect details, so that they *define* things by recording an endless train of impressions. I'm uneasy about that: Distinctions between objective and subjective descriptions often seem to me to be only a matter of degree. You can look at one description when comparing it to another and say, "This is more objective than that." I suppose you would mean that less of the writer appears in that particular piece than in the other. But, as soon as a writer records detail, he's making some judgments about degrees of completeness, about which items to exclude, about which to place first or last in a presentation, about which to stress by means of alternate word choices. Very subtle subjectivity is operating here, one that the writer (be he scientist, news reporter, or industrial manager) may not have identified for himself.

The closest I ever came to "objective" writing was as an undergraduate in a comparative anatomy class at Brooklyn College. In the warm spring months we sat at our lab tables, our white coats smeared and stained, while we examined dogfish lying on black paraffin trays. In those days instructors in every subject looked upon writing as an essential part of a course, and Professor Benjamin Coonfield, an austere Southerner with glasses and a small black moustache, terrorized us with his rigorous vision of language. He demanded a formal report, submitted at the term's end, as a record of our anatomical journey through the dogfish shark. The report had to describe fully the object we had dissected and poked at with cold probes for more than seven weeks.

We spent a full session talking about how to write our reports, during which we laid down his rules for words and sentences. Our writing must be simple; we must avoid overstatement and overexpressive (what he viewed as "poetic") language; we must be precise. For example—and this was the most challenging and difficult part of our task—we could never use the word for an anatomical feature (nose, ear, eye) until we had described that feature fully. It was the size, the shape, the color, the position on or in the body that we identified first. Then we might say: "We will call such an organ *the ear.*" Professor Coonfield insisted that our word choice be perfect: Do veins really *run* down the thoracic cavity? Are there two *pair* or two *pairs* of arteries? We found ourselves scurrying for dictionaries. Though I grumbled without end, this approach did more for developing my sensitivity to nuance and precision of language than any other course I took. His purpose was to approximate inductive reasoning in the writing process: We gathered a number of particular details before adducing some general principle, which in this case might be the word of identification for the described object. But his larger goal was to have us describe the anatomical features of the dogfish so completely and objectively that a person who never saw the fish would have an accurate and scientific description of it.

This was a helpful activity for me as a writer—it forced me to look at words and language in a way I never had before—but I see now how short it fell of its purpose. I remember wondering about the innumerable gray bumps along the face of the shark, bumps that ought to be counted and measured (they were, after all, features of the anatomy). Yet, I decided not to list them because they would take too long to record and because, in comparison to the other features of the face (jaw, eyes, nares, teeth, and so on), those bumps paled in importance. I see now how many aspects of the dogfish anatomy my colleagues and I chose to ignore.

Even though factual writing implies a lack of subjective thinking, all this suggests that even in an intense scientific setting, writers exercise selectivity when they present detail. They do not focus this selectivity by means of some judgment or attitude they have about the object; nevertheless, by *some* process of evaluation they report certain details and not others. The doctor who writes a medical report can make it only as complete as his individual judgments allow. And, I think, reporters of fires, robberies, and murders are deceiving themselves when they think that their view is objective.

I am not arguing against "objective" writing, but I am trying to suggest that it is difficult to distinguish it absolutely from subjective writing.

Subjectivity Leads the Way

When your child writes about a place, help him or her use subjective responses to select and order details. Help your youngster zero in or his or her attitude toward that place. You may have to ask a number of questions and to suggest a few possibilities from which your child may choose, such as "What *one word* would you use to show what you felt about the supermarket we visited this afternoon? Was it *quiet, busy,* or *noisy?*" Once a writer identifies a reaction, he collects only those details that relate to that reaction. Beginning writers should give details of time and place, and they should identify their opinion about what they are describing in the first sentences they put down. Encourage first sentences such as these:

- Our kitchen on a Sunday morning looks messy!
- Sitting here in this basic English class on a rather warm Monday morning, my fellow prisoners probably feel the tension of doing their first writing.
- The library on Park Boulevard is very quiet this Tuesday afternoon.

If these sentences served as starting points, a writer next would add details that support his or her impressions about each place. The writer of the first sentence would add details to illustrate the kitchen's messiness; in the second sentence he or she must support the claim that the class feels tension; and in the third sentence add details to picture quietness further.

As your youngster advances, he can create and sustain a dominant impression without exactly stating his opinion toward the place. Notice how this sixteen-year-old creates a mood of despair, almost imprisonment, as he describes the locker room where he must change clothes for work. Look especially at the last sentence, which summarizes, brilliantly, the impact of the scene.

Five o'clock again and the beginning of another night of work, here at The Kitchen in Green Acres. The punch clock stamps out the time with a thud, like a heavy metal gate falling closed, imprisoning me. The smells of flour and frying fat and the clatter of a hundred dirty dishes in the dishwater fall behind me as I near the dull gray door streaked with grease and soot, the door that leads to the basement and locker room.

The door flies open before I even reach it and Bill rushes out, beads of sweat still on his brow, his face red, his skin shining from body oil, his hand brushing strands of hair into place as he passes. The door closes behind me and before me in a narrow rectangular tunnel descends the long stairway to hell. Halfway down, I feel the heat of the boiler room, and the musty smells hit me, but it's not till I reach the locker room that I first see the inferno. There stretches before me a long, narrow room, with the left side and rear wall covered by broken lockers painted gray, many with doors permanently ajar or completely torn off, and others with their doors jammed shut. The ceiling, once painted white, now stands dirtied by the soot of years past and scarred by the rust of the pipes running parallel and perpendicular across it. The right wall is made of cinder blocks and in front of it stands a clothes rack; no clothes hangers swing here and only one shirt hangs from a joint on the rack's far end.

Behind the open door sits the bin that holds the dirty checkered pants, usually soaked from soapy water. It holds the dirty shirts and aprons stained with food and bearing the colors of red, blue, black, and brown. By the end of the week the bin also holds the only uniforms left, so that I must pick through this maze of dirty rags to find the cleanest of the dirty.

One broken chair sits at the far end of the room, and many worn shoes lie scattered upon the floor. In the corner between the two lockers sits a box of receipt tapes of years past, forgotten and gathering dust.

Sitting down, I pull my shirt off and reopen my eyes to the dim light shed by one feeble bulb. The room hums with the rumble of the boiler in the next room and the clatter from above. A cool drop of water falls on my hand from a leaky pipe above as I gaze down at the floor, its original color smeared with the black of grease and gum.

I look absently over to the gray door standing open to the room, but mainly to the sign pasted on it reading This Is Your Locker Room, Keep It Clean. My eyes now drop to a comment written in reply to the sign and penned boldly in black Magic Marker directly on the door: I Agree.

A roach slowly turns the corner of the doorway, his feeling antennas like hairs blowing in the wind and I feel as though he belongs here more than I.

Cameras and Crayons

Children can command few other mechanical wonders with the ease that they manage cameras. An inexpensive camera lights fires even in the most reluctant writer.

After he or she writes a paragraph describing a place, turn your child loose with a roll of film! Keep your instructions simple: "Take ten pictures that show why you feel this room is messy," or, "Take one picture that shows what each sentence in your paragraph describes." Develop the snapshots and have your child paste them on sheets of paper. Then ask your youngster to write a sentence about the action and details in each picture.

You can even start with the camera *before* your youngster writes. From a five- or six-year-old just ask for photographs that will show different features of a place. Ask an older child to portray his attitude or impression of some place with pictures. You then can use those photos to stimulate your child's written reaction in a group of sentences. Whether you use photos before your child writes or afterward, ask for written words to explain each picture.

Our daughter snapped her first picture at the age of three, and I suspect we might have let her try it even earlier than that. What a thrill when the photograph your child took comes back from the developer! If you have a Polaroid or one of the other instant developers, there's even more immediate reinforcement. A child snaps a picture and watches the scene develop before his or her own eyes. Your youngster can secure these photographs with a sentence of explanation in a scrapbook entitled *Places I Like.* Paste each photograph on a page and write a sentence of explanation under each.

You help your child establish the idea of opinion or attitude as a key to writing by connecting it with some cut-and-paste fun. Make a list of words that one might use to describe a place *(busy, quiet, neat, lively);* then ask your child to cut a picture representative of each word from a magazine. He should choose his favorite picture, then write a description that presents details about the picture he's cut out, details that support his dominant impression. Using a large sheet of paper (8½-by-13 inches), help your child paste the picture on top of the page. Below it he should copy the final draft of his paragraph. An illustration prepared by your child can be used in the same way you used the snapshot with a camera. You can ask your youngster to draw and color a picture of his favorite place either after or before the writing exercise, depending upon how you want to use it.

In both instances you're relating your child's writing with his communication in another medium. This connection opens countless roads to creative expression.

Description Described

Don Wolfe, a great teacher of writing who died in 1976, wrote that the assignment that asks a child to describe a room "has explosive power to raise standards of writing on every level" and that it "calls forth the use of sensory diction in almost every sentence, the gold of communication, the nearest approach to sound and color films. . . . It calls for the realistic and imaginative observation that flows immediately into language. It proves to the child that he can paint pictures in words. . . . [It] shows the way to electric communication of the child's deepest feelings and most profound moments of insight."

9

One Person in the Floodlights

As we've seen, the familiar physical world is a rich source for a developing young writer. The women and men who people that world also make excellent subjects for practicing good writing. If you follow the techniques that focus on sense impressions, you can direct your child to write a simple description of a person. Mother, seated in the green leather chair beneath the window, reading *Newsweek;* Dad scrambling eggs in the kitchen on a sunny Sunday morning; the letter carrier as she strolls from house to house; a bank teller shuffling bills and counting out coins on a wooden counter; the butcher in a long white coat as he cuts a bone with an electric saw; a brother or sister, aunt or uncle, cousin, friend, or classmate in a flash of action or a moment of repose—all these become subject matter for a child writer.

One Person, One Sentence

A simple and pleasant writing exercise for a youngster directs him or her to look at a person and to write a single sentence that describes that person performing an action. The word games you have been playing with your child will sharpen the precision of the image he can convey. Activities in choosing a concrete word for a general one, in capturing movement with exact action, in writing sensory language, in expanding and combining sentences help your child succeed in this exercise. Again, you should offer clear directions: "Write a sentence that tells what _____ is doing. Try to use lively words for action, color, sound, and touch." Read your child an example—one of those below or one you have written to describe someone, perhaps your child himself.

Here are several one-sentence descriptions to show to your youngster before you work together on this activity. You can see how sensory images make the brief portrait come to life.

Momma sits on our squeaky rocking chair with her soft brown hands on her lap.

Robert, the newspaper boy, zips by on his bike and tosses the *Centre Daily Times* onto the porch.

My brother Joseph dribbles on his yellow pajamas as he pokes his teddy in the playpen.

A Party Riddle

At the next party you and your child make, plan to have the guests write riddles as a party game. Every child gets a pencil and a pad of paper. Explain the game: "You all have pencils and paper. We're going to write a riddle. Look around the room and find one person you think you can describe in a few sentences. But don't tell us who the person is. Make your description as clear as you can, so that we can guess from your sentences who your person is. You might want to write about what the person did earlier at the party, something you remember. Be sure to tell us what the person looks like, how she moves, what color her clothes are. Put these four things into your description:

1. Show how the person moves or what he or she does.
2. Use a color and a sound.
3. Show a bit of the person's clothing.
4. If the person talks, tell what the person says and how the person says it.

After you talk about these points, see if everyone understands them. Then read a sample like this one.

> I see a little girl in red pants and a white blouse with red and green flowers. She scratches her short brown hair. In her hands she holds a yellow pencil. She is smiling and her warm brown eyes make me happy. She is my best friend. Who is she?

or this one:

> There is a boy at this party who shouted, "I won! I won!" when he pinned the tail on the donkey. He is wearing brown pants and a gray sweater. He has little brown freckles on his nose. They are hard to see under his blue glasses. He likes green jelly beans only. Who is he?

This games relies upon a child's natural love of riddles and keen sensory awareness. It's sure to be a hit with any child and helps your youngster practice key writing skills.

Photo into Words

That tin oval, the large wooden box, or the tattered scrap-book that holds your photograph collection is an object of delight and mystery for every child. I have watched children sit for long hours, sifting through a maze of pictures strewn about the bedroom floor, studying familiar and strange faces with concentration, laughing at styles, smiles, and actions.

This intense interest in snapshots of family, friends, and even strangers can be used for another stimulating writing exercise for your youngster. Select a picture of some person from your photo collection, and ask your child to study the subject's face and pose, and the setting of the photo. Your goal is to encourage your youngster to write four or five sentences that will give life to the picture. Ask him to imagine action, sound, and color (if the photo is in black and white) and to try to identify the person in the picture. The picture selected can be of someone he knows well or has never met. What is important is the intensity of the appeal the person in the picture has for the writer. With your guidance, your child can write a visual portrait like one of these:

> My daddy's grandfather has a round face. In this pic-ture he leans against a brick wall. A brown cigar is in his mouth. I like his tiny blue eyes. If he could speak, he would cough like my daddy and say, "I have to stop smoking!"

> This is a picture of my mother before she met Dad. She is wearing a blue bathing suit at Rockaway Beach. I can see white bubbles from a wave behind her. Her blonde hair looks messy because a wind is blowing. She smiles at me. I can see her straight white teeth. But she can't talk to me because I wasn't born yet.

A collection of these little word portraits makes a lovely scrapbook of family favorites. Help your youngster mount pictures on colored paper or cardboard and the written portraits on facing pages. Ask friends and relatives to comment in your child's presence on the difference in the descriptive qualities of the visual and the verbal pictures.

Self-Portraits for the Very Young

As much as a child can write accurately in sensory language about a familiar person, I find the self-portrait an even more exciting activity. Young children love to look at themselves, to report what they are and how they look. This first manifests, I think, as little drawings such as the one Matthew drew of himself (see page 53) in order to tell a little story. You must have many paintings that your own children made of themselves.

Look at this self-portrait Melissa did on her own when she was five and a half.

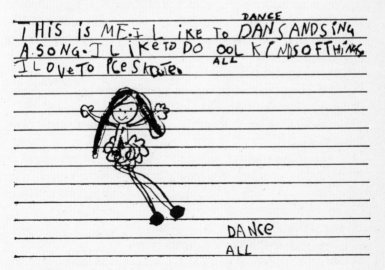

The picture and words are delightful, aren't they? However, I would have guided her to prepare a more sharply visual portrait, set in time and place, and showing much more sensory detail. Nonetheless you see here a child's impulse to define and describe herself, and it deserves great praise. I asked Melissa to read her words aloud, and we both enjoyed her word picture and her little drawing. She told me about the ballerina dress and the dancer's crossed legs. At this point she had not colored the sketch; it was completely in pencil.

After we had talked about her words and picture, I felt that I could help her use her sensory responses to sharpen the verbal portrait. Here's a rough summary of our talk.

"This is such a nice picture! I love the way you told all about yourself in sentences. But I bet you could add some words or ideas that would help make an even better picture of you."

"How? What do you mean?"

"I bet you can add a color word. Where could you name a color to make the picture clearer?"

"I don't know."

"Well, as the little girl in this picture, what color could you see around you, maybe a color of something you're wearing."

"Well, red. Red skates."

"Good! Try to put it in one of your sentences."

"I love to ice-skate in red skates."

"That's perfect. Now, see if you can tell about something you can hear."

"What do you mean?"

"I mean a word that gives a sound—as when you're skating."

"*Errrrr.*"

"What's that?"

"The sound of the skates on the ice."

"That's a wonderful sound! How about a *word* that tells a sound?"

"I don't know what you mean."

"Well, you've given the real sound the skates make. That's very good. But I thought you might want to use a *word* that tells the sound. For example, when someone moves across the floor the person can *thump* or *squeak* or *thud*. Those are all *words* that tell sounds."

"Slip? Slip on the ice?"

"That's a good word to show action, though it's not a sound."

"Let's put it in."

"Go ahead. Put it in."

"I slip on the ice . . . and slide. I slip and slide on the ice."

"That's a fine sentence. But don't you want to put in that sound, *errrrr?*"

"I slip and slide and go *errrrr* on the ice."

"I really like that! Now, can you put in a word that tells how the ice *feels?*"

"That's easy. Cold! No. Freezing. Let's put *freezing ice.*"

"All right. Good. Do you want to try to find a sound word, too? Can you tell how you sing?"

"What do you mean?"

"Well, do you *shout* or *squeak* or *sing* in a *soft voice?*"

"I sing in a soft voice. No. I sing like a bird."

"Okay. Let's put that in. What kind of bird?"

"A blue jay."

"Well, you've complained about how the blue jay makes such loud noises outside your window. It sings in a noisy way. Is that the way you sing?"

"No. A robin! A robin!"

"Does a robin have a soft song?"

"Yes. It's soft and pretty. A little *peep peep peep.*"

You can see through this little dialogue how you can encourage a child to explore words and to select only the most precise words that are concrete and sharp in sensory appeal. Melissa had some trouble understanding the concept of "sound word," and I continued to help her with that concept when she wanted to write. But her wonderful *errrrr* sound was characteristic of a child's original perceptions. I can't see how anyone else would have made that sound! Still, my intent in pressing her further was to try to have her look at legitimate words that name sounds as they show actions. She missed that concept—but she grasped quite a bit, so I didn't worry.

You can see how instinctively she turned to a figurative expression in order to clarify her description. Though not the most original simile from the professional writer's vantage point, it's fine as a child's effort, especially with the highly specific naming of the robin.

As Melissa spoke and made additions to her sentences, I hand-printed each one. This is her new story:

> This is me. I like to dance and sing a song like a robin.
> I love to ice-skate in red skates. I slip and slide and go
> *errrrr* on the freezing ice.

Melissa copied my printing. Then she took the page and made the pencil drawing as you see it.

Melissa was not really describing herself in her story but was instead telling about things she could do. I would have encouraged something more like the little paragraph on page 166. But this was her own work brought to me for reading, and within that context I helped her use the skills she had been working to expand. A week later Melissa announced that her kindergarten teacher, Mrs. Coleman, wanted all the children to describe themselves aloud to the rest of the class. WN I asked Melissa what she planned to say, she recited her self-portrait, and I was delighted with her use of detail:

> I am a white face with nice dark red lips. My teeth are
> shiny and white. My two new teeth are growing in the
> middle of the bottom. I have rosy red cheeks—well, not as

red as my lips. My hair is brown. I usually wear dresses
and in the winter I wear pants."

In my discussions with Melissa I dealt first with ways in
which she could improve the visual quality of her language and the exactness of her word choice. But in the
sentences she first showed me there were some errors with
which I wanted to deal. Since Melissa was offering me a
finished product, I felt it was necessary to talk with her
about some of the conventions of correctness that her sentences didn't follow.

We discussed the expectation that words will be spelled
right and that sentences will be correctly written when
people read someone's work. I reminded Melissa how periods tell readers when to stop. I read aloud her first sentence—"This is me"—and asked if she could tell what
happened to my voice on the word *me*. She heard how my
voice dropped, and I pointed out how I stopped reading
after that word. Together we established a working rule for
the period: It tells when a sentence ends, and it goes where
the voice drops and stops when the sentence is read aloud.
It's almost as if the voice knows automatically about sentence endings. I put a period after the *me*. She made it
darker and rounder. Then I asked her to read aloud from
the word on *I* to see if she could find where the next
sentence ended. She missed it, so I suggested she read
more slowly and take note of where her voice went down
and of where she stopped reading. She found it and drew
in a heavy dot after *song* and again after *things* and *skate*.

A major difficulty for inexperienced writers is keeping
sentences apart. So I advise you to seize any opportunity
to show children how to separate thoughts in sentences
with periods (or question or exclamation marks, depending on the intended meaning).

Next Melissa and I looked at the spelling in her self-
portrait. She had had no formal training, but she was a

first-rate phonetic speller. Our favorite was her spelling of
cucumber in a "vegetable book" she was illustrating. She
labeled it *ququmbr*. She spelled her words from her own
sight vocabulary or by carefully sounding out word parts. I
pointed out her spellings of dance *(dans)* and all *(ool)*, told
her that she had faithfully reproduced their sounds as best
she could, but that those were not the spellings people
used when they wanted to write those words correctly. I
then wrote the words right near hers so that she could
compare the spellings. Then I asked her to write them
correctly at the bottom of her picture (you see them over to
the right) by copying from mine. There was no guarantee
that she'd spell *dance* and *all* correctly the next time, but
the more practice she had the sooner she would be able to
spell them.

In his book for teachers, Don Wolfe offers a word portrait in which a child describes what he sees when he looks
into the mirror:

> In the mirror I see a boy with black hair and snappy
> black eyes. His name is Joe Havens. His chin is a large
> heavy one. On his nose is a bandage where he got hit with
> a tennis racquet yesterday. On his dark face I see lots of
> freckles. One big freckle is on the tip of his nose. When he
> smiles, he shows a couple of big white teeth in front with
> a space between them. I guess this boy needs braces, but
> he doesn't want them.

Notice the wonderful specificity in what for me is the
best sentence: "One big freckle is on the top of his nose."
And there are other fine word pictures: "black hair and
snappy black eyes," "dark face," "big white teeth in front
with a space between them." No child other than Joe
Havens could write this. As such, it is a supremely original
piece of himself that this child lays before the reader.

I often ask young writers to prepare a collage or a
diorama to represent themselves visually. In these efforts,

the young writer-artist tries to answer the question "What Am I?" Look at this illustration to see what I mean:

After the young man or women finishes the visual portrait I ask for a word portrait to answer the question "What Am I?" Here is one writer's response:

"What Am I?" is a question that takes a lot of soul-searching for me to answer. Sometimes I am the sound of an undertaker's voice reciting a eulogy for my father who died of cancer when I was four years old. I am the muffled sobs of sorrow I remember from my mother and the white lace handkerchief pushed against her lips. But I am also the confusion of voices whispering and my Aunt Helen's arms lifting me to hold me close and help me through something I didn't understand. I am the mixture of apology and hope in my mother's gray eyes when I first met my new father-to-be. I am the tension of my stepfather as he tries to read a book in Brookdale Hospital while my mother is inside having a baby. I am the rough kiss, the whiskers and cigarette smells when my stepfather hears from Dr. Beck, "Congratulations. You have a little boy." I am Michael Barry's cries in the middle of the night, the egg yolk in his breakfast dish, his dirty diapers, and the clean smell of baby lotion and powder after Mother bathes him. I am the noisy bustle of moving to Bayside, the clatter of dishes, the scrape of our old couch on squeaky new floors. I am the giggle of my friend Bobbi when I tell her about Saturday night's date. I am also the oversized black-and-white poster of Bob Dylan that smiles at me from above my bed. I am the pink-and-white daisies on my bedroom wall, the torn white sneakers in the corner, my vocabulary-building book hidden in the closet. I am the quiet moments in my room when night comes and I can think.

Expanding a Picture of Someone Close

Help prepare your child to write her description of a relative or friend by reminding her to set the person in a particular time and a particular place. Suggest that your youngster record bits of detail using a table of sense impressions (see page 146). She can begin writing while observing the person in the midst of some action. When you look at the rough draft, ask questions as I did with Melissa in order to focus your child's sensory awareness—and remember, it's important to read an example together first. In this sample, a young girl describes her sister:

I remember when my little sister Julia first came to live with us. She was just one week old. She looked like a little round beaver. When she wasn't crying, you could see that her eyes were blue. Her nose was like a little bell. Her mouth was a little round ball. As soon as she got home, she began to cry, and did she cry! When she started to cry, her mouth became a big O. Her hands were tiny, and her fingernails were as thin as eggshells. Julia was always kicking her feet in the air and waving her hands. We were all very proud of our new baby.

You can see here the sharp sensory images painted through this child's own language resources. These are clear pictures indeed.

Yet you can help your child climb beyond this. Once a writer determines the attitude, opinion, or reaction he or she feels toward the subject, it becomes easier to control the details and to make them tell the story as the writer sees it. To do this, the writer eliminates unnecessary details and focuses upon those details that support his or her opinion. Encourage your child to do this by saying, "What is your main opinion about the person? Is she *carefree* or *attractive* or *strong*? Is he *shy* or *bold* or *serious*?" Once your young man or woman expresses that opinion, you can help sort through the details. "What is there about the way he looks or moves that makes you think he is shy? What does he say or do that says *shyness* to you?"

I doubt that any writing skill is more important than description. Every kind of written activity demands description of some kind. In a school assignment a young writer must often explain a process—how a radio works, for example; or must compare two forms of government; or must explain why poverty exists. At some point he will have to turn to descriptive techniques. The training I encourage will sharpen your child's eye, and make him or her a shrewd observer who can transform observation and experience into written language.

A Moment Reborn in Language

Children have a natural ability to tell stories. In school one student's story may send a class on a visit to the supermarket; another's illustrates a principle of gravity; someone else's instructs the class on the roles of community helpers. Unfortunately schools rarely use children's great knack of telling real events as the core of established writing programs. Recalling a shining event from some particular day is an easy way for inexperienced writers to practice writing skills. When a child burns to communicate a story, the problems of carefully thinking out and inventing what to say and how to say it reduce themselves in a flow of language, a parade of scene. You can stimulate good writing at home, once you understand narrative techniques and how a child responds to narration.

What Is Narration? What Is a Moment?

Narration is relating an event. It is storytelling—but I hesitate to use the words *story* and *telling* because the word *story* frequently connotes *fiction, make-believe,* and *untrue;* and the word *telling* often implies a formal performance defined by behavioral conventions or rules.

I have nothing against imaginative writing, tales woven from a child's fancy, but the best way to stimulate the faithful recording of detail for beginning writers is through attention to real personal experience. When I use *story,* unless I say otherwise, I mean the telling of a real event.

And I appreciate the value of the formal front-of-the-class rituals children often must perform when teacher asks for a story. Yet the prescribed elements of those scenes can hamper the spontaneous flow of ideas.

At home you can establish better conditions for story exchange. As I explain in *Talk with Your Child,* a better term than storytelling is *story talk.* In *story talk* you establish a conversational format. It's less a performance than a dialogue. With the loose elements your child provides when he shares a story orally, you, as the active listener, help shape it through questions, supportive comments, summaries, and other elements of conversational exchange. Thus, as you engage in *story talk* with your young boy or girl, you can heighten linguistic awareness in a relaxed format and can prepare your child for narrative writing, a very important skill. In this chapter I'll point out many story talk strategies; you no doubt noticed a number of them already in earlier chapters. Narration is such an essential skill because it contributes to many other types of writing your child must learn, such as scientific or historical reports, explanations of processes, and argumentation.

In its simplest form, narration is the review of time through language. As such, it may unveil an event that occurred over a long period. Reporters and historians do this when they write about the instances that characterize a crime or a battle. With an enormous base of data at their fingertips experienced writers, by using details, can present an account of an extended occurrence so that readers feel that they are living through the times described.

Inexperienced writers rarely produce effective prose when they narrate events spread out over too vast a period of time. Children usually are given dreadful narrative writing assignments: "How I Spent My Summer Vacation," "What I Do on Saturdays." Can you imagine how difficult it is to squeeze three months or even twenty-four hours onto a single page! To complete such assignments, children frequently string occasions together without detail. They write, "First I did this, then I did that, later I did that," and so on. There's little there in the way of interesting material.

A single narrative moment is a successful approach to narration. By means of sense words, a writer (or speaker) expands the scene and action of a brief period. Don Wolfe first explained the concept of the narrative moment to me, and it has proven its value anew every time I have contact with developing young writers.

What is a *moment?* A moment is a single instance, a flash of time that a writer recalls sharply and can re-create in vivid language so that the event comes alive. Description (which we explored in chapters 8 and 9) must come into play here. The only way to expand a scene that is sharply limited in time is to fill in details of the moment—physical background, characters, actions, and march of events—using concrete sensory language. I see a great overlap between description and narration, although some teachers of writing will insist on "pure description," that is, description that excludes a sequence of events and attends only to physical details about the object, room, or person.

I do not believe that it is possible to write "pure narration" effectively. If the reader is to travel through the writer's moment, only descriptive detail achieves that goal. Certain kinds of writing, for instance, a scientific report that records details of an experiment or a business report that tells the history of a corporation, may have few sensory details. Still, even dry, detached narration uses details of some kind, and a sharp visual image immediately transports a reader into the scene.

So, all your attention to concrete sensory detail until now prepares your child for another leap into writer's territory.

A Moment in Focus

If you have preschoolers or elementary school children at home, you probably can't stop the endless flow of story after story, little narrative jewels, some fanciful, most real, all told with intensity and animation. A simple, "Why don't you write about that" will often send your child scurrying for pencil and paper.

Encourage your child to talk about the narrative so that by creative questioning you can help limit the event to a brief span of time and can stimulate your youngster's memory for details. Ask when the event took place and encourage your child to name the month or season of occurrence. Did it happen in the morning or afternoon, in December, or sometime during the summer? Ask about colors and sounds, about what people said and how they moved. Say, "How did you feel about what happened? Were you scared? Were you happy? Were you annoyed?"

Any occasion that impresses a youngster is ripe fruit for successful narration. A moment at the breakfast table, at the street corner, in the family's old blue Chevy, in the playground covered with snow, at the shelves in the library, in the gym, during snack, at the chalkboard, in the supermarket are all possibilities. (See Appendix A for a number of specific suggestions for good narratives.)

To get your youngster talking, you might ask about your child's subjective judgment on an event in order to establish a focus that will aid his or her insight.

- "Did you have a good day at school—what was the best thing that happened to you there?"
- "What do you like doing most with your baby brother?"
- "When did your friend Karen make you angriest?"
- "When were you embarrassed?"
- "What was the most exciting thing you did in the snow?"
- "What was the best part of the picnic?"

A youngster's inclination to draw also may serve as a solid means for an experiment in narrative. After Melissa's swimming lesson at the town pool, she would rush to me as I wrote at a nearby table and would beg for a sheet of my lined yellow paper on which to draw. One morning I suggested that she write a sentence about the picture she had just finished. I asked how she felt about the lesson, and she told me it was "good." I inserted the word in her original sentence.

This sentence could serve as an effective opening to a group of sentences that tell a story about the lesson. Melissa explained the picture. As she talked I wrote, starting with the left figure. Later we used carets to add details and to sharpen the exactness of her word choices:

This is a boy doing a handstand. This is me doing a

                         in a red bathing suit.
back float. This is Michelle. ∧ She could not float on her

                  with black hair
back. A girl ∧ was trying to help her. The swimming

Liz,
lesson teacher, ∧ taught me how to breathe and to swim.

One could argue that Melissa's writing is more description than narration, but I don't think that the distinction is very important. Despite little sense of sequence, it is the story of a swimming lesson with descriptive details added to show the event exactly as it occurred. Melissa had not pinpointed the action nor had she effectively established the time and place, but I helped her with those elements later on.

A Sense of Sequence

I want to consider the notion of chronology because it is so essential to clear narrative. Children often have trouble keeping time sequence in order; they often bounce back and forth from one part of an event to another. In Melissa's story you don't really know how the lesson proceeded. However, when she told me about the picture she discussed the events from left to right as they appear in her drawing. She was describing the picture she had made rather than the event that occurred. Time is suspended in the drawing as all the figures perform actions simultaneously. Even when young writers suggest sequence more clearly than Melissa did, you often will read a hodepodge of events. For example, here is one confusing narrative:

> On Sundays the whole family has a good time. We usually eat lunch of fried chicken and French fried potatoes at a diner on Route 17. My father and I wash the car after breakfast so it looks new and shiny when Dad zooms our blue Chevy down the street to the Garden Parkway. My mother and sister clean up the house first, and then we're off driving in the sun. Of course, we change our clothes because after an hour of car washing we're all sweaty. When we finally get home we're all exhausted!

This writer needs help in separating one event from another and in arranging events in timely order.

Often a young writer will flash back to earlier times in the midst of a straightforward march of scene. Except in the most adept of hands, the flashback rarely succeeds in riveting the reader to the moment. It is always a digression from a sequence, and even when it is rich in detail, it is a distraction from the main story. Writers usually bog down in a flashback because they use complicated verb forms to keep the time clear, and then imagery pales. One writing teacher calls it "the tyranny of flashback" and sees the technique as an impediment to a writer's growth. An effective narration calls for the focus on one clear moment, which reveals itself through a march of events described in concrete sensory detail.

Here are some suggestions for easy activities that will help your child build skills in commanding sequence.

- Have your child keep a list of the chronological events of familiar actions, such as walking a dog, sitting at the breakfast table, leaving for school. These sharply limited actions compel a youngster to look at a brief time span and to consider in correct sequence the events that make it up.
- Have your child explain some simple process around the house: how to fry an egg, how to make a bed, how to put on shoes. Tell him or her to list the steps in sequence and then to perform them!
- Ask your child to draw pictures on separate pieces of paper about things that occurred in one day. Ask him or her to talk about which came first, second, and last.
- Show your child different photographs of one person—a member of the family. The photographs should show the person at different times. Have your child arrange the pictures in correct time order and discuss each photograph.
- Consider transition words with your youngster. These words serve as bridges from one idea to the next—one teacher I know calls them "sentence glue"—and they help writers tell the order of events more clearly. The important words that bridge ideas through time are: *later, before, afterward, earlier, now, then, some time*

later, suddenly, in the first place, former, latter, in the next place, once, often, next, first, second, third, previously, when, and *at last.* Does your child understand these? Consider your child's age and command of language when judging which words to stress. Ask for an explanation of the words. Discuss those your youngster doesn't know, then encourage him or her to write a series of sentences using transition words.

By learning the importance of correct sequence in his own writing, your child also advances his powers of reading comprehension. A child who knows how to use sequence as part of a story about his own life's moments will respond to the chronology in a story he reads.

When you first ask a child to write about a sequence of events to practice chronology, you might try to follow one of Don Wolfe's good ideas: Ask your child to describe the happenings, one after the other, of the hour after getting up in the morning. Here is one result Wolfe shows:

> I woke up at six-thirty this morning and went downstairs and ate. I had bacon and eggs, milk, and toast. After that I got washed and dressed. Then I went down and read the newspaper. After that I took my dog out. He is black and white. Then I got my water pistols, loaded them, and went outside and shot them. Then I went in and put my water pistols away in my desk. Now it was eight-thirty, and I left for school. At school I played "Catch a Fly" and "You're Up." The school bell rang at ten of nine. Then I went into school.

You can see that this straightforward reporting shows little sensory awareness and weak sentence structure, but it is a product that a parent can help her child stretch toward excellence.

Narration: Sensory Language Leads the Way

The two of you should talk about your youngster's story, then prepare for the writing exercise. Your child's sensory responses will help him develop details to support the narration. Lead your child to record the sounds, smells, tastes, and sensations of touch that characterize the moment through discussion and questions, through bits of detail woven into the sentences after the child jots them down. You might want to use a Sense Table again like this:

Sense Table

Place: Burger King	What I Saw	What I Heard	What I Touched	What I Smelled or Tasted

Where:
University
Drive in
State
College
 	
When:
Saturday
noon
	girls in red
	  suits and
	  yellow hats
	yellow heat
	  lamp
	long French
	  fries
	ketchup
	  squirted on
	  rolls
	chocolate
	  shake
	  filling a cup
	white onion
	  rings
	orange
	  squares of
	  cheese
		hamburgers
		  sizzling
		"Junior
		  Whopper to
		  go!"
		slam of
		  refrigerator
		  door
		ice cubes
		  clinking
		  together
			soft rolls
			crisp hot
			  potatoes
			cold wet cup
			sticky
			  ketchup
			hard
			  countertop
				fish frying
				sweet cola
				smoky oil
				onions

Notice how the writer draws upon those numerous impressions in this narrative:

On Saturday at noon I visited Burger King. As I stood at the counter I saw girls in red suits and yellow hats. One girl squirted ketchup on a soft roll. After that another girl put a sizzling hamburger and white onion rings on the roll. I heard a man's voice yell, "Junior Whopper to go!" Then I heard the refrigerator slam. Ice cubes clinked together in a cup, and a man in a tie handed it to me. When I held the cup it felt cold and wet. When I tasted the cola it was very sweet. I could smell onions and fish frying in smoky oil. Finally, one girl put a bag of long French fries on the hard countertop. When I touched them they felt crisp and hot. Burger King is sure a busy place!

This is really a simple narration (again one could argue "description") with an emergent sequence of events. You see how the writer relied upon the table of senses he prepared in order to tell his story of a visit to a fast-food restaurant. The words "I saw," "I heard," "I could smell" help present the sensory images in a clear, straightforward way. Words like *as, after, then, when, finally* move the events along. Notice that the writer's story is limited in time and that the details are intense and drawn in sharp original images. The writer offers his subjective judgment in the last sentence; it has controlled his selection of detail from the first. Another writer might have incorporated the word *busy* into the first sentence to focus the succeeding details immediately.

In the following two paragraphs by eleven-year-olds, see how the opinion expressed in the opening sentence limits and defines the narrative; and see how the time named so close to the beginning of each selection immediately sets the reader in the moment. In the second paragraph the writer takes us into the next day, but until then her story covers a brief span of time.

One of the scariest people I know is the dentist. On a breezy cool day in September, I had my first visit with him. Boy! was I scared. My dentist lives a block away from me so I was there in two minutes. The second I walked through the silver squeaky door, I felt chills running up and down my spine. Then, I heard the loud humming sound of the shiny drill. I wanted to scamper out the door, but I was too scared to move. As my turn came and I approached the chair, my shoes crackled loudly on the smooth tile floor. My dentist, Dr. S. K. Amazon, appeared before my eyes. He was middle-sized and was dressed in a white outfit. He had very little left of his black hair. He took me to the big blue and white chair, and I sat down. I guess he knew I was frightened. He said, "Relax, I'm just going to look at your teeth." When I went home he gave me a prize. I was very happy. Those fears have left me now, but I'll never forget that day.

On a sunny summer day in July, I went to Palisades Amusement Park for I was determined to go on an exciting ride. When we got there, the first thing I did was to race to the huge gray roller coaster. I was very anxious to go on, but still very frightened. As I plopped down into the rusty brown seat, the humming of the motor scared me half to death! Then, suddenly, the six cars went flashing away up the bumpy hill. When we sped down, I was so scared that I yelled out, "Stop the car," but nobody heard me. As we kept on going, I got over my fear and started to look around. I saw the red Ferris wheel turning around and around and heard the children screaming in back of me.

Finally the roller coaster stopped. As I got off, my mother ran to me and said, "Were you scared?"

I told her, "In that rusty old car all alone, what do you think?" She didn't say anything. We went on to a few more rides and then returned home in our light blue car.

The next day I told my mother that I would never go on such an awful ride alone ever again!

Here is a narrative of a thirteen-year-old's embarrassing moment before a class.

A terribly embarrassing moment came when my best friend, Elizabeth, gave me an April Fools' Day gift in front of the whole class. The old gray room was dead silent when I opened the door with the brass broken doorknob, and I drifted into the class late that hot summer afternoon. Everybody was staring at me as I shuffled in. My first impression was that tall, erect Mr. Smith, my social studies teacher, was going to give me truckloads of trouble! I hesitated as I tiptoed softly to my seat as the brown wooden floor creaked under me. I sat down and my friend Elizabeth pranced to the front of the room and called me up there. I practically tripped up to the front, red-faced and puzzled. She handed me the gift and told me it was for getting the lowest marks all term in that class. The class roared at that. I opened the gift with trembling hands and as I opened the lid, out jumped a giant green bullfrog!! I screamed, I yelled, I shrieked! Boy, was I scared. Again the class burst out laughing with a roar. I slipped into my chair quietly trying to go by unnoticed. But, no such luck. Everybody was still laughing just as hard as ever. I'll never forget that day for the rest of my life!

A fifteen-year-old with a striking command of language brings a moment on a Brooklyn street to life:

The most pleasant memory of my youth in Bedford-Stuyvesant in Brooklyn is the scene of the watermelon man and his crew when he drove into our neighborhood on a summer Saturday. His horse would turn first onto Tompkins Avenue. Straining under the weight of many

green-striped melons, the horse chewed on its leather bit
and heaved wagon forward slowly, each step an effort. The
straw hat it wore shaded its sad brown eyes. Its coat, a
dirty brown and white, rippled with the stress of animal
work, like waves slapping some muddy shore. Patched
leather straps that served as reins ran over its hide and
flicked at lazy green flies; the insects buzzed in the air or
hovered over the shining sample of melon, its pits winking in the sun like a thousand brown eyes. The driver and
his friends too are unforgettable. The hands that held the
reins were calloused and coarse, yet these overly large
hands with square dirty nails held the reins with an almost regal gesture. The veins and muscles in the hands
and arms of this kingly watermelon man looked like the
ropes on an old homemade swing. He wore a dirty vest, a
torn undershirt, and melon-splattered jeans, emblems of
his trade. Suddenly, his sons and nephews in the back of
the wagon laughed and grinned and started the chant,
"Melon, melon, watermelon." The watermelon man, his
gray hair moist with sweat, his wide mouth showing a
perfect set of teeth, now took up the melody. Red ban-
danas and gaudy handkerchiefs waving in slight breezes,
these fine men sang and hummed the chant.

Finally, a transaction began. A woman from a
brownstone window across the street called, "Hey, them
melons fresh?"

"Yes, ma'am," cried the figures in the wagon.

"Well bring me up one," she snapped from above. "No,
not you, ugly. You, yeah, the cute one."

"Anything else you wants 'sides a melon, honey?" replied the "cute" one, winking at his companions in the
wagon, who heckled and howled at this.

"Just a melon!" screamed the hoarse voice of a man
from the same window above.

I, standing in front of Jack's Candy Store on the corner
of Madison Street, must have snapped that scene firmly in
my mind, for I still can hear the cry of the watermelon

man as it struts and dances in my ears: "Melon, melon, watermelon. Git de fresh watermelon. Melon. Melon."

Here, unedited, is a narrative from an inexperienced college writer:

The day I caught a king Cod fish, out by Montauk Point, I will never forget the moment I experienced that spring day out on the ocean. One bright and clear blue morning, my family and I drove to the end of the Island, to do some of the fishing that was going on out in the Island. On the way to the Island, my family and I were talking about the different kinds of fish that were running at that time. My father said, "Cod, Flounders, and Flukes". So I said, "Let's go fishing for Cod fish". My family agreed to go Cod fishing, and we did. At six AM. we sped into the fishing dock area, and my father looked over the situation, and decided to go fishing on a large brown boat, the Mary II. When a fog horn honked at six thirty the boat pulled out, and went for a cruies of eighteen mile ride into the ocean. Then at eight o'clock the boat arrived at the fishing grounds, and Captain Kallous looked over the side and shouted in a deep voice, "All lines down." The person next to me caught a fifteen pounder which fought on the wooden deck. It smacked its white tail from side to side. Shortly after, I got hit with a bite. The pole started to bend, and I could feel the the weight of the cod fish in the pole. It took me about twenty minutes to reel up a fighting cod fish from the choppy blue water. As I was reeling up the fish, it was man versus the elements. It takes a specal skill to reel up a large cod fish, because as the fish is hooked he will tend to pull down. As the fish is pulling down, you do not reel up, because the fishing line will have an excess of tension, and the line will break. By the line breaking you will lose your rig and the main thing, the fish. So I reel up a thirty five pounder, and I entered the fish into the pool. It took first place, and I won twenty six dollars and changes for the largest fish caught that day on the Mary II.

I thought you'd want to see this as it is, because, despite its mistakes, it's a wonderful narrative—the same young man who wrote the weak piece on women's liberation (see pages 127 and 128) wrote this one after studying in a writing program like the one I'm suggesting here. What an improvement this paper is over the other! Here the writer has shared a rich and powerful experience and now can begin to explore and to meet the social requirements of language, convinced that he has something worthwhile to communicate. It's unfortunate that at twenty this young man is just *starting* to learn skills that can be studied and developed from a very early age.

Read samples to your child of what other children write before he or she starts a narrative. You even might help your child prepare a list of aims. In such a list pinpoint several of the key elements of narration. Here's a model; adapt it to suit your son or daughter.

Writing Down Your Story: What to Shoot For

1. Tell your story clearly with one event following the other in order.
2. Tell when the story takes place as soon as possible. Name the month or season. Tell the time of day (morning or afternoon).
3. Show the people in your story. Tell how they move and what they do.
4. Describe what they are wearing. Use color words and touch words.
5. Tell one sound you heard. Tell one smell you remember.
6. Use someone's exact words.

Playing with Dialogue

As one feature of the faithful presentation of a narrative and/or descriptive moment, the writer must rely upon spoken conversation, dialogue between the figures who people the event. The formal requirements of quotations— such as, where the quotation marks go and where you put *he said*—sometimes mystify a child. However, if you are patient in answering those questions you will give your young writer added options for expanding detail. (In Appendix B I've explained a simple way of teaching your child how to use quotation marks.)

You can take one of many approaches to teaching your child how to write quotations. One asks a child to select a simple comic strip from the newspaper and to paste it on top of a sheet of lined paper. The youngster copies the dialogue from the balloons above the characters' heads, using *He said* or *Archie said* or *Doonesbury answered* before or after the spoken words. Another activity has a child pretend that two familiar objects at home are having a brief conversation. Here's an example:

Mr. Scoop said, "Ice Cream, I'm coming to get you!"

"No you're not! I'm too hard," replied Ice Cream.

"Well, how will David have his dessert!" Mr. Scoop asked.

"All right," Ice Cream said. "He's been good all week. I'll soften up."

Such writing can lead to a little playacting between you and your child in which you each read and act out the conversation. Children love acting; encourage your child, alone or with friends, to write a brief original play about some holiday or special topic she has studied. One summer, youngsters of six, seven, and eight had a grand time putting on their own Fourth of July Pageant in King's Park, New York. One of my son Joseph's friends has written plays regularly from eight years old on and the neighborhood children perform in them regularly. Youngsters don't have to memorize their lines exactly, but writing and performing a play is a fine way for children to combine the fun of acting with a practical writing activity. With simple video technology now available in many homes, young children can write, produce, and tape their own plays.

Point out to your child that the use of a quote will add lively detail to a written narrative. As your child learns to use quotations, suggest that she write a narrative that relies heavily upon dialogue. It might be between two people talking to each other. You can suggest to older children that the characters be portrayed in some form of *conflict*. In this example, the dialogue carries the excitement of the narrative moment and the details are sparse but effective:

The gloom of the gray, misty day poured into the bedroom shared by my sister and me, casting shadows into the corners. Clothes lay spread in a misshapen mass upon the two identical twin beds, sorted into two piles on each cover.

"Wait a minute. That's mine," shouted Susan accusingly as I threw a tartan plaid skirt onto the woolen clothes pile on my bed.

"It is not," I countered. "You gave it to me last year when you went away to school."

"Well, I want it back. Now!" she demanded, her brown eyes bulging with anger.

She lurched forward almost falling over the battered black trunk filled with her clothes, which stood in the middle of the room. I backed toward the doorway swiftly sidestepping her three pieces of matching red luggage still unpacked.

"Leave me alone or I'm going to tell Ma," I threatened weakly. "You have enough clothes. Why do you want this skirt?"

The overhead light illuminated my sister's mouth, tight and drawn, as she moved closer and closer. "Because it's mine," she answered simply.

Leaping forward suddenly, Susan snatched the now-crumpled skirt from my grasp. "It's my skirt and I'm going to keep it . . . it's my skirt," she repeated haughtily.

Eyes blazing, I shouted angrily as I slammed the door, "I never liked that skirt anyway!"

A Short Story: Fiction for Thirteen-Year-Olds

The short story combines the narrative skill rooted in reports of sensory experience and the creative act of thinking through an original story. It is a challenging activity for a developing young writer.

Be sure to explore *dilemma* and *conflict* when guiding your child in writing a short story; define the terms and discuss them. Good short stories usually have a dilemma where a character thinks through one side of a problem, then the other, finally making a choice whose consequences the writer explores. The dilemma should be important and meaningful, one rooted in the choices people need to make in their lives. If you're thinking that thirteen-year-olds have no sense of dilemma, you'd be surprised. Even more than older children, the thirteen-year-old has a keen notion of predicament. Perhaps the conflicting loyalties for parent and friend, for obedience and challenge, for remaining a child and growing up, are particularly keen at this age and the pressures a child must deal with foster insights that are deep and passionate.

When I teach short-story writing to eighth or ninth graders, we discuss *dilemma* and *predicament* and give examples of situations in which a person would suffer through a choice. We talk about what might go through a person's mind as he or she considers each side of the decision. Then I ask everyone to write down a dilemma on an index card that I will collect the next day. After I take the cards, I read each one aloud and the youngsters weigh the choices. Here are some typical suggestions that came to me over the years:

- A girl of thirteen wants to smoke. Actually she's not sure she wants to but all her friends do and they are pressuring her. Her father died of lung cancer just last year and she is frightened. There's a Valentine's Day dance this weekend and she knows she'll be tempted there.
- A boy, whose family is poor, wants to give a Christmas present to his little brother. The boy decides that he will steal a baseball glove from Woolworth's. But the manager is someone who helped him out of trouble once. How will he do it?
- A boy has a dog he loves but the dog has attacked two local children who teased him and has bitten them badly. The boy's father says the dog must be put away and the boy must take the animal to the ASPCA. Will he do it?
- A girl who always gets good grades did not study for a science test because her parents had a fight that night. As she sits in her class the teacher leaves the room. The girl has a chance to cheat. Although she has never cheated before, her grades are important to her. Will she do it?

Although these are not exceptionally original dilemmas, the discussions that follow always show that such situations are common and vitally important in the life of a young teenager and arouse intense feelings. Once the writer finds a powerful situation to lay at the heart of a story, I would urge him or her to set down the events straightforwardly, using rigorous sensory language. "The Sabbath Breakers" is a marvelous story from a ninth grader in my writing class. It won first prize in a contest sponsored by the New York City Board of Education many years back.

Mr. Goodman's eyes traced the faded blue pattern on his tallis, folded neatly beside him. It was the same tallis he had worn at his Bar Mitzvah, fifty-one years ago, and it was the same shawl that he would be buried in. His parents had been immigrants from Poland and for sixty years, ever since he was four, he had gone to synagogue on Saturday. The prayers ran through his mind as he remembered the sonorous voice of the rabbi on the first Sabbath he had gone to *shul*. Vaguely, he recalled his mother and older sisters, heads covered as they sat on the other side of the temple in the women's section. Images of his father, rocking in rhythm to the hum of voices as he prayed, flitted through his mind. The strange, awe-inspiring sound echoed in his ears as it had years ago. Mr. Goodman smoothed the fringes on his tallis as he recollected old men reciting the mystical words by heart. A sudden stabbing pain in his hand brought him back to the present. He wondered "Why should I go to *shul*? God's never done anything for me. No family, nothing to do, and this arthritis . . ." He winced as another pain streaked up his arm.

"Never mind *shul*. I'm going to paint my fence. Holed up in that old store all week, I want to get out. Fresh air and the sunshine will do my arthritis good. That's settled."

Fifteen minutes later Mr. Goodman was shuffling down the walk swinging a can of paint. The old man reached his fence, and carefully set down his pail. With gnarled hands he popped open the can of paint. His white hair softly sank to his forehead and the enormous blue-plaid shirt he wore filled with the warm breeze. Dipping the brush into the paint he argued, "I pay my dues to the *shul*. He won't mind if I paint on the Sabbath. Besides, look at the cracks in the fence. Another week and it might split. I have to do it now." He resolutely slid the brush down the picket fence. Deftly, his shaking hand caught a bead of paint before it could drip down the plank.

The sun rose higher in the sky and the wiry old man painted on. His scuffed slippers were dotted with paint and the white boards glistened in the sun. People, strolling home from synagogue in groups, gossiped about the events of the week and stared at Mr. Goodman. The rabbi, swathed in a black coat, strode boldly down the street, very conscious of being the most respected man in the neighborhood. Mr. Goodman hastily turned his back to hide from the rabbi's piercing eyes. He busily swept the stickly bristles up and down the pickets as he reminded himself, "It's a free country, I'm not gambling, just painting a fence."

Slowly all his neighbors drifted into their homes. Mr. Goodman continued painting. Only four planks were still bare. Across the dusty street stood an audience of two boys. They leaned against a streetlamp and solemnly observed every move Mr. Goodman made. The old man was very conscious of the four eyes staring at his back, but tried to ignore them. The boys whispered to each other. One muttered angrily, "He's no Jew. Painting on Saturday. Why wasn't he in *shul*? Does he think he's someone great? God should punish him."

The little one squeaked in agreement, "He's no Jew. He's got nerve. He should be punished."

The fat one took a step forward and his second chin quivered as he screamed, "Old man, God will punish you! Just wait!"

Mr. Goodman shuddered but did not turn.

"Hey you!"

The fat one stooped and grasping a large rock, shrieked, "Nazi!" He took aim and threw with rage.

Blood splattered the glistening white fence and Mr. Goodman fell with a thud.

The pious boys ran to tell of God's punishment.

In this story the main character resolves his dilemma early, and the writer drives home the consequences of that dilemma with ironic pungency. You see how the principles of narration and sensory language help the story: Instead of flashing back to earlier events the writer tells us details by developing a dialogue in her protagonist's mind. The vitality in this piece of fiction comes from the young writer's sharp perception of the physical world.

Your sons and daughters often spill over with excitement at moments of storytelling, of story listening and sharing. You are still working in Tolstoy's domain when helping your child unlock experience from memory and convey that experience through sensory language. A child can write a narrative more easily if his oral tale falls on responsive ears, so you must listen and laugh and question and commend and exchange tales. Then help focus your child's event, and explore its sensory qualities.

Adventures in Make-Believe

What holds more promise than a child's imagination? In wonderful leaps a young mind wanders and connects, dreams and invents, projects and uncovers. Surrounded by a world of fiction—television, fairy tales, movies—a youngster absorbs models for imagined stories early. This delight in fancy is a sea of possibilities for developing writing skills.

The imagined episode about which a child chooses to write depends upon concrete sensory detail, which provides the dimension of reality that helps the reader to suspend disbelief. In familiar fairy tales that your child reads, glimmers of color, bursts of sound, flashes of hot and cold, sweet smells and rank, snatch him into the make-believe world. The same realistic touches should appear in a child's own imaginative writing.

Descriptive skills of place, object, and person move down new roads with imaginative writing. The narrative skill that your child is developing will apply here too. Will the pretend story unravel through a clear progression of scenes? Will the writer identify time and place? Will the sequence of events advance the story clearly and logically? An imaginative tale intensively perceives a *single moment* in sensory language and offers depth and quality of action. Thus, your child can write make-believe while practicing important language skills that you have encouraged all along.

Riddles and Games on Paper

I've taken a delicious model for two-sentence riddles that children can write from the delightful nonsense in Jane Sarnoff and Reynolds Ruffins' *I Know! A Riddle Book* (New York: Scribner's, 1977). Here is a book that offers lively illustrations and silly riddles in easy sentences. For example:

Do fish perspire?
Sure, that's what makes the sea salty.

Eight-year-olds write their own silly riddles. This makes great practice since a child can focus ideas in two simple sentences. In them you can help establish basic notions of correctness and completeness. You can look for end marks and capital letters and can encourage the use of lively action or other sensory detail. To focus your child's thoughts, you can suggest general topics for riddles, such as animals, fruit, machines, or weather. Here are some riddles to share:

- How does the snow fall?
  It falls when it's pushed.

- Does a horse laugh?
  Nay, it does not!

- When is the sky clumsy?
  It's clumsy when the rain drops.

- How does an oak grow bigger?
  It opens another branch.

- Why do cows chew grass standing up?
  Grass cannot sit down.

Most of these riddles demonstrate a youngster's ability to play with words. Though that seems a sophisticated skill, I'm always impressed at how well children pick up on multiple meanings and how they are amused when they apply a meaning that does not suit the context. (Don't insist on the *double entendre!*)

One writer wrote this silly riddle, quite different from the last one:

- Why do cows chew grass standing up?
  There would be no room at the dinner table for the rest of us.

Supervise the writing of riddles carefully, because your young writer may be tempted to offer an *incomplete* sentence as a response to the opening question (see Appendix B). An unguided child might easily write this as the third riddle I mentioned:

When is the sky clumsy?
When the rain drops.

The word group *when the rain drops* is only a piece of a sentence, and that's exactly the kind of sentence fragment I find with alarming frequency on the papers of inexperienced writers. You can see why the writer wrote what he did: In his mind the connection between thoughts is clear, and he is depending upon the reader to relate back to the previous sentence. Conventions of edited American

English, however, demand that written sentences express complete thoughts: Take the opening question away from the riddle and you have something that does not make grammatical sense: *when the rain drops*. The word *when* tells the reader to expect something else that's going on at the same time as or as a result of what follows it. Unless the writer supplies that information *to the sentence*, it does not express a complete thought.

If your youngster writes a riddle with only a sentence piece as the second statement, cover up the first one. Ask the child to read the words aloud. See if he thinks it makes sense. Talk about the idea of completeness, about a sentence needing to say a whole thought between the capital letter and the period. If your child cannot understand the idea after you talk, rewrite the sentence piece so that it is complete.

Another thing to watch for in these riddles is the correct use of *it's* and *its;* explained more fully on pages 304 to 305. Deceptively simple words, these appear often as errors even on college students' papers. Riddle writing often calls for these words, so you should be able to explain that *it's* means *it is* or *it has* and that *its* is used in all other cases.

For the two-sentence riddle game you might use these with your child:

- Why does a dog bark?
- Why does the floor squeak?
- Does a cat read?
- Will the bus be early?
- Can a tree be late?
- Does a shoe talk?
- When does a nose run?
- When does the sun rise?
- Does darkness fall?
- Do dogs laugh?

You can excite the fancy of children six or older by asking for riddles in which a child pretends to be some object. Your youngster must give a clue about herself *as* the object without telling *what* she is. Suggest that your child use words for colors, actions, sounds, smells, and comparisons in the riddle. Read these as examples with your child:

> I am tall. In the winter I am skinny and naked and shake in the wind. In the spring I wear green. In the summer I wear yellow. What am I?

> I am long and yellow. I have an orange top and a black pointy tip. Children always bite me. I know how to write. What am I?

A child could make a wonderful drawing to follow up any of these riddles.

Visits with Make-Believe

A parent can stimulate imaginative writing about visits to or with characters in fairyland, in favorite stories, or on television shows by drawing upon your child's familiarity with fictional characters. Here your youngster brings the character into your home or joins the character on one of his or her adventures. These paragraphs as examples provide sharp physical details despite the imaginative framework:

> Goldilocks sits on the furry white rug in my living room. She has curly blonde hair and blue eyes. She sits on the floor because she does not want Daddy's chair to break! I ask her if she wants some sweet hot chocolate. She says, "No. I would like some oatmeal." I want to play outside, but she says she is afraid of the bears.

> I played in Toftrees Woods with Little Red Riding Hood yesterday. We picked buttercups in the warm sunshine.

any sparrows chirping in the blue sky. Suddenly I saw a wolf leaning against an oak tree. I said to Red, "Sh! Follow me." On tiptoes we sneaked out of the forest.

I visited Sesame Street yesterday. I brought one dirty sneaker for Oscar to eat. He crunched it with his teeth. "More! More!" he yelled. He rolled his big brown eyes. I pushed him back into his home in the garbage can.

I was sitting on the couch and Peter Pan was sitting on my new yellow chair with orange spots. He was wearing a green hat, a green jacket-shirt, green pants, and green shoes. He has dark brown eyes. I said to Peter Pan, "I wish I could grow up with you in Never-Never Land." Peter Pan said, "You forgot that I am not going to grow up." He moved his lips over his teeth. Then he flew out the window.

I visited Sesame Street yesterday. I saw Big Bird and he was all yellow. I asked him to play ball with me. "Sure," he yelled. He caught the ball with his orange beak. But the ball fell out with a boom because it is slippery.

Ask your child questions before writing in order to draw out details: "You saw Peter Pan?" "What was he wearing?" "Where did he sit?" "What did you say to him?" "What did his face look like?" Make up a list of pointers for your child to mention in the visit to make-believe:

Writing About a Make-Believe Visit

1. Tell where you are. Show what you see around you.
2. Tell what your visitor looks like and what he or she is wearing.
3. Use a word to tell sound.
4. Use words to show color.
5. Show lively actions.
6. Tell what you and your visitor say to each other.

Help the more mature writer expand an episode from a book during which a child puts himself squarely into a scene. Here is a thirteen-year-old's exuberant (if somewhat over-described!) tale of Marc Antony's oration:

> I, a lowly Roman commoner, stand amongst crowds of grumbling plebians as they irascibly huddle about in the Forum. My ragged clothes cling closely to my body as people lunge toward the pulpit. The sound of children bellowing and women screeching echo through my ears. My robe which drapes loosely about my body flaps sprightly in brisk breezes. My shoes are worn and battered. And as my feet stand weary, I feel them touch the trodden earth. My neighbors mumble quietly as they slouch over, facing the roaring crowds. Frantic women chatter noisily, flinging their filthy arms into the air. Pushing and jostling halt. Whimpering, growling, shrieking and murmuring: all cease. Antony marches toward the bare and lonely pulpit to deliver his eulogy for Caesar. He stands erect upon the platform. His red robe swoops over his brawny shoulders and flowingly drapes about his body. Brown leather sandals are tied about his calloused knees. His rapid brown eyes gaze about the silent crowd. "Friends, Romans, countrymen, lend me your ears; I come to bury Caesar, not to praise him," starts Antony with a hoarse voice. As I sway on my torso to the side, I give great heed to what is said. As I scan the crowds of people, I realize that they too are swayed by Antony's speech and wish revenge on Caesar's body. Tears trickle down the flushed faces as some bend their heads in a silent prayer to ask for forgiveness. Yes, vengeance is fluttering in the air.

Ask a child who has a special interest in science, art, or mathematics to write about a pretend visit with some great figure in the field that excites the youngster. In the following piece, a thirteen-year-old has read a biography of Gregor Mendel and has studied about heredity in science class. She pretends she is a newspaper reporter and interviews the great scientist, setting the scene in time and place.

On a blustery day in 1857, I arrived at the Modern School in Austria to interview Mr. Gregor Mendel, discoverer of the laws of heredity, for the *Daily Post,* the local newspaper. Anxiously, I scurried up to the oak door of his quarters and meekly took the brass door knocker in my hand and knocked three times. Quickly Mr. Mendel, his merry blue eyes twinkling, opened the door and softly murmured, "Please, do come in."

As I entered the small room, I noticed a high riser bed covered with a blue bedspread, a mahogany dresser, and a desk overflowing with notes, among other things. I situated myself in a plush purple chair and viewed Mr. Mendel. He wore a navy blue suit and a blue striped tie. His gray hair appeared to be receding, his eyes were kind and soft, and he sported horn-rimmed glasses. "Mr. Mendel," I queried, "What made you so interested in heredity?"

He stroked his long chin thoughtfully. "Well, I have been interested in the field ever since I was a child. The laws of life and the mystery of an ordinary garden pea constantly racked my brain. To satisfy my curiosity I have begun research and I have come up with a theory. I am now in the process of collecting data on my peas. Would you like to see them?"

With much excitement, I replied, "Oh yes, sir. I would like to very much." He rose slowly and motioned to a huge door. The room contained thousands of crystal-clear test tubes and millions of peas. Hanging on the white walls were many charts containing scribbled data.

Mr. Mendel's short round face beamed with pride. "These," he remarked, "are the F_2, or second filial, generation. As you can see there are both green and yellow peas in the pod in the ratio of three to one."

He went on and on with explanations, and after many

hours the time arrived for me to leave. I gratefully babbled, "Thank you, Mr. Mendel. It has been very informative and exciting. Thank you again. Good-bye." That ended a wonderful afternoon for me and brought a good story to the *Daily Post*.

Another exciting leap into imagination asks a child to pretend his way into a photograph or a painting. Use a famous art reproduction, such as *Christina's World* by Andrew Wyeth, one of the Rockwell paintings, a lively scene by Degas or Renoir. Ask your child to imagine that he is part of the painting and to write what he would see, hear, feel, and smell if he joined the scene. A photograph from a book or magazine or one from your home collection serves well here, too. You might ask your child to look at a snapshot of some family member and to write a tale about the person. Your child can draw upon bits and pieces of family stories told about relatives who lived in times past. This short tale was written by a ten-year-old about his great-grandfather who was born in Italy:

> Since the time my great-grandfather was a little boy he lived in Italy and loved it there. One fine day when the sky was blue my great-grandfather went to the market for his mother. Lovely things were at the market: toys, food, everything you can think of. But my great-grandfather had just enough money to buy bread. As my great-grandfather was walking, he saw a man with a silver knife in his hand. He told my great-grandfather he could have the knife for the money he had in his hand. So he gave the man the money, which was two shiny coins, and started for home. When his mother saw him with the knife and not the bread, she took the knife and didn't let him go to the market again.

This simple, lively narrative framework can serve to build important language skills. A parent would say, "I love the colors *blue* and *silver*. Can you use a more specific word than *toys* or *food*, though? Can you use a better word than *walking* to show action? Can you add a sentence to tell what the man Great-grandpa met looks like?" Because there is confusion about the way the child uses the word *he* here, on a later draft you have a ripe opportunity to talk about pronouns, and how they must always clearly refer the reader back to someone or something. It's a good idea to remind your child that sometimes it's better to repeat a word instead of using a pronoun which might be confusing.

Animals on Parade

The intense interest a child of any age shows toward animals builds another treasurehouse of writing activities. This interest in pets leads easily to straightforward and real narratives of moments with animals, such as this one:

It has been almost seven years since the first breezy March afternoon that we took our dog home from the kennel to live with us, yet it seems like only yesterday. Excitement bubbled up inside of me as we rushed into the modern building, and the sounds of pitiful yelping reached my ears. It didn't take long before a soft, fuzzy, sable ball of fur leaped into my awaiting arms. Carefully, I parted his soft white hairs of what I imagined to be a face, and a small, pink, moist tongue emerged gingerly to lick my arm. His warm, friendly, brown eyes stared up at my face while I felt his long tail, with the beginnings of what would someday be a great mass of fur, glide slowly back and forth with a swishing sound. Carefully, I placed him down on the floor and immediately he scurried after some withered leaves somehow left on the floor. They crunched under King's small, snowy white paw, but they got no mercy from him! Soon he tired of this game, and he quietly snuggled up against my leg and fell asleep. It didn't take long for me to realize that I was hopelessly in love with the little ball of fur, and with a happy nod of my head and a smile I watched my father pay the man.

But it is the fanciful excursion into animal land—where dogs talk, chickens carry pocketbooks, and cats sip coffee—that sets a child's fancy racing with limitless possibilities for writing.

Children delight in Aesop's fables. Perhaps you and your son or daughter can take a short trip to the library and read some of these together. Then your child should try to write an original animal fable, complete with moral. Here is an eleven-year-old's tale of a fox and chickens:

There once was a red fox who loved to eat chickens. He did not have enough money to buy them. So every night he would sneak into the dark barn and steal a chicken. He always had more than enough chickens for many days, but he still snatched one every night. Farmer Brown bought a big black dog to guard the chickens. One night the dog hid behind a maple tree and waited for the fox to come to steal a chicken. When the greedy fox sneaked toward the barn, the dog growled, "I've got you now!" and jumped on the fox and ate him. The moral of this story is to be satisfied with what you have.

Do you remember Rudyard Kipling's *Just So Stories?* Children love writing their own "just-so" tales in which the writer reveals the secret of some animal's behavior or physical appearance. Your youngster might want to explain

- why flies fly
- how the giraffe got a long neck
- how the monkey got a long tail
- why the lion has a mane

- why the tiger has stripes
- why the elephant has a long nose
- why dogs bark
- why cats lick their fur
- how the canary got a beautiful voice
- how the kangaroo got his pouch

For seven- and eight-year-olds you can give the opening and closing sentences of the tale and can ask your child to tell an original narrative using clear sensory detail. For example, you might offer these:

You may not know that elephants once had noses just like you and me. _____

_____

_____

_____

_____

_____

_____

And that's why the elephant has a long trunk.

or:

Dogs once talked like people. _____

_____

_____

_____

_____

And that's why dogs bark.

Here are some to read and discuss as models:

You may not know that elephants once had noses just like you and me. But elephants were always butting into other people's business. One day a large gray elephant tried to listen in on a conversation. Two tigers sat in their living room drinking hot chocolate and chatting. One tiger said, "My, there's a draft in here." She stood up and slammed the door shut. But the elephant's nose was stuck! Did it hurt! He tried pulling his nose out by backing away. He pulled and tugged and pulled some more. Finally his nose came loose, but it was badly stretched. It looked like an ugly gray snake. And that's why the elephant has a long trunk.

Once Joe Turtle was taking a walk over to Clem Rabbit's briar patch. Clem was pasting a new set of thorns on the thornbushes. He always changed thorns every spring. Joe told Clem that he thought there was a fish in the paste pot. Clem said to look again. Joe looked very hard and then, ploof! He fell in. The paste dried on his back. And that is why all turtles since Joe's time have had hard green crusts or shells on their backs.

Your child shouldn't limit to animal tales his or her excursions into fantasy. Suggest that your youngster expand upon other ideas such as:

- why leaves turn yellow
- why the grass is green
- how the ocean got waves

- why roses smell
- how the sea got salty
- where thunder began
- how the stars got bright
- why mountains are tall
- how glue got sticky
- why the wind whistles

Here's a fine example of a child's myth on thunder:

One day a giant up in the sky was moving the furniture in his house. He just couldn't make up his mind where to put the furniture. He started to throw the furniture around the house with a loud banging noise. He began to get raging mad. Lightning spurted in green streaks out of his eyes. He threw more furniture around the house and heaved some out the window. Crash! came the thunder. The furniture he threw out the window fell on the white clouds and made the clouds break. Then it rained.

"I Am a Pizza": Personification and Delight

When I explained personification in chapter 5, I pointed out that it was a good way for a child to add liveliness to his writing. By giving human qualities to nonhuman beings a writer can tease out an image with figurative language:

The car sputtered and coughed along Mitchell Avenue. Leaves whispered secrets to the cold, unfriendly ground.

Sputtered, coughed, whispered, unfriendly: These words name human acts or qualities but here they're used to enliven and clarify the picture of an inanimate object.

I've already mentioned the personification-riddle game in which a youngster tells what it's like to be some object. Now, ask your child to pretend that he or she is an object or animal who can speak. Ask your youngster to write a more extended piece about a brief moment in his life as that object. You might suggest:

- a moment in the life of a Ping-Pong ball
- my breakfast cereal speaks
- what it's like to be a doorknob
- I am a comma
- a ball goes bouncing along
- a vacuum cleaner's life
- the sink speaks out
- the troubles of a toothbrush
- a record's racket
- the ketchup bottle talks

Discuss some pointers that your child should consider when writing:

- tell what your make-believe name is
- tell where you are
- show what you look like
- tell a sound that you make
- tell sounds that you hear
- tell what you see around you—colors, actions, people
- tell what somebody says

These samples by writers of different ages show the enchantment and humor of "Pretend-You-Are" writing:

I am Karen's doll Bessie. I live on top of a white dresser in Karen's bedroom. I have short brown hair, brown eyes, and red cheeks. Sometimes I drink make-believe tea from little cups at Karen's tea party. I always wear my pink party dress. When Karen lifts me I feel warm and I squeak, "Mama, Mama, Mama." At night I sleep on Karen's cool soft pillow.

Thump! Here I am in Angelo's calloused hands ready for a dunking into a can of bloody tomato sauce in the Avenue T Pizzeria. Why does my floppy, powdery dough have to be attacked by lumpy herbs? Yes, the life of a pizza can be frustrating. There is an enormous crowd tarrying to thrust their fangs into my luscious body. First I'm pounded, tickled, and then s-t-r-e-t-c-h-e-d to three times my size. A flying saucer ride around Angelo's head follows, with prayers that his butterfingers don't release me. Spicy, fiery sauce drowns my nose as tickly cheese crumbles over me. My trip to the Sahara Desert begins as Angelo shoves me into Maestro's 550-degree oven. My flat skin rises to an auburn bubble as I'm swirled around the scorched wall of the oven. Bing! I'm done. "One slice!" Vivian yells above the mob. Begging and pleading not to amputate my eight slices, I feel Angelo swish the knife, breaking my cheesy heart in two. Gulp! Vivian drools over my tantalizing flavor and aroma. In vain, I hope for crumbs to be left, so I can rebake as another slice of pizza in Angelo's Avenue T Pizzeria.

Flash! Flash! Flash! My life as a glittering green and orange neon sign may not be exciting, but it is a lot of fun. Many people hurry past me on a wintry night with their heads bent and their collars up as they battle their way up Avenue U. Some stop and come into Enrico's Kosher Delicatessen where I live. It is a cozy little restaurant with candles melting in wine bottles which are on top of gaily covered tables. At five o'clock, when Enrico turns me on, I feel proud to be a part of the shimmering sea of light that dances over Avenue U's slush-filled streets. This morning a man named Maxie came and polished my fluorescent tubes; it tickled as he picked up the worn brush and gently passed the bristles over the O in Enrico's. After he had finished, he carefully poured the soapy water from the bucket into the streets and picked up his tools and packed them in the trunk of an old Oldsmobile. Maxie is a kindly old man with sparkling gray eyes and a patch of silvery hair; the back of his faded blue uniform loudly proclaims in black letters—Maxie's Window Washing and Sign Cleaning Service. Sitting here behind the sparkling plate glass window, I get the chance to notice many things. There's Mrs. Rosen's daughter, Paula, playing hopscotch on a thin chalk outline which barely stretches against the cracked gray cement. As she jumps, her blond ponytail bounces up and down, and her gray-and-red jacket streams out behind her. Oh, oh, she'd better be careful! Billy, her mischievous, red-haired brother, creeps up behind her with a cracked peashooter tightly grasped in his mitten. Just in time, their mother sticks her head out the window. She calls, "Billy, Paula, come in for dinner!" Whirling around and seeing her brother's grin, Paula gives him a hard kick in his skins and me a sly wink. Now I'm alone again. I wish my brother Charlie were here, but a mean little boy, with hard black eyes and a good pitching arm, threw a snowball at his face. He was sent to the hospital for repairs, but now his face will always be scarred by a long, twisting crack. Sometimes I wish I could be human and roar through New York's jungle of glass office buildings. But, my own life has its rewards too; it was just yesterday that my flashing light saved a little boy from stepping in front of a car whose headlights were turned off. The life of a neon sign is fun and rewarding; why don't you try it sometime? Flash! Flash! Flash!

On Your Own in Fantasyland

Who knows better than a parent her own youngster's sense of make-believe? Invent writing games to excite your child's pretend world. When holiday seasons approach, ask your child to assume the identity of a familiar object and to write about his feelings: a Christmas tree, a menorah, a Thanksgiving turkey, a holiday candle, or a pumpkin. These make wonderful identities for tales of fantasy. When a child buys or makes a gift for a member of the family, let your child pretend that he is the gift and ask him to write about himself. Make a cassette, in your youngster's voice, of the story that she has written; give it to Mommy, Daddy, or Sister along with the gift. Encourage your youngster to write fairy tales of his own design. Some children love to write continuations of familiar stories, legends, or fairy tales: "Snow White's Family," "When the Little Engine Couldn't," "Goldilocks, Part II." And the "tall tale" is another exercise in delight; it's the kind of dizzy silliness children adore in romps through make-believe.

A Child's Message Through the Mails

If the whimsy and joy of traveling through make-believe add wings to a child's writing, a message mailed and answered also can set his or her skills and interests soaring. First help your youngster see how the post office works. Look at the process through a youngster's eyes: a trek through the snow to a blue metal box; a pull on a squeaky handle; a flip of the wrist; a letter diving into darkness. Then the enchantment: a phone call ("Yes, I can come") or a note in response ("Thank you for your letter. . . ."). Why, some man or woman actually brought that message to Sacramento or Phoenix, Martha's Vineyard or Brooklyn!

Using the Mails

In chapter 2, I showed how little notes to members of the family were a painless writing practice for a child. The notes that a child leaves on the refrigerator door or bathroom mirror for Mommy and Daddy have their own reinforcement in the immediate response of a smile or nod. Letters and postcards bring responses *in writing*. Watch your daughter's eyes when she watches for the letter carrier stepping up the path; see your son's electric grin when Mr. Bloom pauses in his rapid sorting of letters at the tin maze of mailboxes in your lobby and says, "Here's one for you, David!"

Use the mails! So much of a child's school letter-writing activities is hopelessly unfulfilled: Term after term your child painfully writes letters to fit the school's demands. The teacher examines the class' letters, then the children take their letters home and throw them into the trash bag. Letters need envelopes. They need stamps. They need mailboxes, postal clerks, and letter carriers.

It's incredible how many teachers have eliminated the only step that justifies so much letter-writing practice to a child—mailing the letter! Of course, letter writing is a good activity for building skills and a short easy-to-grade exercise, often no more than five or six sentences. A child can establish good patterns of social behavior by sending and receiving invitations, thank-you's, and mannerly requests for help. Even the *form* of the letter is a strong approach to correctness: A period must go there; a capital must go here; a comma must *not* go there. Red pen in hand, the teacher can quickly check off a child's violation of the code.

You can alter such an unpleasant approach for your child. Point out the requirements of the letter format, but explain that they simply are conventions that people expect, and that these conventions simplify the reader's task. Demand form only when your child intends to *mail* the letter! Then, you have his attention and interest, because his message is worth laboring over—someone will receive it, read what your child has written, and probably write back.

Creative Letter Writing

Think of the last letter you enjoyed receiving. What made it a pleasure to read? Perhaps it was something you would want to read again in the quiet of the living room after the children are asleep, or you might want to quote a word here and there to your spouse. Aside from the joy of hearing news from far away, and from sharing the experiences of men and women you love but often cannot see, you respond to the words that mirror an image of the writer's personality. That sounds just like Suzy, you might think. "Isn't that just what Mom would say," you murmur. "Why, that's something only Michael could write."

Messages reflect a child's personality, become documents of his or her perception, and serve in a youngster's program of creative growth in writing. I define creative letters as messages written in the child's own language that convey necessary information to people in his or her real world.

"Come to My Party"

A letter of invitation is a good message to begin with. For your child's next party, set aside a few afternoons so the birthday girl or boy can write original invitations to the guests. Depending on your youngster's age, help out as much as necessary. Don't insist on too much writing at once, especially for very young children. Talk about the message you need to send, and encourage your child to write a brief note that will highlight all the important information guests need to know. Make a list with your youngster to remind him or her of what to include:

What We Need to Tell in the Invitation
- What time the party will start
- What day the party will take place

- Where the party will be
- What kind of party it will be
- One special thing about the party

Work on scrap paper to plan the simple message, reminding your child that he'll have to write the same note for each guest. You don't want to overtax the youngster, so help out significantly if your child gets too tired. In at least a few of the cases, however, your son or daughter should follow through on the whole process: writing the message, folding the letter, addressing and stamping the envelope, and, finally, mailing the finished invitation.

Here is the message for one birthday invitation that a parent and child prepared together.

> Please come to my house for my
> birthday party
> on Sunday, March
> 2, at one o'clock.
> We'll have chocolate
> cake with whipped
> cream, and my daddy will
> show cartoons.

The little detail of what the guest might expect reveals the child's special delight at this party and is perfectly fitting to include in the message.

Once the message has been composed, your child should make a final draft. Your youngster will use the final version as a model to copy as he writes out all the other invitations. If you want to, you can write in the return address and the opening sentence, then have your child print the message. Point out the information the return address gives. Name and explain words that a writer might use instead of *Love* (*Sincerely, Fondly, Your friend*) before he or she signs the message. Here's a model to present:

9899 Cricklewood Drive
Boalsburg, Pennsylvania 16801
December 8, 1989

Dear Susan,
   Please come to my house for my birthday party on
Sunday March 2, at one o'clock. We'll have chocolate cake
with whipped cream, and my daddy will show cartoons.

                    Love,
                    Audrey

You might also take the time to explain RSVP, if your
planning requires responses to the invitations. Many parents expedite replies by offering a phone number, but it's
better to ask for written responses, so that your child can
anticipate receiving return notes.

I've included in this section a reference form for writing
the friendly letter (the correspondence we're considering
here is called a *friendly letter;* I'll discuss the more official
business letter in a while). In the sample, I've pointed out
trouble spots, places children often make errors when following the format. Because I think it's unnecessary, I've
omitted the terminology used for the various parts. Notice
the labels and the spacing for clarity. There are wide borders; and spaces are left after the address, the greeting, the
end of the message, and before the signature. This model is
a good reference tool for older children; they can keep it
available as they write. You can use it as a model to consult
when making concrete suggestions to your child about
correctness in written responses. Know your own child;
never bear down on right and wrong to the extent that his
or her creative efforts flicker and die, and never push the
very young too early to obey these letter-writing conventions.

When it's time to address the letter, be sure you have
selected an envelope that's large enough for your young

child's sprawling print. Addressing the envelope must be done carefully, because without clearly written words and numbers, the letter may go astray; but with the parent's supervision even a six-year-old should be able to write clearly enough.

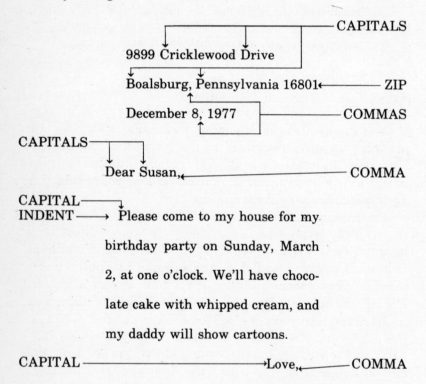

Here's a model envelope that will guide you as you help your daughter or son with the party invitations.

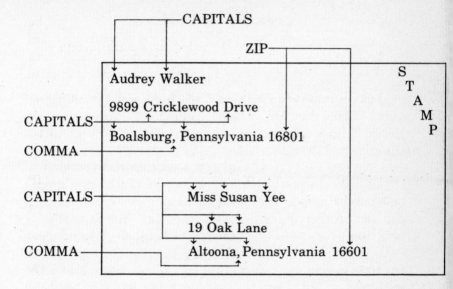

Some parents draw wide horizontal lines on the envelope for youngsters to write on. That's a good idea: The lines hold a child's print to reasonable size. If you're wondering about abbreviations and when to use them, sticklers still insist that all words, including *Street, Avenue,* and even the name of the state, be fully written out, but the Post Office Department says that two-letter abbreviations for state names (*PA* for Pennsylvania, *CA* for California, and so forth), accompanied by zip codes, speed up the mails. Make your own choice; but use the official abbreviations listed in the zip code directory at your local post office if you decide on them.

A trip to the post office during the letter-writing project may hook your child on mail forever! Watching those enormous canvas crates squeaking down an aisle, eyeing a clerk stuffing mail into pigeon holes, and standing in line and paying for stamps add an exciting dimension to a child's letter-writing experience.

Let's Write Letters

You have numerous opportunities for using letters in a realistic context.

The Homemade Postal or Greeting Card. With unlined index cards that are roughly equivalent to postcards in size a child uses scissors, paste, crayon, and paint to become a card designer. On one side of the card your youngster can draw a picture and add a written-in word or two. Or an original photograph or a picture cut from a magazine can be pasted onto one side of an index card and then can be protected from rough handling in the mails by painting over it with a thin coat of lacquer or some clear nail polish. *Voilà!* You have an original picture postcard. On the reverse side your child can draw a line down the middle and put a brief message on the left side, and the address and stamp on the right. To make a homemade greeting card, your youngster should cut a thin piece of cardboard a little less than double envelope size; folded over, the cardboard forms a greeting card upon which your child can draw a picture on front and can copy a message inside. Who knows, maybe Mr. Hallmark started this way!

Thank-you's. Etiquette demands a note in response to a gift, and parents who are concerned with their children's growth in writing skills should start using this kind of letter for good practice early. A present from Grandma, a gift from Mommy or Daddy, toys from the neighboring children at birthday party time all provide realistic impetus for letter writing. Encourage your youngster to use language that shows his or her unique personality in all these friendly letters. Your child can show the giftgiver his appreciation of the toy or game by mentioning some special joy it has brought. Don't be elaborate; if there are many notes to write, use the same message, except perhaps for the last sentence.

The freshness of a child's perceptions speaks out in these messages:

Thank you for your gift.
I love Sindy's brown hair
and her soft pink skin.
Will you come to play with
me and her soon?

I love the softball you
gave me for my birthday.
Dad and I tossed it around
in the grass at Sunset Park.
But we had to snatch it away
from little Tommy. He likes
to sit on it!

How did you know that calcu-
lator was what I wanted? I
like the way the numbers
flash in red on the little
screen. Thank you for helping
my arithmetic.

Thank you for the
money for my birthday.
I am going to buy a
pair of white boots
and bubble gum. Please
visit us soon.

The tone of these will warm the giver for having chosen the gift so well. Your youngster learns an important social obligation and at the same time practices writing.

Letters, Notes, and Cards to Shut-ins. Your youngster should send brief notes to classmates or relatives who are ill at home or in the hospital. It's letter writing for a *reason*, sent to people whom your child can cheer with a message.

Fan Mail Many children's television programs like *Sesame Street* encourage viewers to send in mail to the characters. Often the actors simply request drawings, but you can urge your youngster to write a brief message to his favorite star. Often the stars respond, and your child has a letter to cherish. As your young writer grows up, encourage him to write to his favorite stars or heroes: You'll be amazed how many take their fan mail seriously. Years ago a twelve-year-old in one of my classes wrote to John Steinbeck and delighted the class when she read aloud his handwritten note of response.

Letters to Faraway Friends and Pen Pals. If you have a cousin or friend who has recently moved out of state, or if you and your family have been uprooted because of a job change, or if an older sister has gone off to college, try to encourage your child to send letters every week to those who are far away. Here is a letter to a child who moved to State College, Pennsylvania, from a nine-year-old California friend back home.

Ellen mentions specific details about her new move and asks questions about activities and family members, inviting a letter in response. Hillary's mother says the breezy style of the letter is very much like the child herself. I can't tell whether or not her parent helped Ellen compose the note, but I know how I would have helped if she'd asked my advice. I wouldn't tell her what to say or what questions to ask, but I might say, "What a wonderful letter. You've told Hillary such good things and you've asked fine questions. Why don't you add a sentence that shows what our lovely beach looks like, maybe tell a sound of the ocean or give a picture of the sea." Or, "I think Hillary would love to know a little more about Spot. Why don't you tell her what he

> Jan. 4
>
> Dear Hillary
> I miss you. I liked your
> card. We moved to we
> live six miles from the
> ocean. It is nice here.
> We had a nice Christ-
> mas. Did you? Did you
> have snow?
>
> I have a new cat his name
> Is spot and he sleeps
> with our dog. I am
> learning to embroider.
> Do yo like your new
> school? I like mine.
>
> How is clair?
> Write to me.
>
> from
>   Ellen

looks like and one funny thing he did last week." Or, "Tell your friend what you are embroidering." Thus, I might coax out sentence groups like these:

- I have a new cat. He is brown with big white circles on his paws and back. His name is Spot and he sleeps with our dog. Yesterday he knocked over Mom's coffee cup. When it crashed to the floor, he jumped into my arms!

- We live six miles from the ocean. The water is blue and warm and we see sailboats.

- I am learning to embroider. Now I am making pink-and-green roses on the border of a pillowcase.

In my concern for correctness I'd ask Ellen about using a capital *S* in Spot's name. I'd suggest she read the second paragraph aloud slowly so she could hear her voice drop after the word *cat*. I'd ask how she should show that one

sentence is over and another about to begin. I'd discuss the
letter format: the absence of her return address, the small
letter in *from* (I might suggest possibilities for other clos-
ings), the placement of her signature to the left, the abbre-
viation of *January*. Her age and temperament would
determine my pursuit of these matters; I would not want
to overwhelm her. Knowing that the letter will travel thousands of miles to sit at a friend's breakfast table excites any
child and encourages concern for correct expression.

If you're lucky enough to have friends or relatives in
another country, try to find a correspondent about the
same age as your child. Help start pen pal communications that will assure frequent letters and provide an opportunity for you to influence your youngster's writing
growth. As your child grows older, she'll be less likely to
want you reading her letters! If you can't find a pen pal on
your own, help your child write a letter to Washington,
D.C. to the embassy of some country where he'd like to
have a correspondent. Or, write the American Junior Red
Cross in Washington for pen pals names. You might ask
around your own neighborhood for likely correspondents
for your son or daughter—children who live in other cities
here in North America or in Africa, Europe, or Asia.

Business Letters for Homebred Dynamos

Everyone likes something for nothing and children are no
exceptions. Innumerable public and private institutions
are ready to send pamphlets, booklets, photographs, and
free samples to anyone who writes asking for them. This is
precious motivation for your boy or girl to write business
letters.

The business letter is like the friendly letter in regard to
matters of courtesy, clarity, and correctness. The differences are in tone and purpose. The letter to a company
or an agency is straightforward and more formal. This

does *not* mean one uses Dreadful Big Words, such as *here-tofore, forthwith, pursuant to your letter,* and so on, that often appear in bad letters that we adults must suffer through. Business letters explain, demand, apologize, and inform; all these goals are action-oriented. Someone is being asked to fill a need the writer has.

The conventions of the business letter are much stricter than those of the friendly letter. In the sample one I've given I've labeled the parts of a business letter so that you can point them out to your child. The letter makes its point and supplies critical information quickly; a busy respondent can act easily and decisively to fill the writer's request.

1550 Winthrop Street
a.   Brooklyn, New York 11203
January 7, 19___

b.

Information Office

c.

Williamsburg, Virginia 23185

d.

e. Gentlemen:

f.

My family and I are planning a vacation this year during my school Easter vacation, April 3 to 10. We would like to know more about Williamsburg.

g.

Will you please send me information about hotel rates, restaurants, and sightseeing? I would also like to have a map of the city. Any other information you can send would be helpful, too.

h.   Yours truly,

j.

k.   [*Signature*]

l.   Richard Siskind

m.

a. *Child's address*. Note these trouble spots:
1. Capitals for name of street, word *street* or *avenue* capitalized as well.
2. Capitals for city, state, month of year.
3. Comma between city and state, between date and year,
   and no place else!
4. No abbreviations.
b. *Space* between child's address and next part.
c. *Address of people the child is writing to*
   1. Capitals for name of office or company, for city and
      state.
   2. Name of person—if you know it—goes first in this
      address with *Mr., Mrs., Miss,* or *Ms.*
d. *Space* between business address and next part.
e. *Greeting*
   1. If you know the person's name, say *Dear Mrs.
      Santini* or *Dear Mr. Davis*. Otherwise, *Gentlemen*
      or *Dear Madam* or *Dear Sir* is fine, if you're not
      addressing one person in particular. Since the
      reader is just as likely to be a woman as a man,
      however, you might want to address the company
      in the greeting: *Dear Information Office* or *Dear
      McGraw-Hill Book Company*. Notice the capitals.
   2. A colon follows the greeting.
f. *Space* between greeting and rest of letter.
g. *Letter* itself. Brief, clear, courteous, important
   information included, to the point, correct.
h. *Space*
i. *Closing*. Watch these trouble spots children often
   miss:
   1. Capital letter only for the first word in the closing.
      Other choices: *Yours very truly, Respectfully
      yours*. Less formal choices are *Sincerely* or *Sin-
      cerely yours*.
   2. Comma after the closing.
j. *Space* here.
k. *Child's signature*

l. *Child's name* printed clearly (if the letter is typed, this will be typed, of course).

m. *Margins*. Notice the spacing—wide borders, clear layout—for easy reading.

The business envelope follows the same conventions as the envelope for the friendly letter. You'll want to take some time explaining how to fold the letter into thirds horizontally. A standard sheet of stationery for business letters is 8½-by-11 inches, unlined, but you may have to rule lines to aid your young child in printing clearly.

You may be wondering who will answer a letter from a child. Which companies might you suggest to your sons and daughters as likely correspondents? Let me say that, increasingly, businesses recognize that answered letters develop goodwill. Children usually live in a house with a mother and a father who are consumers; and, as he grows, each child is a potential consumer with his own money to spend. Public relations offices in the private sector, business, and industry exist to disseminate information about their organization, their products, and their concerns. I will suggest some possible recipients of your child's business letter, but the list of free things to write for could fill the rest of this book. (In fact, a book you might want to buy for sources is *1000s of Free Things* by the editors of *Consumer Guide* (New York: Beekman). To avoid disappointment—companies go out of business; letters get lost; poor public relations departments ignore requests—I suggest you encourage your youngster to send off three or four letters to different corporations. Discuss with your child the possibility that a company might not answer, so that your youngster is not too disappointed if he or she receives no replies at first.

All right, here are more than two dozen ideas for business letters, which children from six to nineteen might consider:

- Write to the chamber of commerce of your town or city—any town or city—and ask for information about vacationing, historic landmarks, and places of interest.
- Write to a publisher to ask for a catalog of children's books.
- Ask for a book about how to care for your animal from the company that makes the pet food you use.
- Write to your local Internal Revenue Service for a social security application or to your local motor vehicle office for an application for a learner's permit.
- Write to your local savings bank for an application for a passbook savings account.
- Write to the local board of education for a list of summer activities for children.
- Write for a free catalog of roses from Jackson and Perkins Co., Rose Lane, Medford, Oregon 97501.
- Write for a catalog of toys from

Fisher-Price Toys
East Aurora, New York 14052

The Ertl Company
Dyersville, Iowa 52040

- Write for free recipe books to

California Table Grape Commission
Fresno, CA 93755

Campbell Soup Co.
Campbell Place
Camden, NJ 08103-1799

Rice Council of America
Box 740121
Houston, Texas 77027

Almond Board of California
P.O. Box 15920
Sacramento, CA 95808

Fleischmann's Yeast Co.
Standard Brands
625 Madison Avenue
New York, NY

Betty Crocker Kitchens
1 General Mills Blvd.
Golden Valley, Minnesota 55426

Morton Salt Co.
110 Wacker Drive
Chicago, ILL 60606

- Write for pamphlets on baby care and feeding from Gerber Products Company, Fremont, Michigan 49412.
- Write for a catalog on planting and farming, consumer affairs, historic sites, or health care from the Superintendent of Documents, Government Printing Office, Washington, D.C. 20402.
- Write for a book about rubber to B. F. Goodrich, 3925 Embassy Parkway, Akron, Ohio 44318.
- Ask for a list of their free publications from John Hancock Mutual Life Insurance Company, Hancock Place, Boston, Massachusetts 02117.
- Write for hints for good picture taking from Eastman Kodak, Rochester, New York 14603.
- Write for information about the Girl Scouts to Girls Scouts of the USA, 830 Third Avenue, New York, New York 10022.
- Write for a booklet about artificial food additives (*Today's Food and Additives*) to Miss Peggy Kohn, V.P., Con-

sumer Affairs, General Foods, Consumer Center, White Plains, New York 10625.

With all those built-in excitements about letter writing encourage your child to pick an idea and to get started first thing tomorrow!

Words in Focus:

Creative Definitions for Your Young Writer

A substantial vocabulary increases your child's potential as a writer. I'd like to describe some challenging games and activities that will help advance your child's use of language.

What Does It Mean? How Does It Feel?

One of the exciting—and often troublesome—features of words is that they arouse both intellectual *and* emotional responses. It's comfortable but not correct to believe that for every word there is simply one (or even only several) definition stored in a dictionary. Words evoke a range of feelings and associations that no dictionary definition can accurately suggest.

The exact definition of a word is called its *denotation*. When your child copies the meaning of *night* from a dictionary, his definition draws upon what the word *denotes*. The *connotation* of a word is its suggested meaning, the thoughts and feelings (in language) aroused by the word. If when your child thinks of *night* he feels *fear* or *comfort* or *quiet* or *warmth,* those words are what night *connotes* for him.

The connotative meanings for words are no less legitimate than the denotative ones. The dual conditions of meaning act together, enriching our language possibilities. However, you can see why it's important to keep these different qualities of words clearly in mind. Otherwise it's possible to substitute associated feelings, definitions, and ideas for actual meanings.

A good example of this idea is the word *shark.* The dictionary tells us a shark is any of numerous, chiefly marine, fish with a skeleton of cartilage and tough skin covered with small toothlike scales. But is that what leaps into mind when most people hear the word *shark?* The associations of *shark* are overpowering: fear, blood, massive jaws biting limbs off innocent bathers, terror as a gray, winglike fin races through the waves. Peter Benchley, the author of the book *Jaws,* knew he could rely upon our connotative responses to sharks; in some respects he developed his story through connotations, that as you may have learned, are not really accurate. Very few sharks are interested in humans for Sunday dinner. Yet we will continue to shudder, cringe, and despise this maligned creature of the sea—the *shark!*

When you explored word meanings using a dictionary and thesaurus (in chapter 7), you worked with denotative meanings. When you encouraged definitions in images (the associations a child has for words like *red,* for example), you highlighted the connotative.

To understand better these characteristics of word meaning, children of nine and ten can play together in a variation on the old parlor game of word association. You're not interested in instant associations, however.

Rather, you are going to ask your child to think about what a word means and what it suggests. On a sheet of paper folded into three columns ask your youngster to write down a word that you provide in the first column. In column 2, ask for a definition of the word; and in column 3 request thoughts and images suggested by the word. You might encourage your child to use a dictionary for practice, but don't ask him to copy the word's meaning. Your aim is to help your child distinguish the *definition* from his *feelings* about the word. Here are some examples:

Word	Meaning	Suggestions and Feelings
summer	warm time of year from June 21 to September 20	fun at the beach cherry ices heat no school roses and lilacs water sprinklers
alone	not with other people	lonely friendless sad my dark bedroom

Stimulate the awareness of a word's *shades of meaning*—the differences between what words denote and what they suggest (frequently based upon how they are used)—by looking up the words that a dictionary says are similar in meaning but that arouse different feelings and attitudes. Look at these pairs:

bad	evil
heavy	fat
bright	vivid
cry	sob
big	enormous

tasty	delicious
weak	helpless
active	restless
tall	lanky
tired	exhausted
intelligent	brilliant
dry	parched
car	jalopy
doctor	physician
thin	slender
little	petite

Heavy and *fat* mean pretty much the same, but *fat* is a more negative word when it is used to describe a person. When you list and discuss these words, ask your child to write sentences for each one after he understands the meanings by checking the definitions in a dictionary. Your child's age and level of comprehension determine which words to examine.

Another exercise that will help your child appreciate the variety and economy of words focuses on words with multiple definitions. In *The American Heritage Dictionary*, *dark* has more than ten meanings; *dead* has fifteen, *horn* eleven, *light* more than *forty* depending on whether it's a verb, a noun, or an adjective. There are many such simple words with various definitions: *lift*, *mind*, *moral*, *bad*, *bat*, *limit*, *fast*, *blink*, *civil*, *class*, and *drop* are just a few other examples. Look at some of these words with your son or daughter; discuss the various definitions; and ask your child to practice by making up a sentence for as many words as possible. Each sentence should demonstrate a different meaning. Here are some sentences written for the word *dark:*

It was dark at six o'clock.
Mother wore a dark brown hat.
I am not allowed to go out in the dark.

Sally's idea kept me in the dark.
He had a dark reason for sneaking into the house.
The Dark Ages is a period of history.

Work with a dictionary that suits your child's ability, and try to excite her delight in how words sound, in what strange and interesting words mean, where they come from and how their meanings came about, and in how to use them. Try working on some of these:

fiddle-faddle	unicorn
muscovado	papyrus
porringer	polonaise
popinjay	loon
lemming	dromedary
dandelion	bonsai
crazy quilt	aqueduct
boomerang	Amazon
longhorn	zeppelin
zircon	porcupine fish

Suggest that your child make an original dictionary. Your child's age will determine the scope and intent of this homemade wordbook; but here is an activity that children of most age groups enjoy. For younger children you can combine the verbal and the visual. Ask your child to write a word on top of an unlined page and then draw a picture beneath it (or cut one out of a magazine and glue the picture on) to illustrate the word's meaning. Supply a binder and dividers marked with alphabet tabs; make twenty-six sections and insert lots of loose-leaf paper. When your youngster finishes writing and illustrating each word, ask her to insert the page in the correct section. This is also a wonderful opportunity for your child to practice alphabetizing. Make sure each new entry goes in the correct place. The words the younger child selects for illustration will be essentially concrete objects like *ball, oak, lilac, airplane, pen, refrigerator,* and words suggesting clear actions like *skip, drip,* and *fly.*

As your youngster grows older, propose a variation. For each word, your child will write a brief definition to go with the illustration. A sentence should appear beneath each drawing, using the word in a statement about the illustration. Older children who choose not to illustrate words can prepare a private dictionary of new words they hear or read. Using a loose-leaf binder, they would include a sheet of paper for each letter and might rule or fold the paper into three columns: one for the word, another for its definition (in the child's *own* language, even if he looks the explanation up in the dictionary), a third for a sentence that uses the word correctly. Some parents encourage a fourth column that indicates the pronunciation of the word. Part of a typical page in this kind of home dictionary might look like this:

Word	Meaning	Sentence
brawny	strong and having muscles	I saw his brawny arms.
biped	animal with two feet	Humans are bipeds.
bleat	cry of an animal like a sheep or goat	The lamb bleated for its mother.

For a new word to join a child's vocabulary it must be practiced in a variety of contexts: The word must be read, spoken correctly, written, and used in a sentence to demonstrate understanding. The private dictionary provides opportunities for a youngster to practice those stages in small doses, as the words crop up in your child's experience. Encourage your youngster to read through his or her dictionary once or twice a week in order to renew acquaintanceship with personal vocabulary.

This homemade dictionary advances skills on important fronts. As a writer your child expands resources for presenting ideas with precision; as a reader, your child expands resources for understanding your child's ideas expressed by others; as a speaker with an increased supply of words, your child expands his capabilities with oral language.

Writing Clear Definitions

Despite practice with words and a dictionary, your child may not always be able to put the knowledge he has about a word into a coherent statement. That's true for everyone. Remember those occasions when your son or daughter asked you the meaning of some word you knew but were helpless to put into language? I once saw a humorous television segment in which men and women tried to define *scruples*. Twisting, squirming, and stammering accompanied their incredible statements. (One man said the word meant a kind of meat, and that you ate scruples with spaghetti.)

It is important to master the skill of constructing a solid definition if your child is to succeed as a versatile writer. Beginning with the basic exercises in grade school that ask a child to define words from a list supplied by the teacher; to the complex activity of telling the class the meaning of a concept in history, mathematics, or science; to the rigors of writing a report, memo, or letter on the job, the ability to state the definition of a key term succinctly and clearly is essential.

Well-constructed definitions have four critical parts. A good definition:

- Names the word or term (sometimes in more than one word) that will be defined.
- Uses the word *is, are, was,* or *were.*
- Tells what general group of things or ideas the word belongs to.
- Names the special qualities that make the word different from other things in that group.

For example:

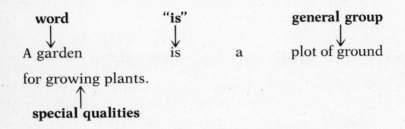

If you use this definition, with its arrows, as a model, explain the various parts to your child. Help your child understand that naming the general group to which a word belongs does not sufficiently establish the meaning of the word. Not every plot of ground is a garden. What other plots of ground can your child name or describe? Here are some other samples to look at:

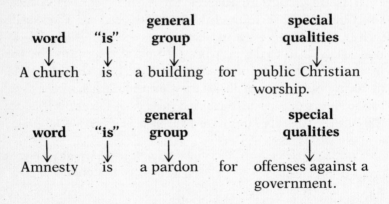

For children who are just learning this skill, you might want to try a different visual approach. With colored chalk, pencil, or crayon draw four rectangular boxes of different sizes and colors on a page. Each one must correspond to a feature of the definition. Write the feature over the box. The page should look something like this:

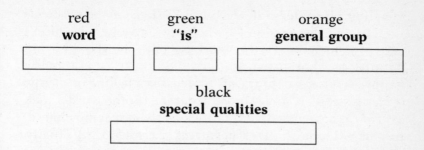

A child fills in the boxes with their correct parts; if you have colored pencils, your youngster can write the words in the same color as he has drawn the box.

Another way to present this is to make a grid, in which you list the various parts of several definitions in ruled columns.

word	"is"	general group	special qualities
A silkworm	is	a caterpillar	that spins a fine thread to make a cocoon
A handbook	is	a manual	of information on a special subject
A nail	is	a pointed piece of metal	hammered into wood or other material as a fastener
A pogonip	is	dense fog	of ice particles
A bracelet	is	a band or chain	worn around the wrist for decoration

Caution your young writer about definitions. First, she must avoid using the word itself or a form of it in the meaning she offers. If she wrote "*Division* is to *divide* something" she wouldn't be helping someone who didn't know the meaning of the word. Second, she should avoid definitions that use negatives. "Sadness is not being happy" is a weak definition; "Sadness is a feeling of sorrow or depression" is much more accurate. (Some words, such as *widow,* have negative qualities as their specific characteristics—in those cases negatives are all right.) Finally, remember that it is not gramatically correct to use *when* or *where* after the word *is.* Your child should write, "A closet is an enclosed place for storing clothing, food, or tools," not "A closet is where you store. . . ."

Here is a list of words you might want to try for good one-sentence definitions; but you'll have more fun if you and your child come up with words based on your own interests:

- summer
- ink
- prejudice
- Buddhism
- union
- calculator
- Goth
- drizzle
- evaporation
- isobar
- tide
- fear
- diary
- matzo
- penguin
- rayon

You can help your youngster expand one-sentence definitions to fuller efforts by pointing out the kinds of questions to ask about the object being defined:

- What size is it?
- What does it look like?
- What shape does it have?
- What color is it?
- What might the object remind us of?
- Does the thing look like anything else?
- What materials contribute to the object?
- What is the object used for?
- How is the object made?

Here is a brief definition of *rayon,* which was built from significant features the writer discovered after thinking about some of those questions:

> Rayon is a fiber produced from cellulose and used to weave fabrics. Chemicals dissolve the cellulose (wood pulp or short cotton fibers) which machines then force through tiny holes. The dissolved material, hardened in warm air or liquid, forms filaments which may be either twisted into threads or cut and spun. Spun filaments of rayon may look like wool, linen, or cotton. Because yarns with new features are developed all the time, rayon now has a variety of uses: It appears in automobile tires, in grease-proof cellophane sheets, in sponge rubber as a substitute for cellulose, and is special glass that cannot be shattered.

Definitions like this one clarify words and expand a child's facility with language.

Personal Meanings, Personal Words

When I wrote of the denotative and connotative meanings of words, I stressed the glorious variety those qualities give to our language. I want to close this discussion of creative definitions by celebrating those private, personal, and associative attachments people make to words and ideas.

Here is a definition rich in sensory diction and highly personal in the response it arouses:

> *Green:* a row or unripened tomatoes sitting on the kitchen table; the dirty old blotter on my desk filled with doodles in pencil and red ink; wood velvet carpet in the living room; hundreds of pickles floating in the barrel at Mike's Delicatessen on our corner; the large, round, sparkling eyes of my cousin Elizabeth; ivy clinging to the side wall of the quaint old schoolhouse on Mill Road in Brooklyn; diced scallions peering out of a container of cream cheese, small clumps of lettuce, and a handful of olives all at Sunday breakfast; a slippery trail of seaweed stretching at the water line along Brighton Beach at low tide; a statue of a smiling Buddha sitting on the roof of the Ho Sai Kai Restaurant on sunny Pitkin Avenue.

This is the work of an eighteen-year-old who is an advanced writer: There are riches of original detail and of sharply drawn, specific images in the descriptions. Here you have proof that a good writing exercise goes beyond age limits. The child who listed sensory images in response to the word *red* (see page 65) though many years younger and less practiced than the writer who defined green, used the same skill, drawing upon her own powers of observation and linguistic resources.

When I face a group of inexperienced writers with limited vocabulary, I often turn to a visual technique that can help a child explore words and meanings. I ask the youngster to select a word that is rich in definitions—either a concrete word such as *summer* or *Thanksgiving* or an abstract term such as *fear* or *love*. The child then makes a collage that visually represents the meaning of the word without using written language. When we put the collages on display, we note how difficult it is for someone else to guess the word the creator of the collage had in mind. This is especially true of abstract words. One person's representations for *love* or *loneliness* vary widely from another's; even representations for concrete terms like *spring* or *school* are hard for an observer to crystallize in the same word that artist had in mind. This shows how inadequate visual means often are in conveying precise information. Despite their problems in communicating ideas accurately, words are often more exact than pictures in saying what we mean.

Word exploration has a number of possibilities for other visual reinforcements. A young child who examines concept words *(love, tenderness, anger)* can illustrate them with drawings. You might suggest that your child cut photos from a magazine and mount them to illustrate the word. These visual exercises interact nicely with the verbal skills you are trying to advance.

As a final experiment in personalized meanings, I suggest that you ask your young writer to select some word that can be defined through his or her own experience in a single moment. It should be an experience that helped the writer understand the complex meaning of some important word.

Language users constantly seek new meanings and applications for words they already know. You could all look up *ghetto*, for example, and think you understand its meaning. (*The American Heritage Dictionary* says, "A slum section of an American city occupied predominantly by members of a minority group who live there because of social or economic pressure"); but it's not until you experience ghetto life that you really can see the fullest implications of the word. Someone who experiences a ghetto for a short time (as in the example you will see), although his understanding of the word has been advanced, still has a weaker sense of what *ghetto* means than does the child raised in an urban slum. Furthermore, a child who seeks out the meaning of *ghetto* in books beyond the dictionary will ripen his conception, but his vision will still lack the personal, indelible meaning that only experience can as-

sure. Youngsters perceive language as a living, vital entity
when they write definitions that grow from experience.

This sample of a ghetto relies upon descriptive and
narrative skills, but the writer's redefinition stretches language beyond its limits.

I learned what *ghetto* meant after my first drive down
Washington Street in Brooklyn one December morning. A
dozen empty buildings in one side of the street had broken windows and large black smears from a fire. I saw
boarded-up doors, overturned garbage pails, and clumps
of newspapers along the sidewalk. Three black children
without coats played with the stuffing of an abandoned
couch on an empty lot. A scraggly mutt stretched out on
the corner. Everything looked so old and depressing and
worn out. No dictionary ever gives that idea in its
definition.

Here are some words to offer your young writer for
extended definitions. Use the more abstract ones with mature children:

- hope
- joy
- friend
- old age
- success
- teacher
- courage
- money
- hero
- a child
- American
- fun
- happiness
- fear
- sports

14

Language Singing:
YOUR CHILD AS POET

■━━━━━━━━■

In recent years, agencies like the National Endowment for the Arts have worked along with state and local art councils to sponsor artists in the schools. Children learn fiction, poetry, and painting firsthand from men and women with creative skills. One of the most exciting of these projects is the Poet-in-the-Classroom Program where poets work in residence alongside young children in school settings. Through poetry workshops, individual writing, group and collaborative poetry, youngsters in many parts of the country experience the thrills and delights of creating their own poems. Under the wings of these poets a child's efforts grow close to the spirit of poetic experience.

Children love poetry; they delight in rhythms and sounds, in sharp visual images, in the emancipation of spirit through language. Kenneth Koch's impressive book *Wishes, Lies, and Dreams* (New York: Chelsea House, 1970) is a source of great inspiration for those who love to see children feel the force of language through poetry. Read Koch's book; he's an exceptional teacher who describes countless ideas for writing poems with kids and offers wonderful examples of their work.

Your child's home library should include a shelf of poetry books, which you can read aloud together. The sound of the human voice breathes excitement into written language.

In this chapter I'd like to point out some activities that will delight the waiting poets in your family. I'd also like to share ideas about what to stress when your child writes a poem, and to mention some techniques poets use when they write.

Talk-to-Me's and Word Whackies

No one can deny the hypnotic delight in rhyming language. In fact, when they think of poetry, many think only of rhyme. Recall those poems you learned as a child: the nursery rhymes, "Hiawatha," "The Highwayman," "Evangeline," and, perhaps, some from Robert Louis Stevenson's *A Child's Garden of Verses*. Reading specialists use rhyme to teach reading skills, and rhyming plays an important part in a child's use and recognition of word families.

Children respond to rhyming; they sway and bounce as they savor the melody of a poem that trips along. In the exploration of language, rhyme tickles a young child; and there is the chance to make those sallies with words permanent in *writing* poetry.

A good, simple way to involve young children with rhyming is to play with couplets, two lines that rhyme at the end of each:

I take a drink
from the kitchen sink.

Somebody sat
on my red hat.

I like to talk
when I take a walk.

Some parents will leave out the last word or two of the
second line of a couplet they write so very young children
can add the rhyme themselves before they try to compose
their own couplets. Practice for three-line rhymes in similar ways:

Into the sky
I saw a kite fly
Waving his tail good-bye.

There's a maple tree
Would you like to see
How it stands beside the house with me?

Rhyming works best when the subject of the poem is
not serious. Encourage your child to write silly rhymes
that play with words in improbable situations. Lovely couplets appear when children write "If I Were" rhyming
poems:

If I were a brown cow
Would I know how?

If I were a table
Would I be able?

If I were a pen
What then?

If I were green
I'd be mean, I'd be mean.

If I were a cloud
How could I talk loud?

Another way to involve your child in little rhymes is by
encouraging him to write "Talk-to-Me's." In a Talk-to-Me
rhyme, your child speaks to some inanimate object:

Ice cream, ice cream, take my hand
We'll play in never-melting land.

I like you, white refrigerator.
Do I get my apple now or later?

Older children might try a game of Word Whackies.
These rhymes have two or three lines too, but they repeat a
particular sound made by letter combinations in words.
The results are delightfully ridiculous, as in this rhyme
which uses the *h* and *m* sounds.

Ho, ho, ho, I have a happy heart
I helped a hippopotamus
To make his motor start.

Here are some others:

Fo, fo, fo, I'm funny Freddy Frog
I fight with flies and frankfurters
Then flip into the fog.

A tree told me on the telephone,
"Take me to a taxicab and help me home."

When children have trouble selecting words that
rhyme, you can build rhyming word groups in lists for
your youngster to use as she writes. Guide her as she
composes, seeing that she rhymes at the end of each pair of

lines. Encourage your child to suggest her own words too. These are some examples:

shoe	hat	try	still	away
blue	cat	fly	frill	hooray
new	fat	why	will	delay
true	bat	by	bill	array
due	rat	cry	hill	today

Parent and child can prepare groups of words with repeating sounds as well.

chill	snake	over	light
cheap	snoop	oven	lazy
Charlie	sneeze	ox	lettuce
chime	snarl	olive	leaping
chair	snap	orange	loon

After the two of you prepare the lists, make sentences using the words with similar sounds, adding words where you need them:

An orange ox opened olives over a lake.

Come up with a silly line to complete the couplet in rhyme:

When he finds all the pits, goodness sake!

By combining a rhyming exercise with sensory language, you'll be helping your child work as a poet. An excellent activity suggested by Don Wolfe uses one of Christina Rossetti's poems "What is Pink?" to build from. Here are the first few lines:

What is pink? A rose is pink
By the fountain's brink.

What is red? A poppy's red
In its barley bed.

What is blue? The sky is blue
Where the clouds float through.

Using this delightful model, urge your child to ask his own question, starting with a color:

What is gray?

Then, your youngster must think of something he remembers that has the color. He repeats the color word at the end of the line:

Smoke is gray.

In the next line, your child expands upon the idea he just expressed, offers details of setting, action, or place, and rhymes with the color word at the end of the line:

As it curls away.

Thus, the three lines look like:

What is gray?
Smoke is gray
As it curls away.

You need not confine your child to color—sound, smell, taste, action, and touch work equally well.

What is loud?
My cat was loud
When she meowed.

What is dry?
My garden is dry
In hot July.

You also can encourage your child to see this as an exercise in metaphor, selecting an abstract term for concrete definition:

What is hope?
A puppy is hope
On a long, long rope.

What is sorrow?
A dream is sorrow
When it ends before tomorrow.

These little games in rhyming and writing improve a young child's facility with words and his pleasure in them.

What's Wrong with Jingling?

But rhyme is not poetry!

William Slaughter of the University of North Florida in Jacksonville, an author and a poet in the National Endowment for the Arts Poetry in the Schools Program, recently named a number of ways to get children to write poetry. The first point he insists on is that children must be helped to overcome the notion of poetry as rhyming. Yes. *Overcome* it.

Does that shock you? If you've seen *any* poems written by school children, you've no doubt noted the jingling:

Nice turkey roasted well
Pilgrims and Indians got along swell
Thankful for good things past
A day to celebrate at last!

In the summer I go to the beach
There I like to eat a peach
In the sun I bake and bake
And after that I have a milk shake.

Mr. Slaughter is not a lone voice. Another poet-in-the-schools in New Jersey tells of a school being rhyme-crazy, the children starved in self-expression. I agree that we should move children away from rhyming in poetry.

First, rhyme can make trivial the thought and experience a poem attempts to convey. To me a poem is the honest communication of experience compressed in intense, concise, and electric language. If the young poet is groping for words to rhyme with others, and feels compelled to rhyme in order to make a poem, he is forcing experience into prescribed language rather than using language to report experience.

The youngster who wrote about the beach strained to rhyme that word, struggled to stretch out what she wanted to say so that *peach* wound up at the end of the next line. Unless rhyme is used with great skill, it detracts from the meaning of the poem itself. Coupled with a strong rhythm, rhyme bounces along, so the reader crosses the range just to get over the mountains, without any thought to the meaning of the journey.

Keep in mind that the selection of words, the way the poet places them in a line, the sounds made by letter combinations, the stresses required by pronunciation and meaning, and the pattern of sound and word are much more important in the poet's rhythmic skill than rhyming.

Finally, the schools overteach "rhyming poems." Poems in the classrooms frequently mean nothing other than rhyming. Selections read aloud by the teacher, white sheets of children's writing tacked to bulletin boards, original poems filling school newspapers and magazines art products carved in rhyme. A group of thirteen-year-old boys squirms at the prospect of poetry because of the "silliness" of rhyme and because of the preconceived notion that love and flowers and gush define the poetic experience.

This is not to say that rhyme is evil, ineffective, worthless: Rhyme has the power to rivet a child's attention to a tale, to stick ideas in the mind. But if you believe that a poem is the intensification of experience through the language of sense imagery, then you see that rhyme has a subsidiary role. Don Wolfe calls rhyme "an almost magic adjunct to the poet's art . . . a subordinate theme to his music, not the stream of its melody."

The young girl of eight who wrote about her summer day on the beach (see page 250) obscured real experience by forcing rhyme, by pouring honest perceptionlike water into paper bags. Without depending upon rhyme but with a feeling for the flexibility of language, and a sense of the possibilities of poetry to express emotion, she might have written:

> In the summer
> I go to Jones Beach,
> Eat a peach
> In the sun.
> I bake and bake and bake
> Dreaming of milk shakes.

There is a change in thought here, and though this poem lacks instant sensory appeal, it is quite an improvement over the previous effort. The rhyme still remains, but it does not stick out; it works *for* the ideas. The writer forces readers to take in the words "Eat a peach in the sun" by the way she lays out the lines and by the way she has shifted some parts. We barely notice that *peach* rhymes with *beach* directly above it. The use of *Jones* not only adds specificity but also changes the stress on the line, again calling attention away from the rhythm, how *milk shakes* really misses as a rhyme yet maintains some music through the *ake* sound.

Look at the two versions of the poem side by side to see how they speak about similar experience, one using language to advance ideas, the other trapped by rhymed language that weakens the writer's intended thought:

In the summer I go to the beach	In the summer
There I like to eat a peach	I go to Jones Beach
In the sun I bake and bake	Eat a peach
And after that I have a milk shake.	In the sun.
	I bake and bake and bake
	Dreaming of milk shakes.

If a child's poem uses rhyme at all, it should serve the poem's meaning. Notice that the rhyme in the next poem effectively serves the purpose of freedom and delight in love, yet doesn't overpower the other rhythmic qualities. The teenage poet repeats words and sounds of letters, varies the length of the poem's lines, shifts usual word order in the sixth line, and breaks rhythm by commas in the last line.

The grass is green
The grass is high
The sun is yellow in the sky

The air is fresh
The air is sweet
My fingertips the cool breeze meet

The flowers nod
The flowers stand
My love, the spring, now holds my hand

It won't be easy convincing children of six to nine that rhymed poetry has fewer virtues than unrhymed—the singsong is appealing to them as an end in itself. The best way to establish the value of unrhymed poems is to read them aloud to your child at home, or at least to select those whose rhyme does not intrude. Poets like Langston Hughes, Rachel Field, Frances Frost, Vachel Lindsay, Robert Frost, and Walter de la Mare have written poems that avoid rhyme and that children will enjoy.

Language Singing, Sharp and Clear

In attempts to move children along in their writing skills, your main goal has been to tease out concrete language that will impress upon a reader the full sensory impact of your child's responses to daily life. Poetry requires an even more intense expression of the experience than prose does. Poets choose words with even more care than other writers do, each word making an essential contribution to the poem's meaning. In prose the writer can lead up to and lay the groundwork for later elements, but poetry is stream-lined. Every word counts. The words must convey exactly the meaning the poet wants and must also contribute to the rhythmic effect he's trying to achieve. The writer of poetry must be much briefer than the prose writer; this means the poet must compress ideas and observations into as few words as possible.

When you encourage your child to write poetry at home, any subject is fair game. You must mine the same elements that you mined before: the gold of sensory diction, precise action, and figurative language. Simile, metaphor, and personification bring an imaginative dimension to the poem and delight writer and reader alike.

You're not interested in rhyme, but in the sound of words together, the way a voice moves in rhythm as it reads the lines aloud. Offer these guidelines to your young poet:

- Use a word picture in every line.
- Use color, sound, smell, touch, and taste.

- Try to show an action on every line.
- Make a comparison.
- Don't use words that sound harsh together; read your poem aloud to hear how it sounds.
- Don't use rhyme.

These aren't rules; use them loosely depending upon your body's or girl's age and interest. An eight- or nine-year-old can look at and understand those pointers and can incorporate many of them as the poem takes shape. For other children, use the guidelines to ask constructive questions: "Why don't you use a color in this line?" "Why don't you use a word that gives a better picture of action than *is* or *walk?*" "Are the words in this line easy to say together?" Rhythmic language is a hard goal for a child to achieve. Along with an attention to the sounds of the words themselves, you can suggest repetition of words, even whole thoughts, in order to achieve rhythm.

Start your home poetry writing right away with activities that practice the use of the senses, encouraging your child to spread the words out in varying lines on the page. Pick a sense and suggest a poem that focuses upon it. A color, for example, makes a good starting point. In this selection from *Indiana Writes,* a journal of chilren's writings, notice how Patricia McGraw starts with a color and then calls into play the other senses:

If I could touch dark blue,
it would be soft like a pussycat
or like silk or a baby's hands.

If I could taste dark blue,
it would taste good and sweet,
sugary like cinnamon,
or maybe like bacon.

If I could smell dark blue
it would smell strong
like skunk or like a hot iron.

If I could hear dark blue
it would sound like running water,
running mad
or like rain in the night
or quiet like falling stars.

And nine-year-old Mike Davis, writing in the same journal, takes *red* and in three comparisons calls up taste, sound, and sight.

Red is sweet
like an apple
red is loud
like blood
red is quiet
like the sea
at night
when the tide
is going out.

Use a familiar sound as a starting point and help develop a poem that uses simile as this eight-year-old does:

My heart beats like a bat in a baseball game
And like the thumping of the rain
And like a tornado whirling a rock at a house.

To stimulate poems like this one, give your child the opening part of a line, perhaps:

"My shoes squeak like ____"
"My voice sounds like ____"
"My clock ticks like ____
"Our car coughs like ____

Another good approach to sense poetry is to select a word and to ask for five lines, each giving a picture of that word in terms of a different sensory appeal, as this ten-year-old does:

> Smiles taste like candy
> Smiles smell like cherries
> Smiles sound like laughter
> Smiles feel like lips
> Smiles look like cracks

or

> Hair smells like rosebuds
> Hair looks like grass
> Hair sounds like whispers
> Hair tastes like leaves
> Hair feels like feathers

Here are some words to give you ideas for sense poems of this type: *hands, books,* a *ball,* a *daisy* (any flower), the *wind,* a *table* or *chair,* a *pencil* or *crayon,* a *banana.*

The child's natural world is a perfect source for ideas. Wherever possible, offer guidelines urging your child to look at a single moment in time as he gives his sensory impressions of nature. In these schoolchildren's poems notice how the simple use of comparison joins with sharp and original images. The repetition of words contributes to his rhythm:

> How loud the wind yawns,
> Roaring so hard as it whizzes by
> Weird sounds in my ears.

> The drooping branches of my maple
> Hang low:

The bitter cold of winter
Makes them helpless old men.

Smoky
Smoky-gray
Like a fire when leaves blow in
And billow away;
Leaving behind them
Smoky
Smoky-gray
Like a book I once read
And stored away;

A memory that is
Smoky
Smoky-gray
Like an early fog
On a morning in May
Before the sun clears the web of
Smoky
Smoky-gray
And all the thoughts
In my mind today
Are
Smoky.

The snow melts like syrup
Falling off pancake hill
The flowers bloom like
Ribbons opening

When it rains an angel is crying.
Tears pour like a stream.
Falling gently from her cheeks.
Blessing the world below.
When it rains an angel is crying.

Her tears cool the summer heat.
Making us cool and restful.
Relaxing in our sleep.

Today I saw a leaf
So crisp
So dark
So brown
Yes, I saw my first leaf of the day
Upon this solid gold morning.
Its veins, swollen,
As if it labored hard
Upon this golden morning.
I had to leave this treasure
For there was much of the morning left, so
I quickly let the leaf glide to the ground
And I strolled away,
Still wondering.

The sky is very blue and the clouds are very mean—
And when you touch the clouds the rain begins to
    pour—

And when it drops on me
My hair begins to cry.
The rain has a gray color
And always bends my roses.

A whispering rain
Gently cracking a mirror pond.
Water cries autumn.

Blue sea
with empty harbors,
the sun's rays
carving ripples
into the water.

A child with
a sunburnt face,
shielding his eyes
against the glare.
A lazy breeze
brushing over the sand,
leaving the waves
of unspoken words
and quiet thoughts.

The wind snaps its whiplike tongue and a billowy cloud
    of white sand beaches up and marches over the barren
    beachhead.
The wind shouts a command, and murky blue waters
    churn into a frenzied mass of white foam.
Furious, the wind wrenches an oak from the ground and
    hurls it, howling, "I am King, and no force on earth
    can resist me."

Snow!
Snowballs, snowflakes, snowmen.
Scattered round the world like a blanket.
Good snow.
Bad snow.
Little snow
Dark snow
Light snow
Doing things, each different
Twirling, swirling, swaying with the wind.
Then sun:
The enemy,
The feared
No more big, little, bad, dark, light,
Twirling, swirling snow.

But do not worry
It will snow again
Very soon

Fall:
The dead leaves,
Red, yellow, and brown,
Rustling
As the breeze winds through the yard,
Swirling
In the driveway
Skipping
On the sidewalk.

Fall:
Winter's coming,
The cold wind blowing raindrops
Like frozen steel daggers in my back.
The sky,
Gray and dark with thunderclouds
Pouring down hail,
Like a child throwing pebbles at an ant,
Forcing it into the ground.

Fall:
Back to school,
Yellow crossing guards
Sloshing through puddles near clogged-up sewers.
The line in the candy store
Waiting for new binders and paper.
Friendships renewed,
New faces,
In the fall.

This list of subjects for nature poems might give your youngster some ideas.

- the lake in the rain
- thunder at night
- a rose at dawn
- a sparrow on the roof
- the sea in winter
- a frozen lake
- ducks in the sky
- clouds rolling on
- trees in the wind
- summer grass
- bees
- spiders
- fall leaves
- snow
- spring breezes
- a daisy
- dandelions
- climbing ivy
- a brown mouse
- seagulls
- an alley cat
- a stray dog
- a blue jay
- sunrise
- sunset
- a riverbank

In a poem, personification has extraordinary possibilities. Discourage rhyming and look for clear images, strong and appropriate rhythms, and words that roll easily from the tongue. In these pretend-you're-something poems encourage a bit of nonsense and make-believe:

I am a bee
I buzz the roses on the ground
I buzz the grass, I buzz the lamp

I buzz your windowsill
But don't say I'm busy.
I'm buzzy.

I am Arthur's bed
I wear a white sheet
And a white pillow hat
I smell like fall
When he crawls into me late at night
I groan a little
Then I play him a song on my springs
Until he sleeps

Recommend an appeal to one of the senses or a lively action in each line of the personification poem. The subjects suggested on page 207 work fine here too.

A variation on the personification poem is one in which a child and some nonhuman object have a conversation. Look at these two poems by nine-year-olds from *Indiana Writers*. The first, a talk with a beaver, is by Darrin McGowan; the second, a talk with a turtle, is by Karen Sue Evans.

Why are you cutting down trees?
Because I do not like fingers.
Why do you have such a long tail?
So I can play Ping-Pong over spiderwebs.
Why do you have short paws?
I fell in a river and they shrunk.

Turtle, where did you come from?
The water and my mother.
Why do you have a hard back?
To protect myself.
Why do you go slow?
Because I have short legs.
When your head and legs go in you look
like a flying saucer.

Turtle, you are always green.
In the dark just me and you.

There are many possibilities for early experimentation with poems. The whole world of experience lays topics at your child's feet: glittering moments of pleasure and love; sudden bouts with pain; an emotion at once sudden and powerful; the objects that pass daily before your youngster's eyes.

Shapes and Rhythms for the Poet's Song

One of the reasons I suggest moving away from rhyme is that poems rely upon other qualities of language to play their music. The marriage of rhythm and image is the hallmark of poetry.

Many poems insist upon an exact form: Lines must have so many syllables, so many stresses, and must be grouped in a certain way. Rhymes must appear in prescribed places. Poems with these exact and specific rules for composition based upon rhythmic qualities help children develop their powers as writers.

The Japanese *haiku* gives even a seven-year-old the opportunity to measure and use the rhythmic qualities of words. Haiku is a three-line poem that offers an observation upon one moment in nature, usually relating to a season of the year. It has strict requirements in form: The first and third lines must have five syllables each; the second line, seven. Look at these haikus written by children; count the stresses; and note the succinct statement, the rhythmic flow, the use of image, and the absence of rhyme.

Fields of blue meadow
A lone star twinkling above
A thousand wishes

Monkeys swing from trees
They watch the sweet falling leaves
Chee Chee Chee they say

The snow falls slowly
On the cold and lonely fields
A flower withers

A little bird perched
On a tree stripped of its leaves
Whistled death's sad tune.

A gusty wind blows
Trees quiver; leaves toss and shake
Stillness. A white dove.

The day is silent
Birds and flowers are asleep
Come and wake them up.

First read these haikus aloud to your child. Count the syllables, and write numbers beside each line or put check marks or *X*'s so that young youngster can count the syllables at the end of the line. Treat this like a puzzle: Can your child write one line about a tree? a flower? the wind? The line must have only five syllables all together. Help out with words and ideas wherever necessary. (Remember the old trick of holding your hand beneath your chin and saying the words; when your chin drops, count a syllable. The technique is not foolproof, but it's good enough for counting syllables in haiku.) You might want to offer the first line of a haiku, asking your child to complete the rest. Try some of these as starters:

Winter whips the trees

_____ _____ _____ _____ _____ _____ _____

_____ _____ _____ _____ _____

A red summer sun

____ ____ ____ ____ ____ ____ ____

____ ____ ____ ____ ____

When autumn leaves dance

____ ____ ____ ____ ____ ____ ____

____ ____ ____ ____ ____

A bud in spring said

____ ____ ____ ____ ____ ____ ____

____ ____ ____ ____ ____

Another kind of poem with precise requirements in its form is the *cinquain*, a five-line poem, each line having this syllable count.

____ ____ (2)

____ ____ ____ ____ (4)

____ ____ ____ ____ ____ ____ (6)

____ ____ ____ ____ ____ ____ ____ ____ (8)

____ ____ (2)

You can develop many variations on these pattern poems. Some people simplify the syllable counting by asking children to write cinquain according to word count. Line 1 has one word, line 2 has two words, line 3 has three words, line 4 has four words, and line 5 has one. Others make arbitrary word requirements for each line, believing any five-line poem with varied word count qualifies as a cinquain.

A lake
Beside an oak,
A sad and silver face
That cries with yellow, yellow leaves.
Autumn.

Cat
Black cat
Yellow beady eyes
Slowly moves the grass
Cat

Endless thread
from a giant spool,
winding over the face of the earth
twisting, turning, connecting—
highways.

Consider the *limerick,* and you move into wonderful choices for humor and imagination. The strong rhyme and rhythm interact to build the silliness children love. Read Edward Lear's limericks and enjoy the complete abandon with which he treats reality. A limerick form has five lines of bouncing rhythm; the first, second, and fifth rhyme with one another, and the third and fourth rhyme with each other. A limerick often starts with "There once was a . . ." or "Said a . . ."

Said a lovely young apple up high,
"I don't like being pretty and spry
When old farmer McGee
Smiles brightly at me
I just know he thinks only of pie!"

There once was a boy from New York
Who tried writing a poem with a fork
He flew into a rage
When he punctured the page
Then erased his mistake with some chalk.

A "pure" limerick requires a specific stress pattern and a specific number of those patterns per line, but don't be rigid about requirements with your child. Make dashes to show where the words would appear on the lines. Or start your youngster off with a line and/or two pairs of rhyme. Or arrange rhyming words in groups before your child starts writing. You might lay the poem out this way:

Then go back and fill in the last words on the line with any of the sets you made, leaving rhymes for lines 2 and 3 blank for flexibility:

Why Poetry?

Poetry demands exact expression of observation and idea, awareness of sound and rhythm in word combinations, and the use of language in a variety of contexts. These qualities are important for all kinds of writing. Poetry has the added dimension of delight and sweetness; it stays in the mind with ease and pleases the spirit. Something happens to a person when he writes a poem. He feels he is on the verge of creation, on the highest, almost transcendent, level of consciousness, groping with a searing intensity for language that will clarify meaning. For children the experience is magical, too. One young writer says:

> In poetry
> the sky's the limit—
> we can be free!

15

A Report for School

During a recent college class I taught, a young woman delivered an oral report she had volunteered to present. She leaned against the gray metal desk in front of the room, holding photocopies of pages from the *Encyclopaedia Britannica* in her hands. As she tried to read those pages aloud—for the first time, it seemed to me—she stammered over the words. Trapped by her own inability to understand the sentences, she couldn't convey her meaning to the class. Later that week, she turned in her paper. It was an exact copy of the *Britannica* article, filled with complicated language and structures. This wasn't an ignorant or incapable student; she had a quickness of mind and a ready intelligence, despite a record of failures and disappointments in school. I've seen sixth graders, eleven- and twelve-year-olds, prepare reports of strength and quality, and I'm certain that poor study skills limited that young woman's abilities and kept her from achieving. She'd learned nothing about gathering information, digesting it, and arranging it in a clear form.

Teachers do not spare reports from children: An endless stream of science and book reports, reports on faraway people and places, reports on animals and fish and natural resources, on outer space and inner earth, wends through the child's homework assignments each week. However, I've seen little to suggest that children learn how to prepare reports in school, how to gather and record information in a fruitful way. You may have stood over a child who is in tears, desperately asking for help.

"The teacher says to write a report on helicopters. I don't know what to do!" he or she may say.

How do you help?

Some parents help too much; they do their child's work—collect the data, put it together, even write the report for their child to copy over.

Parents shouldn't do their children's assignments. But you will want to help your son or daughter understand how to write a report for school. A child works on a report *outside* the classroom—at home or in the library. The teacher sees only the finished product; but *you* share the labor of creation as the project moves toward completion. So it's a good idea for you to begin to understand the kinds of skills your child has to develop.

A Project in Stages

A *report* in its most simple definition is a prepared piece of writing on a particular subject. A child writes using information beyond or supplemental to personal experiences.

Research and study play key roles in a report, and these are enormous concepts for a child; they must be broken down. A youngster must understand the various stages through which he must move in order to write his report. To do this *you* should clarify your own understanding of the components of research and study so that you can help your son or daughter.

These are the steps through which a report writer must move:

• ***Understanding the Assigned Topic or Finding a Topic to Report On.*** Frequently, the language of the assignment is not clear, or if it is, the writer may not understand what the goals are. Often an assignment is open-ended; the child required to define her own area of interest or to select a book to read and to write about.

• ***Limiting the Topic.*** An assignment may be too broad for a report. For example, the subject "Write a report on the Eskimos" would frustrate any child's attempts. There are *shelves* of books in the library on the general topic "Eskimos!"

• ***Finding Information on the Topic.*** What sources can a child find for material on the topic? Which materials serve better than others?

• ***Gathering, Grouping, and Digesting Information.*** Children must learn how to collect data simply and efficiently and how to restate the information in their own words. Even nine-year-olds can learn the rudiments of note taking and simple outlining

• ***Writing the Report in a Clear, Interesting, and Orderly Way.*** The final presentation must offer the facts in a manner that involves readers and holds their attention as it informs.

A parent's role is to direct and to guide a youngster's progress without doing the child's work. You shouldn't serve as ghostwriter or editor for your youngster, but you should aim to help him or her develop self-sufficiency in the written activity.

Let's consider these five parts in the process of writing reports for school.

"What Do I Do?" First Questions First

The problem of finding a reasonable subject for investigation has two faces: Your son or daughter may come to you with instructions that somehow escape understanding. Your role is to help interpret the assignment. Ask, "What do you think Mrs. Coleman wants in this report?" Often a teacher uses part of the day's instruction as the basis of a report and assigns it assuming her students will recall their classwork and will elaborate on the day's instruction in their writing. Encourage your child to talk about the work that preceded the homework assignment. Was it a lesson from one of the classroom books? Was it a poem the children worked on together? Was it an assembly program everyone watched or a neighborhood walk during recess or a television show the class viewed together? Stimulate conversation; ask questions that probe the topic. You often can get youngsters to clear up complications about the assignment. Do not hesitate to suggest a phone call to another child in the class or a brief conversation with the teacher early the next morning.

Sometimes the language of the assignment is not clear—this is especially true as a child advances through the grades. Poorly worded instructions may be too vague or too complicated for your youngster to grasp. A child (or even his teacher) may not understand the meaning of key question words like *analyze, contrast,* and *describe.* These words are often used by teachers to state assignments.

Word	What it means
analyze	break a subject down into parts
compare	show how things are alike
contrast	show how things are different
define	give the exact meaning of something, showing how it's different from other things like it
describe	show what something looks like

explain   tell why or how something happened
illustrate   give examples to support an idea
prove   give factual reasons to show something
                 is true
summarize   give the main points about something

It's possible that one misunderstood word can push a
child off-track, so be sure that he or she understands the
wording of the assignment before work on the report
begins.

Many teachers will state a general idea on which they
want a child to report, but occasionally your youngster has
a free choice. This is especially true for book reports.
Frequently, instructions like "Your book reports are due in
three weeks" are expected to lead a child to a successful
project. Knowing your son's or daughter's interests and
strengths as well as you do has its advantages: You can
help steer your child toward clear goals. "So you have a
book report. Remember how you wanted to know about
children who lived in big cities? Let's go to the library to
find a book about a girl who lives in New York." Or, "You
love kittens. Let's find a book about them. You'd write a
wonderful report about a book on kittens!"

Such direction rescues a child from disappointment
and turns your youngster to productive activity.

Shaving the Topic Down

Related to, and often the cause of, a child's confusion is an
inability to limit the subject of a report. In my experience,
teachers do not suggest adequately limited topics for children to investigate and they don't provide sufficient guidance to help a child invent an original topic.

A youngster who announces, "I have to make a report
on helicopters," needs your advice. First check with your
son or daughter about the *exact* nature of the assignment—

perhaps the teacher did offer a very clear and specific topic; perhaps your child copied the intstructions into a notebook or can retrieve a ditto sheet from his book bag. Read the instructions together. Ask, "What do you think your teacher means? What would she like you to find out?"

Often the topic stands alone: "helicopters." Then you must help your child find a more limited target. Achieve this by phrasing questions that turn attention to a specific feature of the subject, one that is reasonable in scope and interest. Approaches vary from report to report, but I think it's best to try to state a question with a *how* or a *why*. A question can fire a child's interest and at the same time help focus the report itself. You might use one of the words whose meanings I discussed on page 272 in a question or a statement.

"Helicopters. There's so much you could report about helicopters. Why don't you try to find out how helicopters fly? You might try to find out how they are made or why they are used by police or how they are different from other kinds of flying machines." I've by no means exhausted the *how* or *why* possibilities even for helicopters, but I think you get the point.

If your child must write about Eskimos, for example, pose these questions to direct the activity:

How do Eskimos live?

How do Eskimos get their food?

Why do Eskimos live in igloos?

How is an igloo built?

How do Eskimos make clothing?

What are the four Eskimo groups?

How does an Eskimo child spend his or her day?

Describe an Eskimo's house.

What is the Eskimos' religion?

What kind of clothing do Eskimos wear?

Other good questions might ask *when, where, what kind of,* along with the other possibilities I've mentioned. A simple answer to one of these questions might not qualify as a "report" in a teacher's eyes, but one answer leads to other questions, which a child can explore through several resources. Or he can answer three or four questions that, carefully related, can serve as the girders for a well-built report.

There *is* a risk that a teacher who assigns "Eskimos" as a report really wants a comprehensive treatment. But I believe that a child who clearly and carefully limits a topic will earn rewards not blame. You have to help your child find a narrow focus within the broad topic.

With older children (nine and up) ask the youngster to slice smaller and smaller pieces from a general topic. Suppose the report topic is *education.* Children *must* limit so broad an idea for any productive exploration. A youngster can learn to narrow the field by moving through stages as described on the sample chart I give.

Children often prefer *general* topics for investigation because they find comfort in the broadest possible subjects and think there's more freedom in such an approach. Some psychologists have tried to show that thinking first begins on levels of abstraction and that generalizing is a much more basic quality of your children's thought than was once believed. However, cherishing the general is a trap for a writer. If she doesn't limit a subject, her writing becomes vague and insubstantial because there's too much ground to cover and she cannot offer enough detail to support all her statements. The treatment becomes superficial.

Too General	Still Broad	Less Broad	Narrow: Good Report Topics
Education	Education in Russia	How arithmetic is taught in Russia	Elementary school arithmetic in Russia
Examinations	High school examinations	High school essay examinations	The value of essay exams in high school
Teachers	Elementary school teachers	Kindergarten teachers	How kindergarten teachers are trained
Teaching	New ways of teaching	New ways of teaching children	New ways of teaching biology to children

Your Friends: The Encyclopedia and Other Source Books

Besides the dictionary, there's no more valuable and no more misused tool than an encyclopedia. A world of information lies between the covers of its volumes and usually they are easily available in the library or you may even own one. There are many encyclopedias for different age levels, so that even a child of seven or eight may mine the gold and diamonds from these books.

Since an encyclopedia is the first and most complete source for a child who writes a report, you should know about encyclopedias for children, so that you can encourage your son or daughter to use the one that suits his or her needs. Among the most popular for young children (four to eight or ten years) are *Childcraft: The How and Why Library, Compton's Precyclopedia,* and *Child Horizons;* for children from seven to twelve or fourteen are the *New Book of Knowledge* and *Brittanica Junior;* for children from nine to eighteen are *Compton's Encyclopedia, World Book Encyclopedia,* and *Encyclopedia International.* If you want a comprehensive comparative discussion of encyclopedias on all levels, I urge you to examine Kenneth Kister's *Encyclopedia Buying Guide* (New York: R. R. Bowker, 1981). Mr. Kister has strong opinions about encyclopedias, but his reports are so complete that you'll be able to make your own judgments. You should also consult another useful adviser from R. R. Bowker: *Reference Books for Young Readers* (1988). This book provides evaluations of encyclopedias, atlases, and dictionaries for children and young adults.

When selecting an encyclopedia that looks as if its suits your youngster, examine together information under topics that might interest your child. Then, using *how, why,* or some other good question word, frame a question that your child might answer by reading the encyclopedia entry. For instance, if you're investigating *mouse,* ask, "How did mice come to America?" or "Where are mice usually found?" or "Why don't wild mice live longer than three months?"

When your child begins to use the encyclopedia, he is usually hunting for an answer to a specific question. Once he finds the response, reinforce the skills built earlier. As for a whole sentence that repeats part of the question. Suggest that your youngster tell you, in his own words, the information he has uncovered. Thus, you might read sentences like these:

Mice came to America in English, French, and Spanish ships, which arrived here in the 1500s.

Mice are found in most parts of the world. They live in mountains, fields, swamps, and deserts.

Wild mice do not live longer than three months because they have so many enemies like hawks, owls, and rats.

I said earlier that the encyclopedia is a misused tool. First, because children have little training in how to use one, they will often copy a complete entry word for word. Second, because a youngster can gather so many blossoms from an encyclopedia, he rarely ventures into other parts of the garden—the vast reserves of sourcebooks in a library.

Word-for-word reporting is a runaway problem that too many teachers much ignore. A child looks up his topic, turns to the correct page, copies what is before him, submits what he has copied to the teacher, and receives a check of approval. Questions of ethics aside, such practices defeat the whole purpose of the report, which is to teach a child something that he then can convey in his own written language to someone else. A child rarely interacts with what he reads when he copies a full page of encyclopedia material.

Parents should train their children to take notes on readings—nothing elaborate, just a few words in a list on a page; perhaps, a few phrases that a child will group later into a meaningful whole as he draws upon information gathered from more than one source.

Data collected in note or list form should be a common sight to your son or daughter. At school the events of a day are listed on the chalkboard; the bulletin board may hold a chart of weather conditions for a given month or season; the science class writes down daily observations about a celery stalk that the teacher puts in a glass of red ink and water on the window ledge.

At home, establish situations in which your child keeps records of information. A supermarket list is data collection at its simplest level—and it stimulates some action. You also can ask your youngster to record weather observations, seasonal changes, varied activities on the street as the day moves on. All of those should be based upon what your child sees out the kitchen window. If you've followed my advice about preparing sense charts, you've encouraged even more practice in recording data, and you are anticipating the skill of *grouping*, which I'll discuss in a little while.

Let me give some real examples so that you can have a clearer picture of the goals your child should try to achieve. In response to a report on *hibernation*, a ten-year-old turns to that section in an encyclopedia and reads the page. First, she might talk with you about the report, and you'll help her limit the subject. Perhaps she can report on why animals hibernate. Maybe she'll explore the differences in hibernation of warm-blooded and cold-blooded animals. She might want to explain why small animals hibernate. Or, she may simply explain what hibernation is and how animals do it.

Once there's a clear purpose to the report, a child is ready to take notes. (This is not *always* the order: In some cases children who don't know what they will report on will need to take extensive notes *before* they establish a topic; the notes serve as a way to define the broadest possibilities of the subject that a child will narrow down.) The simplest approach demands thinking beforehand in order to determine some limited topic in advance of gathering material.

Here is part of the entry on hibernation that appears in *The New Book of Knowledge* (New York: Grolier, 1988), volume 8, pages 117–118.

HIBERNATION

Many animals pass the winter in a state known as winter sleep, or **hibernation**. This helps them to live through the difficult period of the year in the cooler parts of the world.

In other regions the intense heat and dryness of the summer can be dangerous to life. Here some creatures, such as certain frogs and fish, seal themselves in mud and suspend all activity until the season is over. This is known as **estivation**. ("Estivation" comes from a Latin word that means "having to do with summer." "Hibernation" comes from a Latin word meaning "to winter.")

Hibernation and estivation both serve as means of avoiding death because of lack of food or water during part of the year. Hibernating animals, however, are more familiar to us. The best known are the woodchucks, ground squirrels, dormice, hedgehogs, hamsters, and the small common bats.

A hibernating animal does more than just go to sleep. A true hibernator falls into a state of apparent death during the winter months and comes to life again in the spring. A good example is the dormouse, a tree-climbing, squirrel-like mouse that is common in Europe and Asia. By early autumn the animal becomes very fat. Then it builds its winter nest. It lays up a store of food. And it retires to sleep, curling itself up with its forepaws against its cheeks and its tail wrapped around its head and back. The sleep may last for 6 months, with breathing so slow that it is hardly noticeable. The creature becomes so cold and stiff that it can be rolled about like a ball. When it wakes again, in the spring, most of its fat has disappeared.

The woodchucks (groundhogs) and marmots of North America behave much like dormice. Both of them become loaded with fat before retiring. And this fat forms their only support for life until spring comes. Their close relatives, the gophers and the true ground squirrels, are also hibernators. But before hibernating, these animals lay up large stores of roots, seeds, and berries for occasional feasts, during the winter. (The true squirrels do not hibernate but simply store food in hiding places for winter use.) A good hibernator, therefore, does three things. It stores up as much food as possible, either as body fat or as actual stored food. It finds or makes a suitable winter shelter. And it goes into a long and very deep sleep, during which its body becomes cold and usually stiff. In the case of the ground squirrel, the body temperature drops from about 98 degrees Fahrenheit to a few degrees above freezing; the heartbeat slows from 400 beats to 10 a minute; the rate of breathing slows from 200 to 2 or 3 times a minute.

If the hibernating animal is awakened too fast, it may die—which shows how close to a living death the state of hibernation really is.

• WHY ANIMALS HIBERNATE

In regions where winters are severe, some animals migrate while others hibernate. Migrating animals travel far enough to find food and warmth, and they return in the spring when conditions become favorable again. That is what most birds do, since they can fly long distances, without difficulty. But except for certain bats, the small, hairy mammals cannot migrate over long distances. They must by some means survive the winter conditions right where they are. Hibernation is a way of doing this.

In these regions the question of food is more important than the outside temperature. Birds and mammals, with their covering of feathers or hair, can usually keep warm if they get enough food. Hibernation or migration is necessary if the food supply fails. Birds migrate because the winter kills their food supply—not because they cannot keep warm in a cold climate. Certain mammals hibernate when their food supply fails.

• **PARTIAL HIBERNATION**

Some creatures appear to hibernate but do not really do so. The bear is an example particularly the American grizzly and black bears. The male bears prowl through the woods and find food throughout the winter. The female bear retires to her den in the autumn, with her young already starting to grow inside her body. She then goes to sleep. Yet her body temperature drops only a few degrees. The young are born early in the new year and are able to get milk and warmth from the mother, who is at least half awake at that time. All winter long she lives on her own fat. She wastes no energy on unnecessary activity. And she is easily awakened and warms up quickly. The long sleep of the female bear is a kind of hibernation, for it serves very much the same purpose. Yet it is not true hibernation, which leaves the body cold and rigid.

• **BODY TEMPERATURE**

Scientists have been puzzling over the nature of true hibernation for a long time. They have been trying to understand what takes place to make the body seem so lifeless. Actually, it is in a state of coma from which it can be awakened. How is this coma brought about and how is it ended? As yet, scientists do not know.

Here are the notes one child prepared after reading the selection.

Notes on Hibernation
The New Book of Knowledge, volume 8, pages 121 to 122.

1. Hiber. is winter sleep for many animals
2. Helps animals live through cold weather
3. Hiber. comes fr. Latin word meaning "to winter"
4. Some hib. animals are woodchucks, ground squirrels, dormice, hedgehogs, hamsters, small bats
5. Hib. like death in winter. Anim. comes to life in spring
6. Anim. who hibernates stores up food as fat or actual stored food like roots and nuts
7. Finds or builds winter shelter
8. Goes into long deep sleep. Body gets very stiff and cold. Squirrel's body temperature drops from 98° F to a little above freezing.
9. If anim. wakes too fast it may die

Show this sample as a good model to your child. Notice the differences between the printed selection and the child's notes. When you offer guidelines to your son or daughter, point out that he or she should

- Use a separate index card or sheet of paper for each source (this makes it easier to group information later on).
- Write the name of the source on top of the card.
- Write clearly.
- Write down the page numbers on which the information appears in case its necessary to check back.
- Abbrevitate wherever necessary but make sure that what's being written down is understandable.
- Copy information accurately.

If you've been encouraging your child to use her own language in taking notes, don't worry about explaining the use of quotation marks when she copies down someone's exact words. Later on, when she turns to sources other than the encyclopedia, you'll have to mention the importance of giving credit to someone else's ideas. Techniques of quoting, paraphrasing, and mentioning sources (within the text itself, in footnotes, or in a bibliography) are beyond the purpose of this chapter, which is to help your child prepare a successful report.

Many elementary school teachers will be content with reports based upon a single source, and for younger children I have no objection to that approach. Still, if the encyclopedia prevents a child from looking beyond it and into other resources, that defeats its purpose. I used the encyclopedia as a starting point: It's where *I* go for an overview of something I need to research. It outlines the broad dimensions of the issue; in it I find the subject that I will investigate further in other books and in periodicals.

Ten-year-olds can see the encyclopedia in the same light. On a topic like *hibernation* a youngster who looks in the subject card catalog in the library will find named a number of interesting books that can expand the information a child already has gathered from the encyclopedia. Show your child how to use the card catalog. If it poses too much of a problem, don't worry. Librarians are trained to help children use the tools of research. Don't be embarrassed to ask librarians for help. That's one of the the things they get paid to do. Bother them—if they're good, they'll love it!

Getting Things in Order

Once you have helped your child find and check a variety of sources and he or she has gathered sufficient information in notes, help your youngster organize materials with some methods of grouping.

Some writers use an outline, which is a formal way of putting information into groups so that the writer has a guide for organization. But at this stage leave the intricate elements of outlining to classroom instruction. Encourage your child to group information even if it's just an informal clustering of details. Any outlining technique is supposed to make the writer's task easy, so don't stress letters and Roman numerals—which very few progressive writers pay much attention to.

When your youngster made sense charts, he or she put details into predetermined groups headed with words like *sounds, colors* and *actions, smells*. Now you're going to help your child look at details, decide on categories, and group the details appropriately.

Remember those shopping lists? Once you itemize the food you need, show your child how much easier it will be to fill the cart if you list the food in related groups. In that way you can gather up items placed near each other on the shelves, and you won't have to run from aisle 5 for soaps to aisle 3 for canned string beans and back to aisle 5 for

bleach. Help your son or daughter made a heading for each
group; base it upon the signs above the supermarket aisles.
Below on the left is a shopping list; to the right is the same
list reorganized so that items are grouped together.

milk	*Dairy*
canned mushrooms	milk
M & M's	butter
laundry detergent	American cheese
potato chips	sour cream
1 lb. tomatoes	*Fresh fruits and vegetables*
1 doz. oranges	1 lb. tomatoes
frozen peas	1 doz. oranges
chicken	1 head lettuce
1 lb. chopped meat	2 lb. apples
paper towels	*Canned vegetables*
canned peas	mushrooms
frozen spinach	peas
butter	tomatoes
napkins	*Frozen vegetables*
American cheese	peas
2 lb. apples	spinach
Milky Ways	*Meat*
sour cream	chicken
1 head lettuce	1 lb. chopped meat
canned tomatoes	salami
hand soap	*Candy and chips*
salami	M & M's
	potato chips
	Milky Ways
	Soap and paper goods
	laundry detergent
	paper towels
	napkins
	hand soap

Using simple, recognizable items like these helps a child to organize materials so that the relations between items in groups are clear. The reason for the groupings is important and should be readily apparent. There are many other lists that you and your child can make: You can organize lists of holiday gifts and chores to be done around the house. Or provide a batch of photographs or magazine pictures and ask your child to group the items in some way—all children, all adult women, all adult men, all appliances. If, after practice, your child can establish his or her own groups, you've done a good job!

These easy activities are not much different from the techniques a youngster must employ when he or she tries to relate bits of information for a report.

After this, by guiding practice in simple outlining, you can help your child write a full sentence outline. Again— don't fuss about Roman numerals and letters. The main topic of each paragraph appears first; subheadings serve as reminders that each topic should have supporting details. Each item is a full sentence.

Outline: What Is Hibernation

I. Hibernation is winter sleep.
   - Hibernation comes from Latin word meaning "to winter."
   - Hibernation helps animals live through cold weather.
   - Some hibernation animals are woodchucks, ground squirrels, dormice, hedgehogs, hamsters, and bats.
II. Animals do many things to hibernate.
   - They store up food within their bodies as fat.
   - They store up roots and nuts for special winter feasts.
   - They build or find winter shelter.
   - Animals fall into a long deep sleep.

- The body may grow stiff and cold, like the squirrel's.
- Animals can die if they wake up too fast.

Enter the Finished Product

With a sentence outline in hand you can see how a report like the one that grew out of this developed. A ten-year-old can easily prepare it. Notice that the writer did not follow the outline slavishly. He returned to his notes for more information in order to expand the paragraph. And see how solid details support the limited topic.

Hibernation is a winter sleep. The word comes from a Latin word meaning "to winter." Hibernation helps animals live through the cold weather. Some hibernating animals are woodchucks, ground squirrels, dormice, hedgehogs, hamsters, and small bats.

Before hibernating, animals must store up food as fat within their bodies. For special winter feast they hide roots and nuts. Also, they must build or find a good winter shelter to protect them in the cold. Some animals use caves. Others dig holes in the ground. Finally, hibernating animals fall into a long deep sleep. Their bodies grow stiff and cold. For example, the ground squirrel's temperature drops from 98°F. to just above freezing. If you see a hibernating animal, don't wake him too fast! He might die.

The procedures I've discussed here will serve, with some modifications, for most kinds of report writing. In a science report, a child might be asked to identify some problem and to plan some method of determining an answer to it. She'd have to explain the experiment step by step in writing and to draw conclusions from it. She might need to read what others have suggested about the problem. A child must practice objectivity in the science report. Her emotional responses to a problem have no place in such an essay.

A book report is perhaps the most frequently assigned report in school. The teacher sometimes supplies the youngster with a list of general areas to cover in a one-page overview. You might observe these as requirements for a child's report on a fictional book:

    I. Name and author
   II. Setting (where the action of the book takes place)
 III. Characters (the main people in the book)
 IV. Plot (a summary fo the main events)
  V. Opinion (what you think of the book)

Under each heading a child puts down a few sentences. I imagine that there are some positive qualities in such kinds of reports: A youngster does learn something about the features of books and the language used to describe them, and if there's any need to refresh his or her memory about a book, it's easy to check back over such neatly devised responses. Besides, reports in this outline format are very easy to grade! Nonetheless, report writing can be a much more imaginative challenge than this.

There is merit in straightforward reporting, whether it takes the form of an outlined book or two or three paragraphs on hibernation, but even report writing can stimulate a child's creative abilities. A young writer in the elementary grades who works with a body of collected data can interact boldly with the materials. Your child can tap his or her own inventiveness for a written report.

If your son or daughter has an open-ended assignment, which, despite a required topic, makes no specific demands about format, why not suggest one of the following ways of writing up the report?

• **Personification.** Ask your child to pretend he's an animal and write about himself as the animal. Your youngster must use accurate information that he or she has discovered by researching. Here's one example reported by Don Wolfe:

> My name is Joey. I'm a canary about five and a half inches long. My head is oval-shaped, and I have black beady eyes. My tongue is long and thin, like a snake's tongue. Most of my feathers are yellow, but when I was young my feathers were gray. I like seeds and cold water. I eat seeds all the itme, but now and then I get the yolk of an egg, a carrot, a tiny piece of lettuce, and other vegetables. I love chocolates, but my mistress says they are not good for me. I hop about on my feet and fly with my wings. I do not fly so well as other birds do. Because I am a male, I have a beautiful singing voice, but my wife does not. I don't want to brag, but we canaries are very intelligent in recognizing certain people. I flutter and make an ugly noise at people I don't like, but I wouldn't dream of fluttering at my wife.

• **Pretend You Are Some Person.** Your child should write as if he or she were one of the main characters in a book or some historical figure. The report will discuss key features of his or her life as the book's hero.

• **Write About a Moment.** For a child's book of fiction or biography or autobiography, write about one single moment that is important in the hero's life. Fill in the moment with details.

• **Pick a Powerful Quote.** As your child reads, she should jot down page numbers on which the author makes interesting, challenging, beautiful, annoying, or unusual statements. Your child then looks back over all the statements and selects one or two key quotations. After copying down the author's statement, your child can write an original paragraph explaining why she made that selection. I find the most interesting responses come when children explain some experience from their own lives and relate it to a statement in the book.

• **Be a News Reporter.** Suggest that your child pretend he's a cub reporter for a local newspaper in order to interview a person. Or, he can write a news report about some key events he's been asked to investigate.

• **Make Up a Character.** Your youngster can invent some character, and then, from this imagined character's perspective, narrate major events in the life of a main figure in the book. That delightful children's book *Ben and Me* is an excellent example. In it a mouse who is a companion to Benjamin Franklin writes about his adventures with the famous statesman-inventor.

• **Write a Play or Dialogue.** Help your youngster write a play based on an important scene in a book she is reading. Or, your child can write a play or dialogue on some moment in history, some discovery or invention.

• **Describe a Moment with a Character.** In this writing activity a child pretends that he visits some famous character (see pages 196 to 197).

• **Make a Book Cover.** This activity combines writing and illustration. Drawing, painting, or cutting and pasting, your youngster can reproduce one scene from a story on a sheet of colored paper that is folded like a book jacket. Then he or she writes a summary of that scene and copies it onto lined paper, which is pasted onto the front and back flaps of the book jacket.

• **Who Am I?** Without naming the character of a biography or autobiography, a young boy or girl writes ten sentences (or brief groups of sentences) that point up highlights in the life of the person. The last line of the report is the question "Who Am I?"

Using Your Willpower

Reread chapter 6, so that you keep your role as helper for school writing in perspective. You must remember that *you* are not the student. I know how tempting it is to give answers, lay out plans, find materials, summarize research, and write the report for the young man or woman you love so much. But it won't help your child—he or she must learn how to do all those things. You are a facilitator, one who frees a task from obstacles, one who makes things easier. Establish a warm home setting that encourages your child to write—but *don't do your child's work!*

16

An Afterword for Too-Busy Parents

In a school district in central Pennsylvania a high school English chairman described the effect of recent cutbacks. Local citizens would not approve higher taxes: The superintendent insisted upon across-the-board reductions. The English staff dropped to eight teachers for 1,400 students! Figure it out: one teacher for every 175 children. Given the usual five-class teaching load, that's 35 in a class.

How much writing will be going on in those classrooms? Developing writers *must* write several hundred words at least once a week, preferably each day. What kind of job can even a specialist in writing do in such circumstances?

In 1968, I left my high school teaching job as an instructor in English: I'd taught five classes a day, and each had more than thirty students. Things have not come very far since then. National organizations have not convinced school officials that the special responsibilities of teachers

291

of writing demand smaller classes and lower child-to-teacher ratios. Unless teachers in elementary schools have reasonable numbers of children to work with, writing skills will suffer. When administrators try to convince the public that statistics show class size has no relation to how well children learn, insist upon seeing the tests that "prove" this position. I'll bet those tests don't ask children to write.

I'm not hopeful that the schools can do what they should to help children develop as writers, in spite of the sudden and far-reaching interest in the skill and some growing graduate programs here and there. Even the college, which once assured close attention to writing, now asks instructors to teach three or even four sections of composition, with as many as thirty students in a class.

All this is to answer your question "Who can find the time to do all this?"

My reply is: "If not you, then who?"

I've given you lots of ideas. You're ready to start things going, so don't put it off! What you do in your home will reward you with delightful proof that any child *can* write.

One Hundred Ideas for Writing at Home

This is a list of specific writing activities for your youngster. They follow the topics of this book. Some ideas are more appropriate for older children, so use your good judgment.

1. Make a list of your favorite toys.
2. Make a shopping list.
3. Make a list of school supplies.
4. Make a list of people you'll invite to a birthday party.
5. Make a list of clothing you want to buy.
6. Write a note for your father or mother asking permission to do something.
7. Write a note to the mailman.
8. Make a holiday greeting card and write a message inside.
9. Make a sign for your room door.
10. Write an absence note for the teacher's records.
11. Draw a picture of someone in your family doing something and write a sentence under it explaining what he or she is doing.
12. Describe your kitchen at breakfast.
13. Describe your living room at night.
14. Describe your bedroom in the morning.
15. Describe your classroom as it looks early in the morning.
16. Describe the sounds of the school yard at three o'clock.
17. Describe a room in the library.

18. Describe the supermarket on a Saturday afternoon.
19. Describe a sports stadium during a game.
20. Describe a visit to a farm or a zoo.
21. Describe a moment at the beach or at a riverbank or at a pool.
22. Tell about one moment on a train ride.
23. Describe the sights and sounds on the school bus on a rainy Monday morning.
24. Describe a busy street in your town during shopping hours.
25. Describe a moment on a car ride.
26. Tell about a visit to McDonald's or Burger King or some other fast-food place.
27. Describe your mother when she's angry.
28. Describe a relative from a color photograph.
29. Describe a dream you had.
30. Describe Dad (or Mother) relaxing.
31. Describe Dad (or Mother) working.
32. Tell about one adventurous moment on your bicycle.
33. Tell about a time you felt proud of your brother or sister.
34. Describe a dinner you remember.
35. Describe your pet at a single moment.
36. Describe the sounds you like (or do not like) when you're lying in bed and waiting to fall asleep.
37. Describe your brother (or sister) playing.
38. Describe your sister (or brother) eating.
39. Look at a famous painting and describe what you see.
40. Describe an exciting moment in a game or sport you played.
41. Describe your street in the winter (summer, fall, or spring).
42. Write about a moment in your park or playground.
43. Write about an embarrassing moment.
44. Write about a job you hate to do.
45. Write about a funny moment.
46. Write about a moment in which you felt happy.
47. Write about a moment in which you felt proud.
48. Write about a moment in which you felt sad.

49. Write about a moment in which you felt frightened.
50. Write about a time you got lost.
51. Write about a moment when you were disappointed.
52. Write about a time you helped someone.
53. Write about a time you had an argument with a friend.
54. Write about a time someone helped you.
55. Write about a moment in church or synagogue.
56. Describe a department store at a moment during Christmas shopping.
57. Write about how to make your favorite sandwich.
58. Write about a time you cleaned up your room.
59. Describe your favorite meal.
60. Describe one of your friends.
61. Write about a moment you got in trouble.
62. Look in the mirror in the morning and describe what you see.
63. Describe your favorite toy.
64. Write about a moment in an airplane.
65. Pretend you are a refrigerator.
66. Pretend you are a washing machine.
67. Pretend you are your mirror.
68. Pretend you are the family car.
69. Pretend you are your bed.
70. Pretend you are one of your own toys.
71. Pretend you are a pencil.
72. Pretend you are a farm animal.
73. Pretend you are Mommy or Daddy scolding you.
74. Pretend you are your dog, cat, canary, or goldfish.
75. Pretend you are the grass talking to the wind.
76. Pretend you are a bumblebee speaking to a rose.
77. Pretend you are a fairy-tale character (Hansel, Gretel, Little Red Riding Hood) and write about one adventurous moment in your life.
78. Write a letter to a sick friend.
79. Write a letter to an author you like.
80. Write a letter to your favorite television or rock star.
81. Write a letter to the editor of your local newspaper.
82. Write a letter to invite a friend to your house for a party.

83. Write a thank-you note to someone who sent you a gift.
84. Write a postcard to a friend when you are on vacation with your family.
85. Write a letter to your teacher to invite her to lunch.
86. Define *happiness*.
87. Define *fear*.
88. Write your definition of *friend*.
89. What is an American?
90. What is poverty?
91. What is courage?
92. Write a poem about fall.
93. Write a poem about a moment at the beach.
94. Write a poem about a moment you felt lonely.
95. Write a poem about a silly moment.
96. Write a poem about a tree or a bush on your street.
97. Write a poem about happiness.
98. Pretend you are a character in your favorite book. Write about an adventure.
99. Describe an exciting moment in a biography you read.
100. Read about the same famous person in history; pretend you are a reporter who interviews the person; write up your interview for the newspaper.

A Parent's Primer on Correctness

This appendix is *not* going to teach you everything you ever wanted to know about grammar but were afraid to ask! At your local stationery stores, magazine stands, and book-shops you will find shelves groaning with books to help adults improve their own writing and grammar skills. Your son or daughter's language arts book from school can serve as a good resource for you about writing. You might enjoy a copy of *The McGraw-Hill College Handbook,* which a colleague and I wrote together.

What I want to do here is to give you an overview of the basics, the main points of correctness, in clear, simple language so that you can:

- recognize serious problems that your child may be hav- ing with correct language use at home.
- help your child understand an error he makes in writing under your direction.
- help your child understand an error the teacher has pointed out in his school writing.

In trying to achieve these goals, I've left out a great deal. For example, I omitted a discussion of agreement of subject and verb because it's too tricky to reduce to a brief discussion. I've also not mentioned commas which, though necessary for clarity, are not worth bothering about in these basic recommendations in the light of other serious problems children have in writing. You have more important work to do!

Sentence Completeness

It's hard to name the exact qualities that make a group of words a sentence because there are so many different kinds of sentences and because there are so many exceptions to the definitions grammarians offer.

Some say a sentence is a word group that has a subject and a verb and expresses a complete thought.

Others say that a sentence is a group of words that name some subject and tell something about that subject.

Whatever definition you use, the point is that you've got to help your child develop a sense of sentence completeness. Help your child test for sentences that make sense.

- Make sure that all sentences begin with capital letters.
- Make sure that all sentences end with periods, question marks, or exclamation points.
- Remind children to read sentences aloud slowly, listening to their own voices. Wherever their voice stops and drops, use a period.
- After your child writes several consecutive sentences, insist that she or he make a conscious effort to look for complete ideas in his or her own writing. If she's having trouble seeing how one sentence should stand apart from the sentence before or after it, have her read the sentences from the last to the first. That will help your child keep the ideas separate.

You want to keep a lookout for two major types of sentence errors.

1. Run-together sentences. In this major error (also called *run-on, fused sentence, comma fault,* and *comma splice*) a child fails to separate sentences correctly.

Sometimes there's no punctuation:

I ate quickly then I rushed to school.

Sometimes there's a comma between the two sentences.

I ate quickly, then I rushed to school.

Sentence sense tells you (and your voice as you read aloud slowly helps, too) that one idea ends after *quickly.* In order to keep the two ideas separate the writer needs a period between them:

I ate quickly. Then I rushed to school.

The comma, though it signals a minor pause, is not a strong enough mark of punctuation to stand alone between sentences. Some writers might choose a semicolon to keep the ideas apart (no capital after it!):

I ate quickly; then I rushed to school.

Though you shouldn't overuse them, semicolons are helpful in joining sentences closely related to each other in meaning.

A child may sometimes correct run-together sentences effectively by combining them with connecting words (notice the comma; here it works along with the connector):

I ate quickly, *and* then I rushed to school. (Other connectors that work in this way, depending on the sense of the new sentence, are *but, or, nor,* and *for.*)

Using a connector that expresses time will help you produce a complete sentence here. The word *then* becomes extraneous in this instance:

> *After* I ate quickly, then I rushed to school. (Other connectors that work in this way, given the sense of the sentence, are *although, since, because, besides, when, while,* and many more.)

2. Sentence pieces. Beginning writers frequently use incomplete word groups that do not qualify as sentences. These word groups, called *fragments,* usually belong to full sentences that go before or come after the fragment. Sometimes these groups require more words in order to make sense as full sentences. Fragments need a parent's patient attention because they are a major error for inexperienced writers.

Look at some examples below; then I'll suggest some ways that you can help your child find incomplete sentences on his own. The words in boldface in the left group of words are fragments. On the right, italics point out the complete sentence, which was formed from the fragment.

<table>
<tr><td align="center">I</td><td align="center">II</td></tr>
<tr>
<td>1. A dog played with a rubber ball. He rushed after it. Over the curb and into the street.</td>
<td>A dog played with a rubber ball. He rushed after it over the curb and into the street.</td>
</tr>
<tr>
<td>2. Everywhere I can hear the wind's howl. Rushing noisily through the trees. It scares me!</td>
<td>Everywhere I can hear the wind's howl rushing noisily through the trees. It scares me!</td>
</tr>
</table>

I	II
	or
	Everywhere I can hear the wind's howl. *Rushing noisily through the trees, it scares me.*
3. One afternoon I stood at the freezer in the supermarket. **When an empty cart shot down the aisle.** I knew a little child was to blame.	One afternoon I stood at the freezer in the supermarket. *When an empty cart shot down the aisle, I knew a little child was to blame.* (The fragment could be attached to the first sentence, "One afternoon . . .)
4. In the street I saw my cousin Steve. **Who really looked ridiculous.** He was wearing his Halloween ghost costume.	*In the street I saw my cousin Steve who really looked ridiculous.* He was wearing his Halloween ghost costume.
5. He cannot tie his shoe. **Unless someone helps him.** He will probably leave his laces open.	*He cannot tie his shoes unless someone helps him.* He will probably leave his laces open. (The fragment might be attached to the sentence after it.)

Help your child learn to find sentence pieces in her own writing. There's no surefire method—fragments keep cropping up straight through writing I examine in college classes—but some strategies work:

- Have your child turn away from her writing for a while, and then come back and read aloud what she's written.
- As she reads, encourage your child to stop for a long breath after each sentence. Train her to ask, "Does this sentence make sense?"
- Encourage your child to read her sentences from the last one to the first one. This helps her see whether or not each makes sense, whether or not each names some subject and gives some information about that subject.

One Hundred Words Most Often Misspelled

As you consider these and keep on your guard for them in your child's writing, remember the pointers I mentioned in Chapter 7.

accommodate	coming	led
achievement	conscious	lose
acquire	definitely	losing
across	dependent	marriage
all right	description	mere
among	disastrous	necessary
amount	effect	ninety
annually	embarrass	noble
apparent	exaggerate	occasion
arguing	existence	occur
argument	expense	occurred
article	experience	occurrence
beautiful	explanation	occurring
become	fascinate	opinion
believe	height	opportunity
benefited	heroes	paid
breathe	huge	parallel
category	interest	particular
chief	involve	performance

personal
personnel
possession
possible
practical
precede
prejudice
preferred
prepare
principal
principle
privilege
probably
procedure

proceed
profession
professor
pursue
quiet
receive
recommend
referring
repetition
rhythm
sacrifice
safety
sense
separate

separation
similar
studying
succeed
succession
surprise
than
then
thorough
transferred
unnecessary
villain
woman
write
writing

Words Often Confused

Some words resist a child's ability to remember how to spell them because they are easy to confuse with other words. I've grouped five sets of the most troublesome of those words together in ways that you might present them to a child. Notice how the sentence example makes the use clear. It's helpful to encourage your youngster to look at one set of words at a time, so that he sees the difference clearly. You might want to check that your child understands by speaking sentences that contain the two or three words under consideration. Ask your youngster then to write the sentence down. For example, if you're checking on the correct use of *too, to, two,* you might read a sentence like this:

The *two* of us want *to* go to the movies *too*.

[too, two, to]

two	means 2, the number
	I see *two* boys.
too	means *also*
	Kiss me *too*.
too	means very
	I am *too* young.
to	use *to* like this:
	Go *to* the bank.
	I like *to* swim.

[it's   its]

it's	means *it is*
	It's Monday.
	(If you can say *it is* you can use *it's*.)
its	shows ownership by some nonhuman thing
	The cat hurt *its* paw.
	(If you can say *his* or *her* use *its*.)

[there, their, they're]

there	means *a place;* it means *not here*
	Put it *there*.
there	also works with *is, was, are,* or *were*
	There is my Father.
	There were three of us.
their	means ownership or possession
	by more than one person
	They lost *their* tickets.
they're	means *they are*
	They're my toys.
	(If you can say *they are,* you can use they're.)

[your you're]

---

your means ownership or possession by *you*
It is *your* book.
you're means *you are*
You're right.
(If you can say *you are,* you can write *you're.*)

[who's whose]

---

who's means *who is*
Who's there?
(If you can say *who is,* use *who's.*)
whose means possession. It asks, "Who does this belong to?"
Whose book is that?
whose may also be used this way
The man *whose* glasses fell picked them up.

When to Use Capitals

More productive than a lengthy list of rules, clear charts
that demonstrate correct use of capitals will serve your
child best. The chart below and this chart of capitalization
are from my book *Creating Compositions*.

QUICK REFERENCE CHART: WHEN AND WHEN NOT TO CAPITALIZE

GEOGRAPHY

Passaic River
Catskill Mountains
not
a tall mountain

New York City
not
our city

Yellowstone National Park
Market Street
not
a noisy street

HISTORICAL OCCURRENCES, NAMES, AND WRITINGS

Tonkin Resolution
Boston Tea Party
Seward's Folly
Fifth Amendment
The Constitution

SCHOOL THINGS

LaGuardia Community College
not
a new college

Mohawk High School
not
our old high school

Coleman Junior High School
not
a junior high school

English, Spanish, French,
American history
not
economics, biology, business

Hint: Languages are always
capitalized. Other subjects are not,
except when specific courses
(usually indicated by numbers) are
meant

Economics 132
History 64

a sophomore in college
the senior class

BUILDINGS AND ORGANIZATIONS

Dime Savings Bank
Sears, Roebuck and Company
Brookdale Hospital
Pathmark supermarket

Republican Party
San Francisco Giants
Girl Scouts

THE WORD I

Always capitalize the word I
    When *I* saw her, *I* was delighted.

DAYS, MONTHS, SEASONS, CELEBRATIONS

Monday
April
not seasons
spring, summer, fall, autumn, winter

Election Day
Festival of Lights
New Year's Eve

RELIGION, RACE, NATIONALITY

God, Lord
Bible, Genesis
New Testament
bless His Name
the Egyptian gods
Catholicism
the Jewish religion
Protestant beliefs
Negro, Indian
Dutch Reformed Church

TITLES
BOOKS, STORIES, SHOWS, POEMS

"Oh Captain, My Captain"
Love Story
A Tale of Two Cities
not
a book by Dickens

The Washington Post
The Ed Sullivan Show
"The Legend of Sleepy Hollow"

PEOPLE

President Bush
Judge Black
Dr. Bracken
He is the president of the company.
Mr. Davis, President of the company

or
Mr. Davis, president of the company

Harriet Parsons, Ph.D.
not
a teacher, a lawyer, a professor

Hint: If the title takes the place of a person's name, use a capital.
The Mayor arrived late.
The mayor's job is difficult.

AREAS AND DIRECTIONS

Lower East Side
East-West relations
Far East
Midwest
lives in the West
but not for directions
New York is six miles east of here.
They drove north across the bridge.

THE FAMILY

I get along with Mom.
or
I get along with mom.
This is Aunt Celia.

No capitals to show relationship:

That is my sister.
Our uncle is generous.
My aunt is very helpful.

WRITING LETTERS

Opening: Capitals for first word and any names.
    Dear Mr. Stevenson:
    My dear Miss Trumball:
    Dear Jerry,
Closing: First word only:
    Sincerely yours,
    Yours truly,
    Very truly yours,

NO CAPITALS FOR PLANTS,
ANIMALS, GAMES

daisies
sycamore tree
an old oak
bananas
a bluebird
six sparrows
a vicious lion
baseball
football
swimming
monkeys
apple

Some Punctuation Pointers

• **End Marks.** The period, the question mark, and the exclamation point end sentences and serve as marks that separate one sentence from another.

The period (.) ends a sentence that makes a statement.

I watched a crow circle above the oaks. It swooped down.
Then it landed on a high branch.

The question mark (?) ends a sentence that clearly asks a question.

Who brought her doll? Did Mary bring Drowsy? Did Carol
bring Raggedy Ann?

Some sentences say that a question is being asked but they do not really ask the question themselves. For those, use a period, not a question mark.

She wondered why he did not call.
He asked who brought the station wagon.

The exclamation point (!) ends a sentence that shows strong emotion, sharp surprise, a forceful command, or strong emphasis.

I hate olives!
I don't believe it!
Just try making me eat one!

• **Quotation Marks.** There are several tricky things about the correct use of quotation marks.

First, your child must learn to distinguish between the part of the sentence that tells about who's talking and the part of the sentence that gives the words the speaker says.

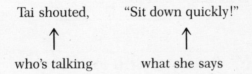

Tai shouted,   "Sit down quickly!"

↑   ↑

who's talking   what she says

Next, he must make the distinction between a sentence that tells exactly what a person says and a sentence that merely summarizes what a person says. The first kind requires quotes; for the second they are incorrect:

Tai shouted, "Sit down quickly!"
Tai shouted that we should sit down quickly.

Last, you need to demonstrate the different kinds of punctuation required by quotation sentences, depending upon where the part that tells who's talking appears—at the beginning, the end, or somewhere in the middle. The best way I know to show this is to show each separately and to use arrows to point out all the marks to remember.

I. EXACT WORDS AT THE END [Quotation marks]

[Capitalize first spoken word]

My mother shouted,"Don't stay out too late, hear,

[comma]

because the alarm's going off early and you'd better be

[End mark inside: priod, quotation mark, or exclamation point]
able to get up for work!",

[Quotation marks]

Hint: If the same person speaks another sentence—without being interrupted—right after his first one, DON'T use another quotation mark. Put the last quotation mark after the very *last* word any one person speaks.

My mother shouted, "Don't stay out too late, hear, because the alarm's going off early and you'd better be able to get up for work. I won't be able to wake you!"

II. EXACT WORDS AT THE BEGINNING

[Quotation marks]

"Don't stay out too late, hear, because the alarm's
[Capital letter]

going off early and you'd better be able to get up for

[Quotation marks]   [Small letter]   [Period]

work," my mother shouted.

[Comma, quotation mark, or exclamation point; no period]

III. EXACT WORDS BROKEN UP

[Quotation marks]   [Close quotes]   [Small letter]

"Don't stay out too late, hear," my mother

[Capital]   [Comma]

[Open quotation again]

shouted, "because the alarm's going off early and

[Comma]   [Small letter (A sentence is *continued*.)]

you'd better be able to get up for work."

[End mark]   [Close quote]

• *Apostrophes.* The most difficult of all punctuation marks to master, the apostrophe, has two main uses.

It shows omitted letters in contractions.

can't	weren't
don't	hasn't
it's	I've
doesn't	I'll

Apostrophes also show possession or ownership. Look at these examples so that you can help your child understand possession.

a. It is the *car of the man.*
b. It is the *car belonging to the man.*
c. It is the *man's car.*

In sentence *a*, the car belongs to the man. Ownership is shown with the words *of the man*. The car is owned. The man owns it.

In sentence *b*, the car belongs to the man. Ownership is shown with the words *belonging to the man*. The car is owned. The man owns it.

In sentence *c*, the car belongs to the man. Ownership is shown by using an apostrophe *s* (*'s*) after the word that tells who owns the thing. The car is still being owned. The man still owns it. But in this sentence the owner is named *before* the thing that he owns. The only way to know the owner is through the apostrophe *s*.

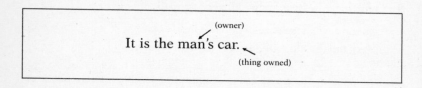

Sentence *a* sounds clumsy and unnatural. You would rarely say or write such a sentence. Sentence *b* is natural but takes too many words to say something very simple.

Sentence *c* is the most convenient and most usual way of indicating ownership. When people speak of *possession*, they usually use this form to show ownership. Because of the misunderstood apostrophe, this method causes many difficulties.

For possession, two separate ideas are involved.

- Somebody or something is the owner. That word will contain an apostrophe.
- Somebody or something is being "owned." That word usually comes soon after the word with the apostrophe.

Apostrophes *do not* show plural. Plurals are formed by adding *s* or *es* or by some special way (child*ren*, g*ee*se, alumn*i*). But apostrophes play no part in showing that the writer means more than one thing. A familiar error children make when they first learn the apostrophe is this:

I saw *turkey's* and *chicken's*.

The words in italics are both incorrect. When an apostrophe s stands at the end of a word it means that the thing the word refers to owns something. What do the turkey and the chicken own? Nothing—at least not according to the meaning of the sentence. Since the writer really wants to show that there is more than one turkey and that there is more than one chicken, the sentence should look like this:

I saw turkeys and chickens.

HOW TO FORM POSSESSIVES: TWO SIMPLE REMINDERS

Reminder I for Possession:
If the word that shows the owner *does not* end in s, add an apostrophe s ('s)

girl   The girl's dress ripped.

[apostrophe s   [This is owned by the *girl*.]
added to
girl]

senator The senator's campaign failed.

[apostrophe s   [This is owned by the senator]
added to *senator*]

Hint for Reminder I: It does not matter if the word is plural or singular. If the word does not end in s, add an apostrophe s.

This word is plural, → *men*   The men's cars crashed.
even though it does   [apostrophe s   [These are owned
not end in s: added to men]   by the men.]

Reminder II for Possession:
If the word that names the owner *does* end in *s*, add only an apostrophe (').

boys   The boys' bicycles broke.

[an apostrophe   [These are owned
added to *boys*]   by the boys]

governors   The governors' meeting ended when the

[an apostrophe   (This is owned by
added to *governors*]   the *governors*.)

chairman fainted.

Hint for Reminder II: It does not matter if the word is plural or singular. If the word ends in *s*, add only an apostrophe.

This word is singular: → *Doris*   Doris' trip was canceled.
it ends in *s*.

[apostrophe   [This is owned
added to   by Doris.]
Doris]

You will note other complications in the correct use of apostrophes to show possession, but they are more advanced skills than those I intend to focus upon here. Your child's grammar book (the upper grades) will point out these special uses of the apostrophe.

Here's a helpful review chart I developed for inexperienced writers who need to think carefully about using apostrophes correctly.

**REVIEW: IF YOU THINK A WORD NEEDS AN
APOSTROPHE BECAUSE IT SHOWS
POSSESSION:**

1. See if you can figure out what is being owned.
2. See if the word in which you want to use an apostrophe is the owner of something. Usually, the thing owned appears in the sentence soon after the owner.

    Exceptions: It is David's.
    We ate at Carl's.

    Here the thing owned is not specifically mentioned, but understood.

    David's (book)
    Carl's (house)

3. Sometimes the owner is more than one. Make sure the word shows plural with the right ending.
a. If the word does not end in *s*, add an apostrophe *s*.
b. If the word does end in *s*, add an apostrophe.

Example: a. You want to show that a boy owns books. The word *boy* does not end in *s*. The possessive is shown this way:

the *boy's* books
[Add apostrophe *s*]

b. You want to show that many boys are the owners of books. The word *boys* ends in *s*. The possessive is shown this way:

the boys' books
[Add apostrophe after s.]

You can find much more complicated rules than these to make possessives. But these I have presented are clear, simple, and acceptable.

Key Books for Young Writers and Their Parents

Children's Wordbooks

You may not be able to buy all these books—some are out of print—but your local library should have copies available for easy browsing in the reference sections.

The Cat in the Hat Beginner Book Dictionary, by the Cat himself and P. D. Eastman (New York: Beginner Books, Random House, 1964). Heavily illustrated in full color, this dictionary for beginning readers (grades K to 6) explains words through simple sentence examples and pictures by Dr. Seuss. An edition directed at children in grades 2 to 3 came out in 1984.

The Charlie Brown Dictionary, compiled by Charles M. Schulz (Cleveland: World Books, 1973). Based on *The Rainbow Dictionary* and recommended for readers in kindergarten through grade three, this picture dictionary is illustrated with over 580 cartoons of the popular "Peanuts" comic series. The 2,400 entries reflect the language that children speak and hear, especially on television.

The Courtis-Watters Illustrated Golden Dictionary for Young Readers, compiled by Stuart A. Courtis and Garnette Watters; consultant on pronunciation, Allen Walker Read (New York: Golden Press, latest edition). Designed for children in grades one through four, this volume defines over 10,000 basic words, including some scientific and geographic entries but none for people, slang, or foreign terms. Entries contain part of speech, simple pronunciation aids, and sentence examples, and are supplemented by over 3,000 black-and-white drawings, a center section of color illustrations, and an appendix of weights and measures, abbreviations, geographical information, presidents of the United States, and rules for capitalization.

The Harcourt Brace School Dictionary (New York: Harcourt Brace Jovanovich, 1972). Approximately 50,000 entires, correlated with modern textbooks for readers in grades four through seven. The entries are arranged attractively and include synonyms, usage notes, some etymologies, and sentence examples. Introductions for the reader explain the use of the dictionary and provide exercises. The two-color illustrations include maps and diagrams.

The Home Activity Series (New York: Dell, various editions). Designed "for parents who want to help their children to learn basic educational skills." The series includes workbooks on handwriting, spelling, phonics, and reading readiness, all based on matching, tracing, copying, and pronunciation exercises, with illustrations. Each numbered book is keyed to the needs of a particular age group, and instructions for parents appear at the bottom of pages when appropriate.

Macmillan Dictionary for Children, edited by Christopher G. Morris (New York: Macmillan, 1982). Designed primarily for readers of middle to late elementary grades, this dictionary contains approximately 30,000 words, including some geographic and scientific entries, each identified by its part of speech, placed in a context sentence, and followed by its phonetic pronunciation. An eight-page illustrated introduction instructs the reader in understanding entries, dividing words by syllables, and using the phonetic pronunciation key, which appears on alternate pages. About 1,100 full-color illustrations accompany the text, along with several hundred brief narratives on the etymologies of interesting words. Definitions are simple and precise but not condescending.

The New Golden Dictionary, compiled by Bertha Morris Parker; illustrated by Aurelius Battaglia (New York: Golden Press, 1972). Recommended for preschool and beginning readers, this picture dictionary defines over 1,200 words, with 880 inflected forms and an additional 450 illustrative examples. Geographic, historical, and biographic names are omitted, and entries do not include pronunciation or part of speech; words are defined in sentence examples and reinforced with full-color illustrations. A parent's guide and a series of dictionary games appear in the appendix. appendix.

The Rainbow Dictionary, compiled by Wendell W. Wright (Cleveland: World Books, 1974). This dated but still respected dictionary for beginning readers contains 2,300 entries based on word-frequency lists and defined in sentence examples from Mother

Goose, Robert Louis Stevenson, Lewis Carroll, and others. Written for five- to eight-year-old children, it omits pronunciation, syllabic division, and word forms, along with geographic and scientific terms, but its framed entries, large clear print, and over 1,100 full-color illustrations make it convenient for the young reader to use without the help of an adult.

The Random House Dictionary of the English Language, school edition, edited by Stuart Berg Flexner (New York: Random House, latest edition). Over 47,500 entries, based on word-frequency lists for fourth to eighth grade students, include biographical and geographic terms and abbreviations; entries give phonetic pronunciation, part of speech, and sentence examples. A substantial introduction for the student, along with a map section and tables of weights and measures, are especially useful. There's a 1987 version of the regular (that is, "nonschool") edition that you can purchase in your local bookstore.

Scott, Foresman Beginning Dictionary (Glenview, Illinois: Scott, Foresman, latest edition). Over 25,000 entries, containing part of speech, pronunciation, sentence examples, and synonyms where possible; includes ethnic, slang, geographical, and scientific terms. Heavily illustrated with approximately 1,000 photographs, drawings, and art reproductions, this volume also includes an extensive series of self-help lessons on skill topics, supported with exercises and review tests appropriate to the needs of students in the middle and late elementary grades.

The Scribbler's First Copy Book: Practice in Writing the Alphabet and Numerals by Joanne Wylie (Racine, Wisconsin: Western, A Whitman Book, 1974) and *The Scribbler's Second Copy Book: Combining Alphabet Letters to Form Simple Words* by Joanne Wylie (Racine, Wisconsin: Western, A Whitman Book, 1974). The Scribbler's series relies almost exclusively on tracing and writing, rather than games and coloring activities, to teach letters and simple words. The *First Copy Book* provides practice in copying basic shapes, letters (upper- and lowercase), and numerals, but does not associate letters and pictures. Beginning with a review of letters, the *Second Copy Book* teaches the child to print groups of words—family, color, number, vehicle, clothing, and furniture—most of which are reinforced with drawings, and concludes with the copying of simple sentences.

See A Word—Say a Word by Joanne Wylie (Racine, Wisconsin: Western, Golden Press, 1974). Designed for beginning readers, this workbook reinforces the recognition of basic words with illustrated exercises and activities, involving matching, tracing, copying, and writing. Word-picture games identify names of animals, colors, toys, and household items.

The Sounds and Shapes of Letters by Adelaide Holl and Linda Segel (Racine, Wisconsin: Western, 1972). Part of the Golden Press Readiness Workbook series, this book introduces preschool children to letters, using tracing exercises, simple recognition games, and numerous pictures to reinforce initial sounds. Activities include coloring, puzzle solving, drawing, word pronunciation, and rhyming, with a cut-out picture section for each letter.

Thorndike Barnhart Beginning Dictionary, compiled by E. L. Thorndike and Clarence L. Barnhart (Glenview, Illinois: Scott, Foresman, latest edition). Over 26,000 words, including a limited number of geographic names and scientific terms, are defined and placed in context; each entry includes part of speech and phonetic pronunciation. Approximately 1,300 charts, diagrams, and black-and-white line drawings supplement the text. Intended for use in grades three and four, it contains an extensive introduction, explaining the use of the dictionary, alphabetization, phonics, spelling, and word forms, with two-color illustrations and review exercises after each section. Etymologies are limited to words derived from people's names and terms that have undergone interesting changes.

Thorndike Barnhart Intermediate Dictionary, compiled by E. L. Thorndike and Clarence L. Barnhart (Glenview, Illinois: Scott, Foresman, latest edition). Listing approximately 57,000 words in a single alphabet, including colloquialisms and biographical, historical, geographic, and scientific terms, the *Intermediate Dictionary* is designed for readers in grades five through eight. Definitions contain sentence examples, part of speech, and phonetic pronunciations, and the text is heavily illustrated with black-and-white line drawings, maps, and diagrams. A comprehensive preface explains the use of entries and provides a helpful guide to spelling, and several pages of endnotes give spelling and phonics rules. Over 1,800 etymologies appear in the entries.

Thorndike Barnhart Junior Dictionary, compiled by E. L. Thorndike and Clarence L. Barnhart (Glenview, Illinois: Scott, Foresman, latest edition). Recommended for late elementary or junior high school children, the *Junior Dictionary* has 44,000 entries, including colloquialisms, foreign words and phrases in common use, and biographical, historical, geographic, and scientific terms; definitions contain sentence examples, part of speech, and phonetic pronunciations, with several thousand black-and-white drawings and charts. A three-part introduction for the reader explains how to use the dictionary, find meanings, and determine pronunciation, followed by a review of the parts of speech, a spelling guide, and numbered exercises and questions suitable for group or independent work. *The Thorndike Barnhart Advanced Junior Dictionary* is similar but contains 30 percent more entries. The entire Thorndike Barnhart series, frequently revised and updated, is a high-quality student set and a popular choice in the classroom as well as the home library.

Webster's New Elementary Dictionary (New York: Merriam, 1981). Written for grades three through eight and junior high school students this volume contains 32,000 entries, with an introduction for the reader and tables of information.

The Young People's Thesaurus Dictionary, compiled by Harriet Wittels and Joan Greisman (New York: Grosset & Dunlap, 1971). A collection of synonyms and antonyms arranged in a continuous alphabet, this work is designed to accompany (but not replace) a comprehensive dictionary for the child of late elementary or junior high school age. An introduction for the reader explains the advantages and drawbacks of the thesaurus format, including some interesting examples of the variety of sources from which English words derive. Its weakness, common to almost all thesauri, is the failure to discriminate adequately among parts of speech and shades of meaning.

Language Skills Books for Parents

Artful Scribbles: The Significance of Children's Drawings by Howard Gardner (New York: Basic Books, 1980). Read this book to discover the meanings behind the pictures that your child draws. You'll also develop insights into how a child grows artistically.

The Art of Teaching Writing by Lucy McCormick Calkins (Portsmouth, N.H.: Heinemann, 1986). A book for teachers, this volume is filled with samples of children's writing and excellent strategies for tapping a child's energy to write. You'll find good ideas here for your own home-learning program in writing. Professor Calkins's work in writing for elementary school children is renowned.

Books, Young People, and Reading Guidance by Geneva Hanna Pilgrim and Marianna K. McAllister, 2nd ed. (New York: Harper &

Row, 1968). Among the somewhat theoretical discussions on the reading interests of junior and senior high school students are several sections useful to parents: Chapters 4 and 5 deal with the social and psychological factors that influence adolescent reading interests, and chapter 6 reviews the basic terms of literary analysis for parents who wish to discuss books with their children. Included is a comprehensive list of sources that evaluate young people's literature.

Children and Books by Zena Sutherland and May Hill Arbuthnot, 5th ed. (Glenview, Illinois: Scott, Foresman, 1977). Valuable chiefly for its comprehensive and up-to-date annotation of hundreds of books for young people, *Children and Books* also includes chapters on encouraging responses to literature, on the child's literary interests and needs, and on contemporary issues of interest to parents: censorship, sexism in children's stories, the influence of television on literacy. An annotated list of adult references appears at the end of each chapter.

A Child's Mind: How Children Learn During the Critical Years from Birth to Age Five by Muriel Beadle (Garden City, N.Y.: Doubleday, 1970). Written in concise, conversational prose for parents and educators, *A Child's Mind* surveys and synthesizes research in children's mental development, providing impartial coverage of cognitive theories and suggesting ways to make the home a good learning environment. Especially useful are chapter 13, which explains how children perceive the written word, and chapter 14, on the acquisition of speaking, writing, and vocabulary skills.

Explorations in Children's Writing, edited by Eldonna L. Evertts (Champaign, Ill.: National Council of Teachers of English, 1970). Intended primarily for teachers, this brief collection of essays and transcripts of recorded discussions provides parents with a comprehensive and provocative survey of alternative ways to motivate and appreciate the writing of elementary school children.

GYNS AT WK: A Child Learns to Write by Glenda Bissex (Cambridge Mass.: Harvard University Press, 1980). With the accuracy of a trained researcher, Bissex traces the development of her son's independent learning to write and read. This is a wonderfully written book and quite illuminating about how a child learns. You'll marvel at the samples of writing and will learn about the value of invented spelling.

Helping Your Child to Read Better by Robert M. Goldenson (New York: Thomas Crowell, 1957). In this informative study for parents seeking to stimulate their child's verbal skills and enrich reading experiences at home, Goldenson suggests games and activities for improving language arts and concludes each chapter with a question-and-answer discussion of the issues. Though the book relies too heavily on anecdotes and hypothetical dialogue, it does provide a wealth of practical information. Several chapters contain reviews of spelling, diction, and sentence correctness.

Home Reference Books in Print by S. Padraig Walsh (New York: Bowker, 1969). This concise, detailed handbook is indispensable for the parent interested in building an adequate home library. Part One evaluates English language dictionaries according to age suitability and size, Part Two rates world atlases in print, and Part Three surveys the numerous subscription books available to homeowners—from encyclopedias to specialized collections on gardening, sports, and religion—with ratings by cost and advice on sales techniques. Each section includes annotations and price information.

The Horn Book Magazine, published six times a year by The Horn Book, Inc., 585 Boylston Street, Boston, Mass. 02116. In addition to articles of general interest in the field of children's literature, each issue reviews children's books and audio-visual materials and recommends new books by suggested reading level. A yearly index lists reviews by author and title.

How to Help Your Child in Reading, Writing, and Arithmetic by Frieda E. Van Atta (New York: Random House, various editions). This series, published in separate workbooks for kindergarten through grade eight, provides explanations of typical verbal and mathematical skills taught in each grade, with review exercises at the end. Somewhat outdated, it still contains useful information on the terms and standards of English usage. Many of the early grade books are now out of print.

The Language Arts in the Elementary School by Ruth G. Strickland, 3rd ed. (Lexington, Mass.: D. C. Heath, 1969). This useful overview, designed primarily for teachers, begins with several chapters on the language development of preschool children and presents writing activities—from dictation of invitations and letters to independent "creative expression"—adaptable to use in the home as well as in the classroom. Chapter 15 is a condensed, intelligent discussion of the value of grammar, usage, syntax, and punctuation (including a review of some basic standards of correctness and the terminology of traditional grammar). Chapter 16 deals with levels of spelling proficiency and the relations between spelling and oral and written English. Other sections help parents understand possible difficulties for a child acquiring language skills.

The Magic Pencil by Eve Shelnutt (Atlanta: Peachtree, 1988). This book provides many ideas for writing at home for children in grades one through nine. Here you will find enjoyable activities in building language skills. The author includes notes to the person who oversees the activity in order to highlight the main concepts.

More Than ABCs: The Early Stages of Reading and Writing by Judith A Schickerdanz (Washington, D.C.: National Association for the Education of Young Children, 1986). This is a valuable resource in helping you understand how to influence your child's reading and writing development in those critical early years.

A Parent's Guide to Children's Reading by Nancy Larrick, 5th ed. (Garden City, N.Y.: Doubleday, 1983). A readable and up-to-date discussion for parents of elementary school children. *A Parent's Guide* includes dozens of activities for stimulating the child's reading interests at home and a helpful annotated list of several hundred selected children's books, organized by subject and reading level. Especially valuable are the suggestions for maintaining a home environment conducive to reading and writing.

Poetic Composition Through the Grades: A Language Sensitivity Program by Robert A. Wolsch (New York: Teachers College Press, 1970). This handbook for teachers includes several sections of interest to parents seeking to promote language sensitivity. Emphasizing the development of precise, evocative language "for improved ways of stating ideas and feelings," chapters 6 and 7 discuss the relationship of writing to experience, and chapter 10 suggests ways to use words with variety, vitality, and precision.

Rose, Where Did You Get That Red? Teaching Great Poetry to Children by Kenneth Koch (New York: Random House, 1974). Emphasizing written responses, Koch discusses ways to help children understand "mature" poetry by Shakespeare, Blake, Whitman, and others, with suggestions for parents seeking to foster the child's appreciation of poetry in general. Like its predecessor *Wishes, Lies, and Dreams*, this volume includes dozens of student poems, along with some perceptive discussion of how children react to imaginative literature, and why.

Talk with Your Child by Harvey S. Wiener (New York: Viking, 1988). This book gives parents a systematic approach to building language skills at home through regular conversation. Among other issues, chapters deal with how children acquire language, how to use reading aloud to children and appropriate conversational strategies about books, and how to use television viewing to stimulate conversation and language growth. An appendix summarizes fifty key books for preschoolers and children of primary school age and suggests questions that will stimulate conversation about the books.

When You Are Alone / It Keeps You Capone: An Approach to Creative Writing with Children by Myra Cohn Livingston (New York: Atheneum, 1973). The author, a noted children's poet, explains a number of techniques that help children express emotional responses in writing, striking a balance between unbridled expression and disciplined creative art. Especially useful to parents are Ms. Livingston's recommendations for adult responses to children's poetry. Chapter 16 suggests activities and topics to stimulate interest in writing.

Why Johnny Still Can't Read by Rudolf Flesch (New York: Harper & Row, 1981). Author of *Why Johnny Can't Read*, Flesch here rails against the "look-say" method that dominated reading instruction in the schools for the last fifty years. He advocates the phonics approach, which is now experiencing a renaissance as one of the most valid ways of teaching children how to read.

Wishes, Lies, and Dreams: Teaching Children to Write Poetry by Kenneth Koch (New York: Harper & Row, 1980). Believing that "the best way to help children write freely is by encouragement, by examples, and by various other inspiring means," Koch describes the techniques he discovered to help elementary school students write poetry and to grow more sensitive to expressive language. Though designed for teachers, the suggested methods and discussions of children's response to words and valuable for parents as well, and the numerous student poems are delightful and useful stimuli for a child.

You and Your Child's Reading: A Practical Guide for Parents by Charlotte Mergentime (New York: Harcourt, 1963). In this informative and comprehensive handbook, Ms. Mergentime discusses some causes of reading difficulties, outlines ways to aid a child in developing spelling and vocabulary skills, and suggests dozens of activities and games to stimulate reading and writing. Chapter 7 presents a systematic and sensitive program for introducing children to word patterns, syllabication, and prefix/suffix rules, with an explanation of phonics and word building for parents. The reading lists are dated, but the suggested activities, including many nonverbal preludes to writing, are varied, interesting, and valuable.

Index

Abbreviations, in addressing
    envelopes, 217
Abstract words, 240–241
    writing images for, 75–77
Action words, 55, 60–61, 62, 65
    Name the action game, 60–61
Addressing envelope, 215–217
Aesop's fables, 203
Alphabet, teaching recognition of,
    15, 17–18, 26, 41, 48
Alphabet books, 14, 125
Alphabet stamps, 15
American Heritage Dictionary, 232,
    241
American Heritage First Dictionary,
    125–126
Animal stories, 202–206
Apostrophes, 311–315
Assignments, role of parents in
    helping with, 91–100,
    272–274
Attitudes
    establishing positive, 17–18,
    38–39
    of teacher, and poor writing
    achievements, 8–9
Audience, for writing, 80
Autobiography, 31–32, 290

Balzac, Honoré de, 58
Ben and Me, 289
Benchley, Peter, 230
Birthday messages, homemade, 23
Book cover, making, 289
Book reports, 273, 287
    finding book for, 273
Books. *See also* Dictionary;
    Encyclopedia; Thesaurus

alphabet, 14, 125
    homemade, 65–66, 233–234
    language skill, 320–324
    picture dictionaries, 125, 126
    word, 14–15, 316–320
Brainstorming, 80
Britton, James, 8
Brown, James I., 122
Build an Image game, 61–63
Business letters, 215, 222–228
    conventions, 223–225
    envelopes for, 225
    format for, 223
    ideas for writing, 226–228

Calkins, Lucy McCormick, 8
Capital letter to begin sentences, 44,
    46, 64
in captions, 45
guide for using, 306–308
Captions, writing, 38, 44–45
Card catalog, 282–283
Career choice, and writing skills,
    9–10
Cather, Willa, 31
Chalk, 14
Chalkboard, 14, 23–24
Characters
    in autobiography, 290
    in bibliography, 290
    and conflict, 187
    describing moment with, 289
    and dilemma, 188–189
    making up, 289
    visits with make-believe, 197–202
Child's Garden of Verses (Stevenson),
    244

Chronology, 176–178
Cinquain, 265–266
Clarity, use of comparison for, 71–72
Collage, 49, 166
Colleges, teaching of writing in, 7
Color words, 55, 56, 62, 65
Colored pencils, 13
Comma fault, 84, 90, 299
Comma splice, 299
Communications, modern, 6
Comparisons. See also Figurative language
    of effective writing and human anatomy, 4
    for solid imagery, 71–78
Composition, 3
    teaching in school, 5–7, 104–110
Computer banners, 22
Computers, 16, 22
Concept words, 242
Concrete language, 114–115
Concreteness, 56
Concrete sensory detail, 56–58, 192
Conflict, 187, 188
Connecting words, 299–300
Connotation, 230, 239
Conrad, Joseph, 57–58
Consonants, 48
Content matter, 2
    teaching, 3
Contractions, 311
Conversation
    between child and nonhuman object, 262
    between parent and child, 33
    dialogue in, 186–188
    fragments in, 41–43
Coonfield, Benjamin, 150
Correctness, 4, 79–142
    code of ethics for, 91–100
    correcting errors, 83–85, 87, 89–91
    proofreading for, 86, 98, 100–3
    of punctuation, 83, 84, 306–315
    sentence completeness, 44, 45–47, 298–302
    sentence structure, 133–142
    of spelling, 83–85, 127–133
    of vocabulary, 112–117
    word usage, 303–305
    writing goals for schools, 104–110
    in writing process, 79–83, 85–90

Couplets, 244–245
Crayons, 13
Creating Compositions, 306
Creative questioning, 33–34, 37, 173
Creative writing, 28–31, 32. See also Imaginative writing
    autobiography, 31–32
    creative questioning, 33–34, 37, 173
    environment for, 32–34
    establishing sentence sense, 41–44
    letter writing, 213
    linking words and pictures, 38–41, 50, 154–155
    as pressure valve for child, 32–33, 48
    role of parents in, 32–34
    sensory language in, 2, 29, 32, 36–41, 55–78
    sharing, 32–34
    speak-listen-write formula for, 35, 37
    story telling, 34–35
Cut and paste fun, 49–50, 155

Definitions. See also Dictionary
    parts of, 235
    writing clear, 235–239
    writing personal, 239–242
de la Mare, Walter, 253
Denotation, 229–230, 239
Descriptive writing
    of actions, 158
    of classroom, 145
    detail in, 55–58
    distinguishing from narrative writing, 175, 180
    expanding, 168–169
    one sentence, 158
    opinion in, 148–151
    portraits, 160–161
    riddles, 158–159
    of room, 143–144
    self-portraits, 161–168
    sense words in, 143–156
    subjectivity in, 152–154
    use of camera in developing, 154–155
    use of sensory diction in, 155–156
Details
    adding to narrative writing, 174–176

build an image game, 61–63
concrete sensory, 56–58
use of questions in drawing out,
33–34, 37, 173
Dialogue
in narrative writing, 186–188
in playwriting, 289
in spoken English, 41–44
Dictionary, 14, 15. *See also*
Thesaurus
children's picture, 14, 125–126
denotative meanings in, 230–231
making original, 233–235
multiple definitions in, 232
role of, in vocabulary building,
123–129
Dilemma, 188–189
Diorama, 166
Dr. Seuss books, 14, 113
Draft
copying final, 97–98
correcting, 86–87
rewriting, 89–90
role of parents in reading, 95–96
writing rough, 82–83, 87–88

Elbow, Peter, 8
Eliot, T. S., 87
Embedding, 136
Encyclopedia, 276–283
taking notes from, 278, 281–282
Encyclopedia Buying Guide (Kister),
277
End marks, 44, 46, 64, 165, 308–309
English, teaching of, 5–7
Envelope, addressing, 215–217
Erasers, 13, 85, 87
Errors, correcting, 84–85, 87, 89–91
Errors and Expectations
(Shaughnessy), 112
Essays, photo, 49–50, 155, 160–61
Examples, setting by parents, 11–12
Exclamation point, 165, 309
Experiences
autobiography, 31–32
building vocabulary on, 112–114
and creative expression, 28–31,
48
creative questioning on, 33–34,
37, 173
daily, 1, 29, 31
environment for, 32–34

sharing of, 32–34
story telling, 34–35

Factual writing, 151
Fairy tales, visits with characters in,
197–202
Fan mail, 220
Felt-tip pens, 14
Figurative language, 72
metaphors, 75–78, 249
personification, 73–75, 77–78,
206–9, 261–263, 288
simile, 72–73, 255–256
Figure, 72
Final draft, parents role in, 97–98
Flashback, 176–177
Focused writing, 81
Fragments, 42–44, 195–196,
300–302
Franklin, Benjamin, 17, 136, 289
Free association, 81
Frost, Frances, 253
Frost, Robert, 253
Fused sentence, 299

Games. *See* Writing games
Get well cards, homemade, 219–220
Ginott, Chaim, 25
Grammar, 3
teaching, 136–137
transformational, 136–137
Greeting cards, making, 23, 218
Grouping, skills in, 279, 285
Guest lists, 17
Guide for the Teacher of Basic Writing
(Shaughnessay), 112

Happiness Is (Schulz), 75
Heavy-duty paper, 13
Home environment, 11–16, 32–34
Homework, parent's role in helping
with, 91–100
Hughes, Langston, 253

Idea(s)
expressing, 5
for narrative writing, 293–296
thinking and talking about, 80
for writing business letters,
226–228

"If I Were" writing poems, 245–246

I Know! A Riddle Book (Sarnoff and Fuffins), 194

Image(s), 57
  as building blocks, 55–78
  building definitions of, 76–77
  children's abilities to create, 129–130

Image building, 61–63
  for abstract words, 75–77

Imagery
  comparisons for, 71–78
  flashbacks in, 176–177

Imaginative writing, 32, 171, 193–210 *See also* Creative writing
  about animals, 202–206
  concrete sensory detail in, 56–58, 193
  describing moment with character, 289
  developing language skills in, 201–202
  fables, 203
  "just-so" tales, 203–204
  making up character, 289
  narrative skills in, 193–194
  personification in, 73–75, 77–78, 206–209, 261–262, 288
  photo essays, 49–50, 155, 160–161, 201
  on photographs/paintings, 201
  Pretend-You-Are writing, 207–209, 261, 288
  riddles and games, 194–197
  sensory detail in, 204
  single moment perception, 194
  on special interest, 199–200
  stimulating, 197–202, 209–210
  visits in, 197–202
  writing about moment, 288

Imitation, 11–12

Impact, use of comparisons for, 71–72

Implements, writing, 13–14

Indiana Writes, 254–255, 262

Ink, 13–14

Invitations, 213–215
  addressing, 217
  RSVP in, 215

It's/its, 196, 304

Japanese haiku, 263–265

Jigsaw sentence, 138–142

Jingling, 249–253

Jonson, Ben, 87

Just So Stories (Kipling), 203

Keats, John, 87

Kipling, Rudyard, 203

Kister, Kenneth, 277

Koch, Kenneth, 243–244

Labeling, 21, 38, 48

Label makers, 15

Language
  concrete, 114–115
  poetic, 150
  rhythmic, 253–267
  sensory, 2, 29, 32, 36–41, 55–78

Language arts, 26, 105

Language experience, 26

Language skills books for parents, 320–324

Lear, Edward, 266

Letter writing, 9
  addressing envelope, 215–217
  business letters, 215, 222–228
    conventions, 223–225
    envelopes for, 225
    format for, 223
    ideas for writing, 226–228
  fan mail, 220
  to faraway friends, 220–222
  friendly letters, 215
  homemade birthday messages, 23
  homemade postal or greeting cards, 218
  invitations, 213–215
  notes, 23–26
  to pen pals, 220–222
  to shut-ins, 219–220
  thank-you's, 218–219
  and use of mail, 211–212, 217

Library
  card catalog in, 282–283
  resources in, 80–81

Limericks, 266–267

Lindsay, Vachel, 253

Lined paper, writing on, 12–13

List making, 16–20, 278, 283–285

Literary appreciation, teaching, 6
Literature, sensory detail in, 72

Make believe. *See* Imaginative
    writing
Manus, Richard, 90
McGraw-Hill College Handbook, 90,
    297
McKie, Roy, 14
Mechanics, 3
Metaphor, 75–78, 249
Milton, John, 136
Moment
    definition of, 172
    describing with a character, 289
    focus on, 173–176
    narrative, 172
    single, 172–173
    writing about single, 288
Murray, Don, 8
My Book About Me, 14

Name the action game, 60–61
Narrative writing, 170–192
    adding details to, 174–176
    children's natural abilities in, 171
    conflict between characters in,
        187–188
    definition of, 171–172
    dialogue in, 186–188
    dilemma and conflict in, 188–192
    distinguishing from descriptive
        writing, 175, 180
    flashbacks in, 176–177
    focus on moment in, 173–176
    goals of, 185
    sense table in, 179
    sensory language in, 179–185
    sequence in, 176–178
    short story in, 188–192
    single moment in, 171–173
    as storytelling, 171
    subjectivity in, 174, 180
    subjects for, 293–296
    transition words in, 177–178, 180
National Endowment for the Arts
        Poetry in the Schools
        Program, 243, 249
Neatness, overemphasis on, 84–85
News reporting, 289

Note taking, 278, 281–282
Note writing, 23–26, 211–212

Objective writing, 149–151
Objectivity, in description, 149–150
O'Hare, Frank, 136, 137
1000s of Free Things, 225
Opinions, focusing on, 148–151, 169
Organization, teaching, 111–112
Orthographics, 39
Outlining, 283, 285–286

Painting, imaginative writing about,
    201
Paper
    heavy-duty, 13
    writing, 12–13
Parent(s)
    helping child's spelling skills,
        130–133
    initiation of, by children, 11–12
    and the question of blame, 5–10
    role of, in correcting errors, 90–91
    role of, in creative expression,
        32–34
    role of, in guiding writing, 1–5,
        11–27
    role of, in interpreting
        assignments, 272–273
    role of, in report writing, 270, 271,
        273, 290
    role of, in seeing school
        assignments completed,
        91–100
    role of, in setting example, 11–12
    role of, in vocabulary building,
        113–114, 117–118
    setting scene for writing, 32–34
    as story tellers, 34–35
    as writing coach, 89, 93
Pencils, 13
Pen pals, 220
Pens, 13–14
Period, 44, 46, 165, 299, 308
Personification
    for abstract words, 76–77
    to add liveliness to writing, 73,
        206–7
    in comparisons, 73–74, 77–78
    in poetry, 261–262

Personification *(Cont.)*
  and pretend, 74–75, 207–209, 288
  in reports, 288
  in riddles, 207
Phonetic skills, 39, 166
Photo essays, 49–50, 155, 160–161, 201
Picture dictionaries, 125, 126
Pictures
  connecting words and, 36–41, 50, 154–155
  expressing emotion in, 25, 38
  writing captions for, 38, 44–45
Places, describing, 143–144, 145
Play acting, 186–187
Play writing, 186–187
Plurals, showing, 312
Person(s)
  autobiography, 31–32, 290
  one-sentence description of, 158
  portraits of, 160–161
    expanding, 168–169
    self-, 161–168
  pretending to be, 288
  riddles of, 158–159
  sensory detail on, 69–70
Poetic language, 150
Poet-in-the-Classroom Program, 243, 249
Poetry, 243–244
  cinquain, 265–266
  couplets, 244–246
  demands of, 267–268
  form in, 263
  haiku, 263–265
  ideas for, 256
  image in, 263
  jingling in, 249–253
  limericks, 266–267
  metaphor in, 249
  personification in, 261–262
  pretend-you-re something in, 261–262
  repetition in, 256
  rhymes in, 66, 244–253
  rhythmic language in, 253–267
  sensory language in, 72, 247–249, 253–263
  simile in, 255–256
  sound repetition, 246–249
  talk-to-me rhyme, 246
  teaching, 6, 250–251
  word choice in, 253–254
  word whackies, 246

Portraits, 160–61
  expanding, 168–169
  self-, 161–168
Possession, showing, 311–315
Postal card, 218
Praise, importance of, 37, 90–91
Precise words, 34, 72–73, 115–117, 150
Predicament, 188
Prefixes, 118–122
Prepositions, 63
"Pretend-You-Are" writing, 207–209, 288
Prewriting, 79–83
  brainstorming, 80
  free association, 81
  parents' role in, 94
  for report, 271–275
  research, 80–81
  subject tie in, 81
Print Shop (Broderbund Software), 16, 22
Proofreading, 86, 98, 100–103
  definition of, 100–101
  of final copy, 101
  marks for, 101
  of rough copy, 101
  techniques in, 102–103
Punctuation, 83, 84
  apostrophes, 311–315
  commas, 84, 90, 299
  exclamation mark, 165, 309
  period, 44, 46, 165, 308
  question mark, 165, 308
  quotation marks, 186, 309–311
  semicolon, 299

Question mark, 165, 308
Questions, creative, 33–34, 37, 173, 198
  responding to, with complete sentences, 45–47
Question words, in report writing, 272–275
Quotation marks, 186, 309–311
Quotations, 186, 187
  in report writing, 282
  writing about, 288–289

Reading and writing, 26–27, 38
Reading comprehension, 178
Reading skills, 26, 105

Reference Books for Young Readers, 277
Report writing, 269–290
  definition of, 270
  finding topic for, 271, 272–273
  limiting topic for, 271, 273–275
  objectivity in, 150–151
  organizing information for, 271, 283–286
  outlining, 283, 285–286
  research sources for, 270, 271, 276–283
  role of parents in, 270, 271, 273, 290
  steps in, 270–271
  taking notes for, 278, 281–282
  topics for, 288–290
  writing final draft for, 271, 286–290
Re- words, 120
Rewriting, encouraging, 88
Rhetoric, 3, 4
Rhymes, 66, 244–253
Riddles
  it's and *its* in, 196
  model for two-sentence, 194–197
  of person, 158–159
  personification in, 207
  sense, 70–71
  word play in, 195
Rield, Rachel, 253
Room sign, 21–23
Roots, word, 118–122
Rossetti, Christina, 247
Rough copy, parents role in, 94–96
RSVP, 215
Rubber stamps, 15
Ruffins, Roynolds, 194
Run-together sentences, 299–300

Sarnoff, Jane, 194
Schedule writing, 19–20
School(s)
  instruction in dictionary use, 124–125
  teaching poetry in, 250–251
  writing goals for, 104–110
School assignment, role of parents in seeing completed, 91–100
Schulz, Charles M., 75
Scientific report, 173, 286–287
Seating plan, 26

Self-expression, linking writing with, 25, 38–39
Self-portraits, 161–168
Semicolon, 299
Sense riddle, writing, 70–71
Sense table, 146–148, 179
Sense words, 55–78
  for description, 143–148
  and opinion, 148–151
  and subjectivity, 152–154
Sensory language, 2, 29, 32, 36–41, 55–78
Sentence(s)
  building, 63–70
  capital letter at beginning, 44, 46, 64
  combining, 136–142, 148
  complete, 44, 45–47, 298
  definition of, 298
  expanding, 50–54
  fragments, 42–44, 195–196, 300–302
  incomplete, 41–43
  pieces, 300–302
  reordering, 67–68, 148
  run-together, 299–300
  spoken, 41–42
  structuring, 134–142
  syntax in, 134
Sentence Building game, 63–70
Sentence sense, establishing, 41–44
Sentence Staircase game, 68–70
Sequence of events, 176, 178
Sharing of experiences, 32–34
Shaughnessy, Mina, 112, 122, 131
Shopping list, 16–20, 278, 283–285
Short story, 188–192
Shut-ins, letters to, 219–220
Sign making, 21–23, 43
Sight words, 62
Simile, 72–73, 255–256
Slaughter, William, 249–250
Smell words, 56, 62, 65
Sound words, 55, 62, 65, 66–67
Speak-listen-write formula, 35, 37
Spect words, 120
Spelling, 83–85
  checking dictionary for, 131–133
  consonants in, 48
  correcting errors in, 96, 97, 103
  developing record keeping system for misspelled words, 130–131
  hints for, 132–133

Spelling *(Cont.)*
  hot spots, 129–133
  ignoring errors in, 39–40
  and list making, 18
  and note writing, 24
  and orthographics, 39
  and phonetic skills in, 39, 166
  problem words, 127–133, 302–303
  rules for, 133
  and use of label makers, 15
  vowels in, 48
Stamp pads, 15
Stationery, 13
Stevenson, Robert Louis, 244
Story talk, 171
Story telling. *See also* Narrative
      writing
  role of parents in, 34–35
Subjective writing, 152–154
Subject tree, 81
Suffixes, 118–122
Synonyms, 127. *See also* Thesaurus
Syntax, 134

Talk-to-Me rhymes, 244
Talk with Your Child, 33, 113, 171
Taste words, 56, 65
Teachers
  role of, in teaching writing, 2–3,
      5–7, 32, 44
  writing notes to, 24
Thank-you's, 218–19
There/their/they're, 304
Thesaurus, 14, 15
  role of, in vocabulary building,
      123–124, 126–127
Timed writing, 81
Titles, incomplete sentences as,
      44–45
To/too/two, 304
Tolstoy, Leo, 28–29, 31
Touchwords, 55–56, 57, 62, 65
Transformational grammar,
      136–137
Transformations, 136
Transition words, 177–178, 180, 30
Typewriter, children's, 12, 15

Un- words, 120
Usage, 3

Verbs. *See*. Action words
Vocabulary building, 112–117, 118.
      See also Words
  on child's experiences, 112–114
  concrete words, 114–115
  dictionary in, 230–235
  guessing at word meaning,
      122–127
  making dictionary, 233–235
  planting words, 114
  precise words, 115–117
  prefixes, 118–122
  role of dictionary in, 14–15,
      123–26
  role of thesaurus in, 15, 123–124,
      126–127
  role of word books in, 14–15
  roots, 118–122
  suffixes, 118–122
  word versatility, 117–122
  writing clear definitions, 235–239
Volkswriter (Lifetree Software), 16

What's the Best Word game, 58–60
Who's/whose, 305
Wishes, Lies, and Dreams (Koch),
      243–244
Wolfe, Don, 155–156, 166, 172, 178,
      288
Wolfe, Thomas, 31
Woolf, Virginia, 87
Word(s). *See also* Vocabulary
      building
  abstract, 75–77, 240–241
  action, 55, 60–61, 65
  color, 55, 56, 65
  concept, 242
  connecting, 299–300
  connecting pictures and, 36–41,
      50, 154–155
  connotation of, 230, 239
  denotation of, 229–230, 239
  determining best, 58–60
  parts of, 118–122
  sense, 55–78, 143–154
  smell, 55, 65
  sound, 55, 65
  taste, 56, 65
  transition, 177–178, 180, 300
  versatility of, 117–122
Word association, 230–232

Word books, 14–15, 126, 316–320
Word play, in riddles, 195
Word processors, 16
Word-for-word reporting, 278
Word usage, 303
  it's/its, 196, 304
  there/their/they're, 304
  to/too/two, 304
  who's/whose, 305
  your/you're, 305
Word Whackies, 244
Writer, relation with written effort,
    28–29
Writing
  assigning blame for poor, 5–10,
    111
  comparing effective with human
    anatomy, 4
  encouragement of, 2–3
  encourage rough, 87–88
  as exploration, 1–2
  guessing at word meaning,
    122–127
  importance of learning, 9–10
  linking with self-expression, 25
  objective, 149–151
  personification of objects, 74–75
  purposes of, 3–5
  and reading, 26–27, 38
  role of in parents in guiding, 2–3,
    11–27
  role of teachers in teaching, 2–3,
    5–7, 32, 44
  for seating plan, 26
  and self-expression, 38–39

  speak-listen-write formula for, 35,
    37
  subjective, 152–154
  words as chameleons, 117–122
Writing activities, suggestions for,
    293–296
Writing games
  book making, 65–66
  Build an Image game, 61–63
  Name the Action game, 60–61
  sense table, 146–148
  Sentence Building game, 63–70
  for sentence combining, 137–142
  Sentence Staircase game, 68–70
  spelling hot spots, 129–130
  two-sentence riddles, 196–197
  What's the Best Word game,
    58–60
Writing goals, 104–105
  for early grades, 106–107
  for high school and beyond,
    109–110
  for intermediate grades, 107–108
  for pre-high school grades,
    108–109
Writing implements, 13–14
Writing paper, 12–13
Writing process, 85–90
  prewriting, 79–83
Writing warm-ups, doing, 81–83

Your/you're, 305
You're a Good Man, Charlie Brown, 75
-*Y* words, 120

About the Author

HARVEY S WIENER was born in Brooklyn, graduated from Brooklyn College, and taught English in New York City's public schools for ten years before receiving his doctorate from Fordham University. As a teacher and father he has worked with young writers of all ages. Currently University Associate Dean for Academic Affairs at the City University of New York, he was for many years professor of English at LaGuardia Community College, having administered the writing program there for a number of years. In 1973 he spent several months in England on a grant from the National Endowment for the Humanities. He directed the basic writing program at Pennsylvania State University for a year. He chaired the Executive Committee of the Modern Language Association's Teaching of Writing Division. In addition to his *Any Child Can Write* he is the author of several writing textbooks, including *Creating Compositions, The McGraw Hill College Handbook* (with Richard Marius), *The Writing Lab* (with Rose Palmer), and *Writing Skills Handbook* (with Charles Bazerman). *Talk with Your Child* was published in 1988. He lives with his wife and three children in Massapequa, New York.